PENGUIN BOOKS
INTERROGATING CASTE

Dipankar Gupta has a doctorate in Sociology from Jawaharlal
Nehru University, New Delhi where he now teaches at the
Centre for the Study of Social Systems. Earlier he was professor
in the Department of Sociology, Delhi School of Economics.
He is also visiting professor at the University of Toronto.

His books include *Nativism in a Metropolis: The Shiv Sena in
Bombay*, *The Context of Ethnicity: Sikh Identity in a
Comparative Perspective*, *Rivalry and Brotherhood: Politics in
the Life of the Farmers of Northern India* and *Political
Sociology in India*. He has edited *Social Stratification* and has
also been the co-editor of *Contributions to Indian Sociology*.
He writes regularly for various newspapers.

DIPANKAR GUPTA

Interrogating Caste

Understanding Hierarchy and Difference in
Indian Society

PENGUIN BOOKS

Penguin Books India (P) Ltd., 11 Community Centre, Panchsheel Park, New Delhi 110 017, India
Penguin Books Ltd., 27 Wrights Lane, London W8 5TZ, UK
Penguin Putnam Inc., 375 Hudson Street, New York, NY 10014, USA
Penguin Books Australia Ltd., Ringwood, Victoria, Australia
Penguin Books Canada Ltd., 10 Alcorn Avenue, Suite 300, Toronto, Ontario, MAV 3B2, Canada
Penguin Books (NZ) Ltd., Cnr Rosedale and Airborne Roads, Albany, Auckland, New Zealand

First published by Penguin Books India 2000

Typeset in *Sabon Roman* by SÜRYA, New Delhi
Printed at Rekha Printers Pvt. Ltd., New Delhi

Contents

Contents

Preface

As always I am particularly grateful to my colleagues and students at Jawaharlal Nehru University, New Delhi. I have also taken the ideas in this book on the road to several institutions of higher learning both in India and abroad, benefiting greatly from these exposures. The list of such places is really quite long, and as I have been at it for several years now, I cannot recall all of them. But it was after one such presentation on foreign shores that I was gently encouraged to write a book-length essay explicating the discrete nature of castes. A short article here, or a seminar there, does not quite have the same impact as a volume devoted to the subject does. I hope that advice was a good one or else it is only my friends I have to blame.

I began reworking my earlier papers and notes on the subject but found it too time consuming. So the job had to be set aside till around 1998 when I realized I should either get on with it or drop the idea altogether. Fortunately, at about that time I was requested to write two separate pieces on the caste system and stratification by different publishers. This gave me the necessary nudge to get on with the work I had temporarily put off. These papers appear as chapters two and five of this book. The other chapters had to be redone extensively and new material added to them. In this process the earlier pieces had to be pared to give the volume greater coherence, and, I hope, cogency. I am glad it has turned out that way for it means that I have also grown with this project. Now that this book is written I can at long last bring to a close a phase of my life that began many years ago in a South Gujarat village. Serendipitously, a poor Dubla woman set me on the task of *interrogating* the caste system, as I knew it, with an account of the origin of her caste. I have discussed this in some detail in the first chapter of this book. After all the time it has taken this is no longer the young man's book that I once thought it would be. Even so, I hope it still carries with it some youthful exuberance.

I tried quite hard to make this book accessible to anybody who has the patience to go through it. I am afraid I have been able to accomplish this only in part. For those who are not specialists I think they can skip chapters two and eight. It is possible to make sense of all that comes in between without being drawn into the theory of social stratification and difference. Needless to say, I would be very disappointed if the professional scholar were also to adopt this advice meant only for the non-specialists. I would like them to read this work from cover to cover, as I always had them in mind while writing this book.

It is not as if a professional academic must always write for specialists. But the fact is that no matter how often one has intervened in the popular press, it is only words of recommendation from one's academic peers that carry the greatest reward. I still think there is little point in being unnecessarily abstruse when there is an easier way of saying things. The difficulty is that it is not always easy to find that route. This is particularly so when a contending point of view has to be formed in theory and not left at the level of popular appeal or linguistic seduction. Without theory it is impossible to transform ideas into knowledge, to convert small change to grand denominations. It is only after such a movement is accomplished that intersubjective communication across cultures is possible on a durable and mutually enriching basis.

Over the years I have learnt a lot from such inter-subjective communications. Marx, Durkheim, Weber and Lévi-Strauss were most helpful in this connection. They were kind friends who helped me grow. I would like my students to learn from them too. I am sure they will make better use of their friendship than I did. Today, the times are propitious as well. Now that the unlearning phase of postmodernism is over, and with it the pretentious posturing of cultural studies where every intellectual weakness became a moral value, there is hope ahead. Sociology and anthropology can once again draw strength from their disciplinary grids and look forward to a grand renewal.

1

Introduction: Why Interrogate Caste?

Anyone writing on caste cannot ignore popular conceptions about the phenomenon. In this case the dominant lay notion of the caste system is also the most prevalent academic view. This is why it is so difficult to dislodge the belief that a single caste hierarchy is universally acknowledged and accepted by everyone in the caste system. In fact, it is more realistic to say that there are probably as many hierarchies as there are castes in India. To believe that there is a single caste order to which every caste, from Brahman to untouchable, acquiesce ideologically, is a gross misreading of facts on the ground.

The truth is that no caste, howsoever lowly placed it may be, accepts the reasons for its degradation. Harijans, of whatever jati, do not accept the upper-caste view that their bodies are made of impure substances. It is quite another matter that other castes insist on treating them as polluting. Yet, while no caste is willing to concede that its own members are defiling, they readily allege that there are other castes that are indeed polluting. This tendency holds even among the so-called untouchable castes. A leather worker (traditionally called a Chamar) is convinced that he has wrongly and unjustly been pushed below the pollution barrier, but has no hesitation in endorsing the low-caste status of other so-called untouchables.

As the 'book view' of the caste system is derived largely from sacerdotal Hindu texts, members of the upper castes find it extremely agreeable. It justifies the caste system in terms of purity and pollution, giving the impression that all castes—high and low—abide by this single, overarching textual hierarchy. Several Hindu texts also imply, when they do not say so bluntly, that a person's position is determined by his or her karma. In other words, the fact that one is born into a certain caste is an outcome of one's past deeds in an earlier incarnation. Thus members of high castes have no reason to feel that they are being unduly over-privileged, as the perks of their caste status in this life are just rewards for their good deeds in their past ones. That this book view has received tremendous ovation in literary circles is not surprising. As the authors of these texts and their believers come from upper castes, what they say and write quickly passes on to academic work.

Nevertheless, the difference between the book view and what actually happens on the ground is quite remarkable and must be attended to. Not only do different castes have different hierarchical elaborations, but in addition, those castes which currently find themselves in extremely humiliating and subordinate positions refuse to accept the theory of karma either, especially when it comes to caste ordering. This makes sense. If they were to acknowledge that their subjugated caste position today is an outcome of misdeeds in their past life (or lives), then they alone are responsible for their degradation. They would then have to accept the Brahmanical dictum that they are indeed made of base substances, stand by the Brahmanical ordering of the caste hierarchy, and a hundred other deprivations that they are burdened with. All this without a murmur. This is indeed how the upper castes would like the lower castes to behave, but evidence around us points to the contrary.

Throughout history there have been caste revolts and caste mobility. From the emergence of Rajput and Gujara-Pratihara kingdoms in medieval India, and the rise of the Jats from the thirteenth century onwards, to the assertion of Izhavas and later of Mahars in the modern period, there is ample evidence to the effect that people do not take their low-caste status lying down. In medieval India again, the entire Bhakti movement lasted several centuries. This could not have happened if the Brahmanical-textual view was universally acknowledged by all in the caste system. Nor would contemporary India be witness to instances of caste wars, Dalit uprisings, and demands for preferential politics. The fact that we see all this unrest around us in the name of caste should amply demonstrate that Brahmanical orthodoxy has only a few takers. And yet, when it comes to theorizing about the caste system it is the book view that tends to dominate.

So deep rooted is the Brahmanical version of the caste system in academic circles that it really requires an empirical jolt to shake it loose. This is exactly what I experienced in 1979 in South Gujarat when a poor Dubla grandmother told me that she was in fact a Rathod Rajput. When I asked her to explain she gave me a long account of her caste origins. Several hundred years ago an ancestor of hers lost a major war and his kingdom, because he was betrayed by his trusted advisor, who belonged to a low caste. After his victory the low-caste traitor occupied the throne and forced his earlier benefactor into a subjugation. My informant, however, was quite sure that a day would come when the Dublas would be able to assert themselves and regain their rightful status in society. This may not be the Dubla story everywhere in Gujarat, but this was certainly what my old Dubla respondent and her family deeply believed.

This story has a few important characteristics, the relevance of which struck me much later. The first is the obvious denial of a prevalent belief in the region that Dublas are made of low-caste material. The second is that the fall from grace was not because of a willful misdeed. Finally, it is not as if the story that I heard denied that low castes do, and perhaps even should, exist—it just stated that the Dublas simply do not belong there. Finally, the sting in the tail! Is it not possible then that all those who strut about wearing their high-caste status indeed have very lowly and unbecoming origins?

This encounter nearly twenty years ago led me to wonder how many other low castes have elevated opinions about their caste origins. The enquiry first took me to the works of British administrators like Hunter, Risley and Enthoven, who recorded a large number of caste origin tales. A new world was revealed to me as I read account after account of those who are customarily called 'low' castes denying their lowly pedigree. Sometimes they said they were Brahmans of a certain kind, on many occasions they claimed Kshatriya (or warrior) status, and frequently their origin myths also suggested that they were the creations of the gods—usually Lord Shiva.

From then on whenever I went on fieldwork I made it a point to ask the so-called untouchables about their origin tales. And each time, unfailingly, I would hear a story that was in stark opposition to the orthodox view. It was not as if members of these poorer castes launched forth into tales of their origin the moment they were asked. It took a lot of persuasion for they wanted to be sure that they would not be ridiculed for what they had to say about their caste antecedents. Like the first Dubla account, these stories too detailed their fall from earlier positions of supremacy. It happened either on account of lost wars, chance misfortune, a little carelessness sometimes, or, as was very often the case, because of deceit. It was not as if these origin tales made the claim that the concerned castes were a rung or two higher on the caste ladder in the past. Far from it: they were always seen as being way on top.

The Kahars, a backward caste of central Bihar, actually trump upper castes in the way they use the Purusa symbol to elevate themselves above the Brahmans. According to the *Purusasukta* legend (also appears as an appendix to the *Rig Veda*) the Brahmans and Kshatriyas emerged from the head and shoulders, respectively, of Purusa, the primeval being. Consequently they merit high-caste status. The same legend goes on to say that the lowly Shudras deservedly occupy a subordinate position because they were born from Purusa's feet. Now the Kahar story presents an interesting twist to all this. The Kahars claim that they are descendants of the lunar dynasty, and that the moon is no less than the eye of Purusa. The corollary, quite clearly, is that in physical and intellectual aspects the Kahars are made up of substances more subtle and refined than the Brahmans, let alone the Kshatriyas.

By now I was quite clear that the reason why the orthodox caste view has such staunch votaries in intellectual circles is because we tend to suspend judgement when it comes to evaluating the intellectual systems of people who are not quite like us. If all of us, intellectuals in India, and elsewhere, were to introspect about our identities we too would be most unwilling to accord higher status to those from different national, cultural, religious or linguistic backgrounds. If we are not ready to accept that people of other provenances can be intrinsically superior to us, why should we assume that the so-called low-caste Hindus should routinely genuflect to upper-caste mythologies that degrade them? This book is not just a quarrel over alternative ways of viewing the caste system. I would also like it to be judged as an attempt at intersubjective social anthropology which self-consciously de-exoticizes the 'other'.

All this prompted me to return to a serious study of Louis Dumont's *Homo Hierarchicus*. This is because I think Dumont systematized the traditional view on caste best, and with great sophistication. This in turn led me to read Marx and Marxism, with special reference to the relation between culture and structure, and of course, to Claude Lévi-Strauss, who is unsurpassed on the theory of superstructures. I can only thank Louis Dumont for all this. Without his work, against which I have tilted for the most part in this book, my understanding of sociological and anthropological theory, would have been even more inadequate.

More specifically, I took a long, hard look at theories of stratification and differentiation. I now realize that stratification and differentiation really complement each other. There is no hierarchy without difference, and every difference implies a hierarchy. This is a lesson I also learnt from the various caste origin tales I had come across. Talcott Parsons too was illuminating in this respect. According to Parsons to give value is to admit hierarchy. I think this is a brilliant observation, scintillating in its utter simplicity. How else can one give value to anything without at the same time devaluing something else? This is how hierarchy, of the most minimal type, perhaps, but hierarchy nevertheless, is inescapable with every judgement of value. Niklas Luhmann, a true disciple of Talcott Parsons, takes this understanding further. While stratification is generally about inequality, it is also true that each stratum is internally characterized by equality. He called this feature *isonomia*, where internal equality presupposes 'inequality with respect to other strata of society'. (Luhmann 1982: 234)

The temptation to understand the caste system in historical terms is too strong to resist. An anthropologist is warned strongly against entering the realm of distant history. I should say conjectural history, for that is exactly how interpretations of ancient material and records seem to most field-oriented sociologists and anthropologists. History can be, however, very insightful even if we self-consciously resist being carried away by it. Most of us usually foray into history like headhunters. We survey a limited area of received knowledge, search for evidence of the kind we like to hear, and then impale such 'facts' and bring them home to the social anthropologist, as fresh food for thought. I too have done just that.

My initial urge to go historical was prompted by the desire to examine the difference between varna and jati. Too often the relation between the two is dismissed as one between the imagined and the real. Marx's study, of 'Oriental' societies proved very useful here as did the works of later Marxists on the subject. I tend to agree with Marx for I believe that for anything to be imagined with such durability over huge stretches of time, there must be something more to it than just an interesting thought. Consequently, when I link varna to the Asiatic mode of production, I do so advisedly for I am also aware that the existence of varna classification was a way of looking at the whole without necessarily assuming that there were only four occupational specializations in ancient India. But the more exciting part is to figure out how culture and structure interact with one another. Or, to put it in a language that makes most people blush these days, what is the relationship between the material base and ideas? Between infrastructure and superstructure? This is where I think it is particularly useful to conjoin Marxism with the Lévi-Straussian version of structuralism, without, however, conflating the two.

An historical excursus on caste cannot but also make one strongly aware of how dependent the jati system is on a closed, localized natural economy. For castes to survive as part of a system, and not just as a number of substantiated isolated identities, a feudal-like social structure is a paramount requisite. Yet not all closed, feudal societies give birth to castes. History again helps in putting in some of the fine contingent points that may have urged Hindu society along to adopt the full-blown caste system. Seen historically the caste system does not appear as pure ideology either. It is apparent that caste mobility and change, conflict and dissension, have characterized Indian history from the earliest of times. All this helps to 'normalize' Hindu society and ideology and prevent it from appearing too distant and exotic.

The central thesis of this book lies in chapters three and five. In these chapters I elucidate the importance of looking at castes as discrete categories which then allow for the formation of multiple hierarchies. These caste hierarchies share many things in common and overlap significantly. For instance, the Rajput hierarchy and the Brahman hierarchy would unanimously place the so-called untouchables at the bottom of the pile. These two hierarchical formulations might also agree that the merchant, or Baniya, occupies slot number three. The dispute between the Brahman and Rajput would then be: which of them occupies the premier position. If we accept, for the time being, that castes are discrete categories, that they have enough diacritics and substance within them to stand independently, then it would be unwise to logically limit the number of possible models to two—viz., the Brahman and the Kshatriya ones. Even if there is a paucity of evidence in extant literature about other models of caste emulation and mobility, we cannot ignore the Baniya variant. If the Baniya variant can be accepted it is possible there may be others too, if not now, perhaps in the future! It is not all that difficult to imagine the Baniya model as a real possibility. Baniyas are proud of themselves and clearly abjure a Kshatriya meat-eating, animal-sacrificing life style. Today, with large parts of India going very commercial, it is not uncommon to find the Baniya model of caste emulation in evidence. Some of that has been discussed in the chapter entitled 'Brahman, Baniya, Raja'.

The primary reason for emphasizing the discrete character of caste is because without such an understanding it is impossible to understand caste conflict, caste politics and caste mobilization today. It is true that such things happened in the past as well, but because pre-modern history moved at a glacial pace, ideologies hardened even before the transformations were completed. Today we can no longer ignore the plentitude of evidence on caste tensions, and indeed on social dynamism too, in the subcontinent. Against this background it appears quite unreal to still rely on the Brahmanical version of an unchanging India, wedded to karma and the doctrine of *sunya*, or nothingness.

If orthopraxy is what people do, then on most occasions there is a great gulf between it and orthodoxy. This is where the notion of the 'invention of tradition' comes in. This invention does not begin with pure introspection over thought, or *doxa*, but justifies emergent practices made necessary by a host of pressing contingent factors, in the name of tradition. Caste politics and mobilizations in India today force traditional forms of thought to yield new meanings in order to justify social action dictated by contemporary secular interests. This is why it is possible for strange bedfellows like Ahirs, Jats and Gujars to come together in a caste block, or for Kshatriyas aligning with Harijans and Muslims to form the well-known KHAM front, and so on. In each case it is not caste logic but the force of secular interests that bring these castes together for political reasons. They would still not inter-dine, and any suggestion that they intermarry would be met with horror, incredulity and, perhaps, even violence.

Chapters three and five could stand on their own but they would do better with theoretical and conceptual supports. This is why it is important to begin our study with a somewhat lengthy examination of the theory of social stratification. This I do in chapter two only to show the close relation between hierarchy and difference. In order to flesh out this distinction, it is necessary to detail the divergence between open and closed systems of stratification. Only then can the dynamism between the two be understood, as also the play between hierarchy and difference. No society today can be characterized as being entirely closed, yet there are many societies where the ideology of a closed society is still not a historical relic. India is certainly one such society and the manner in which the caste system is constantly manipulated for sectional and personal advantages is good enough reason to examine the relationship between closed and open systems of stratification in some detail.

This point is buttressed in chapter five by examining election results in three regions of India and matching them with caste figures. If caste loyalties are so unswerving and rigid as they are claimed to be then surely they should manifest themselves in elections. Contrary to popular beliefs, there is just no correlation between caste numbers and voting results. What needs to be pointed out in this connection is that there is hardly any region in India where any one caste predominates. There are a few places in Bihar where the Yadavs, or Ahirs, make about 20 per cent of the population. But in most of what passes off as areas under Yadav hegemony they only constitute 10-15 per cent of the total population. Likewise, in constituencies considered to be Jat strongholds the Jats are rarely more than 6 per cent of the population. I point out at some length that if caste loyalty and the hegemony of Brahmanism were all that strong then electoral fortunes would not swing as widely as they do in India today.

This book ends with a plea for de-exoticizing the 'other'. I hope that the interrogation of caste so far has given enough reason to entertain the view that what seems distant and unfamiliar can be made familiar through empathy. By sharing our common humanity, and by letting *imagination* guide our fieldwork, we can move on to a different realm of sociological analysis. Now no longer do exotic items interest us simply by their otherness. Instead, they challenge us to see human universals in spite of their manifest strangeness. Belief in a common humanity begins with an act of faith. Facts as they present themselves impress us with their obvious diacritics. The temptation to stop here is great. But to be able to record in painstaking detail the many facets of what is new and different is instantly rewarding. The popular mind loves to separate the world on a perennial basis and a detailed account of pure difference feeds into that mindset straight away. All differences are made to appear as if they are naturally ordained. This is why when the specialist insists only on recording details of strangeness then the work falls in line with popular constructions of reality. Prejudices get a certain respectability, for now an academic work can be cited in its favour. Consequently, humanity takes a little beating each time a territory is ceded to unexamined biases.

Look a little closer and these same diacritics which were so startlingly different at first sight assume a new meaning. These 'trophy facts' now come through as evidence of the universal human mind straining to make the most of specific histories and contingencies. The facts then lose their otherness. The call of the hour cannot be just for sympathy; that is easily done—it is no challenge at all. Sympathy and benevolence are attitudes of superiority. But to be able to empathize and stride alongside others requires an immersion in imagination.

In course of time this imagination is duly rewarded. Only then can we all stand within the arc that humanity traces across cultures, peoples and climes. Only then will we realize that we share the same failings, the same talents, and the same drive to make the best of a given situation.

The idea of human universals has a long history in anthropology. It was first linked with the evolutionists and later by relativists. The problem with the evolutionary version was that it assumed that certain cultures had already climbed the ladder of development and that other cultures would follow but after a considerable lapse of time. As things stood, therefore, some cultures were superior to others, which made empathy across humanity difficult. If other cultures were strange then they had yet to grow. The pressure to see them in us was postponed till the hour of universal history finally brought about a unity of races and cultures.

The relativist view of human universals was problematic in a different kind of way. Each culture was supposed to have its own standards of validation. As these standards were largely incommensurable it was improper to judge one culture from the standpoint of another culture. This relativist position certainly helped to chip away at racist ideologies of cultural superiority. But while it made all cultures equal it was difficult to empathize with the 'other'.

From Bronislaw Malinowski onwards, through Evans-Pritchard, and finally with Claude Lévi-Strauss, the understanding of a common humanity has received more concentrated attention. The emphasis is now on the capacity of mind and not the content of mind. As I try and elucidate in chapters three and nine, the real challenge in anthropology is to see the 'them' in us, and make the unfamiliar accessible in familiar terms. But before we get to that, a little hard-nosed discussion on the theories of stratification and difference is called for.

2

Social Stratification: Hierarchy and Difference

The Scope of Social Stratification: Order and Mobility

There are all kinds of utopias that people have imagined and written about. But by far the most common kind is a society based on complete equality: no division between the rich and the poor, no suffering from want or malnutrition, and a high level of fraternal goodwill characterizing relations between people. What these utopias forget to mention is that equality does not mean sameness. If that were to be the case then most utopias would be dreadfully boring places to live in. In a true utopia people should be equal but also different. Hunters, fishermen, inventors, musicians, doctors, would be practising their craft, but without any feeling of superiority or inferiority. This would demand a complete transformation of sociology and anthropology as we know it. Among other things, such a society would also make the study of social stratification completely redundant.

From what we know, with the aid of sociology, anthropology and history, it seems more or less indubitable that nearly everywhere in the real world there is stratification of one kind or the other. For a long time it was believed that tribal hunting and gathering societies were still innocent of stratification. We now know a little better. These societies may not have such deep notches in their stratificatory systems as the more developed agricultural or industrial societies have, but stratification exists there as well. There are ranked orders separating cadets, young adults, mature married people and elders. Then there is always that ubiquitous divide between men and women. It is often argued that in such hunting and gathering societies it is not so much inequality as difference that is being exhibited. The separation between men and women in these societies is not so much one of inequality as of difference. There is no unanimity on this theme, but nevertheless it is an interesting point. It alerts us to the fact that hierarchy and difference ought to be considered together but as two separate concepts, in studies of social stratification.

Most contemporary societies, whether developed or developing, give evidence of a high order of stratification at various levels and of various kinds. There is the question of inequality of course, that looms large in much of our thinking of stratification, but there is also the issue of cultural diversity. The prevalence of tensions between diverse languages, religions, colours and sects arise because of the conflicting ways by which each community wants to rank the others in real operational terms. Unlike our utopia people are not always prepared to let differences flourish for their own sake without hierarchizing and labelling them in terms of good and bad, refined and crude, or civilized and uncivilized.

It should also be borne in mind that the categories employed in the study of social stratification are the creations of the analyst. These categories may sometimes coincide with popular concepts, but most often they do not. For example, the term class is used in everyday language, but a student of social stratification would give it a meaning quite different from what would be a lay rendition of it. A sociological treatment of class would differ depending on the scholar's theoretical predisposition—Marxist, Weberian or functionalist (Ortner 1991: 168).

Even if the sociologist, or the anthropologist, gives a technical meaning to concepts such as class or status, the material of analysis comes from how people interact with one another, and how they conceive of the divergences in their station and in their life chances. Occasionally, an entire chart of stratification might be based entirely upon how people rank themselves and others (Warner, Meeker and Eels 1949), but the ultimate choice of categories that the scholar or analyst would employ must be succoured by a well-thought-out theoretical rationale. This would hold true whether or not the data comes from subjective and 'warm' facts (such as what people think of each other and of themselves) or from impersonal and 'cold' facts (like the amount of land owned, or money in the bank). The material, in either case, would undergo self-conscious theoretical and analytical transformation at the hands of the sociologist, or anthropologist.

Social stratification is not just about categorizing or differentiating people into diverse strata. That would be a purely mechanical exercise, unworthy of conscientious sociological analysis. Though social stratification most obviously stratifies a given population, the principles of stratification tell us a lot more. Properly understood, social stratification provides an analytical basis for comprehending both social order as well as social mobility. Looked at this way, an understanding of social stratification tells us about the principles of social stasis and of social dynamics at the same time. In this sense it offers a unique window to comprehend the liveliness and vivacity of social reality. To be able to see dynamics in what appears as a static ranked order, and, by the same token, to be able to discern order in flux, surely constitutes the greatest challenges in any disciplinary pursuit of knowledge.

Natural Differences and Sociological Categories

There are various criteria on the basis of which people are stratified. However, not all of them are of sociological significance. A sure way of testing the validity of a study on social stratification is to ascertain the extent to which it tells us about social order and of social mobility. If a form of stratification tells us nothing on these counts then it has little relevance for either sociology or for social anthropology. For instance, to distinguish and categorize people on the basis of height or weight or the length of their hair has no sociological salience at all. This should not give the impression that perceived natural differences have no sociological significance. We all know how colour was used as an important aspect of social stratification in apartheid South Africa. Even though racism may have been dismantled as official policy all over the world, and its scientific pretensions debunked repeatedly, the sad truth is that in reality, colour and racial categories still exercise a powerful influence over the minds of many. Consequently, race-inspired thinking affects the way people of different colours relate to and interact with one another. This is why distinctions based on popular conceptions of race cannot be ignored in studies of social stratification.

The relationship between natural differences and social stratification is thus not an uncomplicated one. There are some natural differences that have no sociological significance, and then there are others that are laden with sociological valency. The fact is that natural differences by themselves do not naturally make for categories of social stratification. If some natural differences, such as colour, are highlighted, it is also true that in the same society there are many other natural differences that are not. The reasons then for emphasizing colour as a potent category of stratification do not lie in nature as much as they do in the specific character of that society that considers colour to be significant.

The odd thing is that very often there are no natural differences that can be discerned in any tangible fashion, yet members of a society may believe that such differences in fact do exist. The caste system is one such example. Though there is no way by which those in a caste society can actually distinguish unfailing natural markers of difference, yet they justify caste stratification on the ground that different castes are built of different natural substances (Marriot and Inden 1977).

We have, therefore, two diametrically opposite ways by which nature is forced by culture to act on its behest. In the case of race, a specific physical difference is picked on to substantiate, justify and perpetuate economic and social inequalities among people. But in caste societies where no natural differences can be discerned by the naked eye, it is imagined that such differences exist and elaborate care is taken so that the substances that constitute each caste do not co-mingle. Hence the elaborate rules prohibiting inter-caste dining, or inter-caste marriage.

Stratification does not depend solely on real or putative natural differences. Class, status, and power are some of the other axes on which stratification takes place. These could be considered as purely social categories as they are substantiated on markers that have nothing to do with either nature or with natural differences. Even so, every sociologist should be sensitive to how these eminently social features tend to be naturalized at the popular level. We thus come across seemingly natural justifications as to why poor people deserve to be poor, or why those who follow a different lifestyle have a natural propensity to do so. By acknowledging the persuasiveness of such ideological justifications for social categorizations we realize the passion that is expended to either maintain the status quo or to overthrow it. In a later section we shall have occasion to return to this very important aspect of social stratification. For now let us move on to a closer examination of the kinds of strata that social stratification is concerned with.

Hierarchy and Difference: Social Statics and Dynamics

It was mentioned earlier that a test of relevancy for the categories of stratification is the extent to which they contribute to our understanding of social order and change. If this be the case then the understanding of social stratification cannot be limited to ranked gradations whether they be of power or wealth, status, purity, pollution, or colour. This is because such ranks tell us only about the order and very little regarding the potentialities for social mobility and changes within and of that order. To be able to factor this element into the studies of social change it is necessary to think in terms of differences as well.

Differences can be said to exist when it is difficult to rank diversities. Wealth, income, status, and even power can be ranked in terms of there being more or less of a single variable. But there are other forms of strata differentiation that cannot be hierarchized or ranked in this fashion. For instance if an attempt were made to rank different languages or religions or aesthetic preferences in hierarchical terms then it would not only be incorrect but also very offensive to many. Differences of this kind are incommensurable and are not amenable to ranking in terms of possessing more or less of a particular attribute. As languages, or religions, or cultures, are incommensurably different, they are logically of equal status. For this reason when attempts are made to hierarchize them, as in sectarian mobilizations, one is immediately alerted to the power dimension, as well as to the unbridled prejudice, that always accompany such drives.

Social stratification thus includes both hierarchy and difference. If one were to talk only of hierarchy then one would be partial to order. If, on the other hand, only differences were to be emphasized then the social imperatives of order would not be appreciated. Instead—change, instability and dynamism would become the focal points of research. That studies of social stratification are usually conceived in terms of the geographical model (Béteille 1977: 129) has limited our understanding of how stratification systems undergo change, and also of the tensions that exist within any given stratificatory order. When classes, for instance, are seen along the geographical model then we only observe the passive layering of crust upon crust. Our attention is riveted primarily to the quantitative dimension of variance between different classes. This quantitative factor is premised on a certain kind of unanimity. So there is a general acceptance by those included within the hierarchy that the positioning within accurately reflects the criterion on which the gradations are based. It is impossible to argue that a person with a lower income belongs to a more affluent class than the person whose income is much higher. There can hardly be a disagreement on matters of this kind. Likewise, a manager has more power than the foreman, and the foreman has more power than the worker on the shop floor. Much as one may chafe at this kind of power hierarchy, its existence cannot be denied.

The fact that posting such quantitative hierarchies is possible in some instances sets the tone for the establishment of social order. Once drawn into a system of stratification which employs such quantifiable criteria of stratification there is little scope to challenge hierarchical rankings from within. It would be absurd for workers to say that they have more power than the managers. Likewise, it would, be nonsensical for a beggar to claim more wealth than a millionaire. While it is possible to arrive at such a consensus in hierarchies of this kind, it is nevertheless also true that there are often disputes in the relative rankings of grades that are contiguous to one another. This is especially so in the case of rankings with respect to power or status, but not quite as obvious in rankings of wealth. This is primarily because the criterion in the case of wealth is so easily and ostensibly quantifiable.

There can, nevertheless, be social mobility within a ranked order provided it is one that is allowed for by the hierarchy in question. The gradation based on class in a capitalist society is considered to be one such open system of stratification. Care should be taken not to conflate all class-based hierarchies as belonging to an open system. In feudal societies class boundaries were firm and mobility across them often invited severe reprisals. This is where the distinction between open and closed stratificatory systems becomes relevant.

Open and Closed Systems of Stratification: Variations in Mobility Strategies

In an open system of stratification mobility within is an accepted property of the system. On the other hand, in a closed system of stratification, mobility is strongly discouraged. In such cases determined ideological wars have to be waged by the aspirants in their bid for upward mobility. In doing so the basis on which low rank was accorded earlier has to be delegitimized. This would imply that a hitherto low-ranking class must necessarily step out of its location within the ranked hierarchy and energize an ideology of difference in order to justify and legitimize its quest for upward mobility. In an open system of stratification it is possible to move up by simply obeying the internal order of rank differentiation.

An open stratificatory system may have a fixed and firm hierarchy, but individuals can go up, or even down the hierarchy. For example, in a modern bureaucratic establishment a person can rise from being a clerk to a manager, a manager to an executive director, and so on. Biographically, there are no reasons why a person cannot aspire to the highest position if the stated qualifications required to fill a position in a hierarchy are satisfied. In a closed system of stratification, however, a person may be strong and brave and yet, because of the accident of birth, not considered as a rightful member of the warrior class.

Debarring mobility within a system of stratification is possible mainly when ascriptive criteria (for example: caste, colour, religion etc) are employed as the basis for ranking. This being the case it is quite clear that the issue of whether a system of stratification is open or closed also tells us whether this system is one that draws sustenance from quantitative hierarchies or from qualitative differences. In a closed system of stratification the first principle of distinction is a qualitative one which is then sought to be hierarchized. Hierarchization does not come naturally where distinctions are qualitative to begin with. When the differences between the various estates, or castes, or races are elaborated there is no scope for movement from one race to the other, or from one caste to the other. Thus when these castes or races or estates are hierarchized, the criterion of hierarchy has to be imposed from outside and can have no justifications within.

The significance of this is not easy to grasp as there is a pervasive belief that the ordering of estates or races is primarily hierarchical. It is because such a view has been prevalent for a long time that the nature of social mobility within closed and open systems of stratification has not been fully appreciated. Once it is realized that closed systems of stratification are premised on differences first which are hierarchized later, then that explains to a great extent why mobility in such systems is always so strongly ideological in its thrust. It has never quite occurred to most of us that the march of upward mobility in a closed system of stratification must wade through strong headwinds that are built on differences. These differences, once again, are basically incommensurable and unrankable in character.

This point needs to be constantly reinforced if a

comprehensive understanding of social stratification is to be arrived at. In a closed system of stratification the hierarchy does not have the complicity of all those who are deemed to be within it. In an open system of stratification, as the basis for the hierarchy is quantitative, one's inclusion at whichever level is above dispute. The only way it is possible to dispute a quantitative hierarchy is to reject it entirely and oppose it in the language of difference. To make the claim of being rich or powerful without actually occupying these positions would only be self-delusionary. But it is always possible to reject the power of the rich or of the powerful by claiming alternative standards of morality, probity and social order. To do this the language of difference needs to be invoked.

Before we go further down this road, it is necessary to take stock of our earlier claim that stratification must include both hierarchy and difference. This is because it is not just a quantifiable ranked order that is being discussed. Very often, ranked orders are imposed on what is inherently incapable of being ranked. The reality is that differences posit logically equal categories whose intrinsic relationship is horizontal in character. To then force them into a vertical hierarchy requires an extraneous agency—which is usually that of political power. Blacks can be characterized as occupying a lower station not because black is an inherently inferior colour, but because in a racist society the White population control power and use colour as an ideological weapon of subjugation. Likewise, in the caste system, or in the division between estates, there is nothing inherently superior in belonging to one estate or to the other, in belonging to the merchant caste or to the warrior caste. Logically these castes are separate and equal, but it is political power that decides which castes will be superior to which other castes, or which estate shall have precedence over other estates.

We find the justification for including differences and not just hierarchy in our study because it helps us to understand how closed systems of stratification are different from open ones, and how mobilization strategies in one must necessarily diverge from the other. As the divergence between open and closed systems of stratification lies primarily at the level of mobility the conceptual distinction between hierarchy and difference is crucial. It tells us at once why mobility is far from routine in closed systems of stratification, but built into open stratificatory systems. Hierarchy and difference help us to be faithful to the raison d'être of different kinds of stratification and at the same time elucidate their divergent mobility paths.

Open and closed systems of stratification are not always discrete historical stages but can be closely intertwined at the empirical level. This is because in every open system of stratification there is a point beyond which mobility is made extremely difficult. As this is often in defiance of the system, so obviously, at this point, elements of difference have entered the picture. It is often believed that closed systems of stratification give way to open ones as we move on from feudalism to modern industrial capitalist economies. There is no doubt that modern industrial societies are what they are because of the tremendous dynamism and social mobility they allow. Even Marx acknowledged this enormously liberating role of capitalism. Yet as there are always imperfections in every system, as there are always attempts to protect one's bailiwick from competition, and as there is always the search for security in an insecure world, attempts are constantly made to ensure a closure in what is legally and formally an open system.

By the same token, closed systems of stratification have also witnessed tremendous upheavals and dynamism, but these have usually gone unnoticed because of the glacial pace of change. In contemporary times, however, this change can no longer be concealed largely because of the dominating forces of modernization and industrialization. Modernization has not only brought machines but, more crucially, changed relations between people. This is why the presence of such contemporaneous forces has given a fillip to mobilization within hitherto closed systems of stratification. The most important effect has been the opening up of the village economy and the concomitant freedom of the lower order from economic bondage to rural oligarchs, or to members of the ancient regime.

That modernization and the breakdown of the natural economy have enabled communities, classes and castes to move out of earlier categories of stratification does not mean that these earlier strata have lost their ideological force or sentimental power. Caste identities are still very strong even as castes are no longer locally confined. Legal justifications for upward caste mobility may be drawn from the liberal language of political democracy, but the emotional charge behind such drives is derived from strong caste loyalties. The fact however remains that caste mobility is now much more of a routine affair than it was ever in the past. What one must then pay attention to in any concrete study of stratification is how the open and closed systems are played off against each other. This does not deny the fact that one form of stratification is probably dominant at any one point of time in any society. It could, however, well be the case that different sectors of a society may well diverge from one another in this respect. In which case it becomes all the more important to see the interaction between open and closed stratificatory systems and not confine them to separate slots in any empirical investigation.

Caste Mobility: Re-Examining the Renouncer

India and America are usually seen as exemplifying closed and open systems of stratification respectively. Caste in India and the open, mobile class structure of America are paradigm cases of the two contrasting systems of stratification. Though the caste system is a prime example of a closed form of an ascription-based system of stratification, it is not as if mobility did not ever occur in Indian history. But every time this happened it aroused great deal of opposition and resentment from the entrenched powerful castes. The Rajputs and the Gujar Pratiharas between the eighth and the tenth centuries, and the Marathas and Jats between the thirteenth and the eighteenth centuries, fought their way to the top by conducting a series of wars. Warfare was a route to upward movement in the caste system. Protest movements also gave impetus to and facilitated claims to a higher position in the caste hierarchy. Some of them were straight caste-based confrontations, but more often a religious sect emerged that promised salvation by breaking caste norms. In each case, however, the existing social arrangements were threatened and delegitimized by such attempts at caste mobility.

In the open system of stratification by classes, mobility is an accepted characteristic of the system. The movement up and down, and even horizontally, does not challenge the ideological basis of the hierarchy though there may be some resistance to particular individuals making it to a higher grade. This brings to our attention yet another interesting contrast between open and closed stratification systems. When mobility is an accepted feature of the hierarchy, then it is individuals who move up or down or horizontally within the system. When mobility is not an usual feature in the hierarchy, then it is groups, or categories that generally move in unison. This is because, in closed systems of stratification hierarchy is forced on to incommensurable differences between communities, castes, races or religions. To reinforce what was said earlier, in such cases what are logically separate and equal categories are hierarchized by the force of political power. This explains why in such a situation individual mobility will just not do. An individual is never a single person, but a representative of an ascriptive community. An individual is thus not a person in his or her own right, but owes membership loyalties to a larger category.

It is often said that Hinduism allows for individual mobility provided one becomes a renouncer (Dumont 1960). Hindu society thus holds a renouncer in the highest esteem regardless of the person's actual caste origin. Though there is something tempting about this postulate there is really a logical obfuscation here. A renouncer does not climb up the caste hierarchy after renouncing the world, but becomes a true 'outcaste', and literally moves over to another world where caste rules do not apply. Indeed the renouncer is deemed to be sociologically dead. On occasions even funerary rites are performed to signify the renouncer's departure from the quotidian world. In this sense a renouncer leaves the world and cannot return to it. What is more, a renouncer, by virtue of having renounced, cannot influence or prejudice the functioning of the caste order with all its political implications.

But all this is legend and not what is really practised. Renouncers are known to be actively involved in this-worldly affairs and often start movements that promise an alternative social order towards a parallel society. In such situations the renouncer is opposed by those who abide by the rules of a caste society. Many Bhakti saints in medieval India faced this kind of resistance. The renouncer may have seen the light and may have ambitions to lead a mass of devotees and followers to a caste-free world, but it is not as if the renouncer can lead from the front. The renouncer in such cases is a subversive agent.

Alternatively, evidence from both anthropology and history reveals that the renouncer does not always give up being involved with this-worldly affairs, and, in fact, actually thrives on patronage from political patrons. In ancient India the Kalamukha Sannyasins 'claimed Brahman status and took the name of pandita deva, and were often the defenders of the *varnasrmadharma* (or the caste order—D.G.)'. (Ibid: 85.) The Kapalika sect too had its own patrons that allowed it to survive and win adherents in a hotly-contested atmosphere (ibid: 75). A closer look reveals that these renouncers were technically not renouncers at all for they often upheld the caste system quite overtly, and, in addition, were closely tied to the compulsions of power and politics.

In ancient myths too there are revered sages like Dronacharya and Bhishma Pitamaha who may have had the outer appearances of renouncers but were deeply implicated in the politics of their times. Perhaps it is also important to distinguish between the renouncer and the ascetic as Romila Thapar advises (ibid: 64). The ascetic is constantly venerated and lauded in sacerdotal texts and more 'frequently described in literature than encountered in reality.' (Ibid.) An ascetic leads a life of loneliness and austerity and is lost to his family, kin and friends. The ascetic is a lonely figure working out a charter of individual salvation. The renouncers live in collectives and form sects, and they are personages of considerable repute in this-worldly caste society. Such renouncers are also popularly known as sannyasins.

From history if we move on to anthropology we again find sufficient instances along the same lines. Richard Burghart successfully pointed out from his anthropological field studies how certain sannyasin sects are closely integrated with the caste system, and indeed use it as an organizing principle of their monastic life. The Dashnami Sannyasins only recruit the twice-born, clean castes to their sects (Burghart 1996: 290). The Ramanandi sect is somewhat more liberated from caste restrictions in that it admits people from all castes. Within the sect, however, caste rules of commensality are observed so that the caste status of the sannyasin is not compromised (ibid: 291, see also 151). In addition many of these sects are not just hostile towards Muslims (ibid: 126), but also carry out violent and hostile campaigns against each other (ibid: 126–28). Surely, these so-called men of religion can be considered as far from having really renounced the world and all its seductions. On the other hand, the ascetics who live in isolation are so few and so distant that the notion that they have won social acclaim by renouncing caste is hard to realize in practice. It is true however that sannyasin renouncers have tremendous social appeal and prestige. But as they have never really given up 'this world' it would be incorrect to say that their status gets elevated because they have opted out of the caste system with all its implications. The fact that the sannaysins and the ascetics have a similar outward appearance has led to a descriptive conflation of the two with rather unfortunate analytical consequences.

Class Mobility in Open Systems of Stratification: The Case of Class in America

In an open system of stratification a single variable must be held in common by all those included in the hierarchy. For example, if we take landownership, then the amount of land owned from zero acres upwards is placed in a hierarchy and in such cases this hierarchy is a continuous one. The gradations do not yield categorical distinctions from within. If we are to separate the upper-middle class from the lower-upper-middle class then it is done on analytical considerations that are not intrinsic to the hierarchy. Thus at one point anybody with fifty acres of land may be termed rich, and on other occasions twenty-five acres might be sufficient for a person to make the same grade. It all depends on what the analyst would like to do with the gradations, and accordingly distinctions and cut-off points are made within the hierarchy.

Sometimes a continuous hierarchy can be constructed by having a composite of a number of variables as in the Socio-Economic Status Indexes. Here a variety of factors like occupation, education, schooling, housing, source of income are considered for the purpose of constituting a quantifiable measurable scale. Once weightage is given to each of these variables such a scale is quite amenable to fine gradations. This is precisely what was accomplished by Lloyd Warner and his associates in a number of studies on social stratification in America. In their classic and oft-quoted work *Social Class in America*, Warner, Meeker and Eels constructed such a composite index and stratified the sample population into upper class, upper-middle class, lower-upper-middle class, upper-lower class, and lower-lower class (Warner, Meeker and Eels 1949:107). But one of the persistent criticisms against the Warner school of stratification is that the criterion or criteria for making these class distinctions remains unspecified. For instance, why should there not be a further elaboration of categories to include the lower-upper-lower class, or a middle-upper-class and so on?

In fact, composite socio-economic indexes such as the one employed by Warner can lead to a lot of disagreement among those studied and also amongst other scholars. Disputes arise because the values given to the variables are often contestable. For instance, there may be a lot of disagreement regarding what kind of weight should be assigned to diverse occupations. A self-employed plumber may take umbrage if slotted below an office clerk, a shopkeeper may not agree to being placed below a school teacher. Quite clearly, when weightage is given to what are inherently different and incommensurable entities, the basis for this weightage is being grafted from external sources even though the hierarchy has the semblance of continuity. If one were to rephrase the criticism against the socio-economic index studies of stratification, then it would perhaps be appropriate to say that such studies run into difficulties as differences are being forced into a hierarchy. The end result is, therefore, bound to be capricious.

If, on the other hand, the hierarchy is established on the basis of a single quantifiable variable, such as wealth, power, or land owned, there is hardly any scope for dissension. A study that emphasizes a hierarchy that is composed in terms of a factor whose distribution can be seen in terms of more or less, cannot be interested in studying social change, though there might be quite an active interest in social mobility, as with Warner (ibid). The emphasis is more upon order and not upon sources of dissension within that order. In this case all those in the hierarchy have something in common though some may have more of it than others. An open system gets complicated once elements of incommensurable differences are superimposed on it. Such incommensurabilities rigidify structures and thwart mobility.

This tells us why America is seen as such an ideal (almost paradigmatic) case of an open system of stratification. More than the industrially advanced Western, European nations, America takes great pride in the fact that it has undermined all the privileges and estates of the Old World. In America the unencumbered individual is supreme. This makes it the ideal locale for the presence of an open system of stratification. Further, it suggests that Americans ideologically acquiesce to this system of stratification for they essentially see themselves as being very similar to one another. It is on the basis of this presumed similarity that we can later talk about a graded hierarchy.

Continuous Hierarchies or Discrete Castes: Comparing the Systems

There are other graded hierarchies too which may not have the same kind of popular approbation. The caste system is often considered to be a graded hierarchy based on the purity-pollution scale (Dumont 1988).

This statement may seem quite unproblematic at a quick first sight, but it conceals many complications. Firstly, the hierarchy that the caste system posits can be seen as uniform and universal, provided one takes on the prejudices of the particular caste that is elaborating this hierarchy. The truth is that there is no agreement over who should occupy which position in the hierarchy. It is not as if the Brahmans are universally acknowledged in Hindu India to be the most superior community. There are powerful Kshatriya or warrior castes who consider themselves as the most superior castes (Hocart 1945: 31-35, see also Quigley 1993: 3), and belittle both the Brahman's status and occupation. (See Gupta 1997: 84-86.) Thus while there is an agreement that castes should be hierarchized on the basis of natural substances there is no agreement as to how these supposed 'coded substances' can be quantified along a gradational scale (Marriot and Inden 1977).

At this point it is important to proceed cautiously. To begin with, while there is an overall agreement that castes should be hierarchized there are strong disagreements regarding the positioning of jatis of the same status (Gupta 1992: 119-130). Even among Brahmans there is no consensus on the relative status of different Brahman castes (Quigley 1993: 62, Fuller 1984, Parry 1989: 89-91).

Further the scale that is always referred to in the case of the caste system is the one based on a putative purity-pollution hierarchy. This scale is itself problematic for it is understood differently in different contexts. When it comes to taking food there is a scale of purity that is often observed (Marriot 1959). But here again there is no unanimity between castes regarding who can take water or food from whom. Usually the implementation of such a hierarchy depends on political power and less on straight ideological acquiescence (Gupta 1992). When it is not a question of food or inter-dining then the hierarchy of purity is not so much in evidence as the distinction between us and the others. The 'others' in such cases are ranked in order of the degree of distaste from the point of view of the caste in question. In this case it is not a scale of purity that is being invoked but one of pure otherness. In fact it is also possible to say that in such circumstances what is more significant is that the unalterable character of the other be maintained more than anything else. If a gradation of the other occurs it is not from any practical point of view for neither occupations nor women are likely to be exchanged across caste boundaries.

The reason then why America has an open system of stratification whereas India's caste-based society has a closed one is because in the former there is an ideological acceptance of a certain degree of similarity (Lipset and Bendix 1957), whereas in the latter there is an enormous investment in keeping differences alive. Whenever differences dominate, the system tends to get closed. Contrarily, whenever there is an agreement over the possession of an attribute that can be quantitatively scaled one can see manifestations of an open system of stratification. Social mobility cannot be fully understood if studies on stratification only pay attention to hierarchy and not differences.

There is yet another advantage in emphasizing both hierarchy and difference while examining social stratification. As a continuous hierarchy in an open system demands and depends upon an agreement over a base-line similarity in that a certain attribute is possessed by all in the hierarchy except that some have more of it than others, there is no room for prejudice in the making of the ranked order. When, however, inherently incommensurable differences are placed in a ranked order we are immediately sensitized to the fact that the ordering is obeying a criterion that is imposed from outside. This imposition can only be an outcome of prejudice. When logically discrete and incommensurable entities are ranked then this always implies real or potential conflict and disagreement. It is this lack of accord that predisposes the stratification system towards being closed in character.

As differences are emphasized in closed systems of stratification, the group rather than the individual becomes the unit of mobility. For individuals to be mobile there must be an agreement on certain base-line similarities between them. Further, mobility is found to be justified when individuals acquire a higher quantum of a stated attribute. As the attribute itself is not being changed but is being graded any instance of social mobility does not damage the position of others in the hierarchy.

A gross demonstration of this can be seen when those who are sectarian claim that certain languages are inherently superior to other languages, or that certain religions are more civilized than others. An infinitely more subtle expression of prejudice, but it is prejudice nevertheless, is when it is calmly assumed that there is a clear, unanimous caste hierarchy based on the notion of purity and pollution. This ignores the vital reality of castes refusing to accept low status and claiming elevated origins of their own (Gupta 1992). That these non-Brahmanical texts have been ignored in the main has given the impression that castes can unproblematically be placed along a continuous hierarchy.

Any change in a closed system of ranking would automatically entail that some other group (or groups) lose status. This is a point that Murray Milner made very effectively when he said that status hierarchies are zero sum in character (Milner 1994: 29). When a group comes up in a closed system of stratification it must necessarily displace either in fact or in imagination the privileged and superior position of some other group or groups. For example when the Jats, or the Rajputs or the Marathas rose to ascendancy they displaced the earlier ruling castes in their respective regions. When a Harijan who is disparagingly called a Chamar, claims to belong to a Brahman caste there is a vicarious displacement of the position of the actual Brahmans and other better-off castes in the imaginings of this community. This imagining is not a lie, nor a pure fabrication. The claim to a superior Brahman status by Harijans is real as far as this community is concerned regardless of whether or not it can actually remise this status in practice. So for Harijans to claim Brahman status, somewhere in their imaginings, the Brahmans that are around must necessarily undergo some status diminution.

In caste conflicts which have been politicized this characteristic is plainly visible. The non-Brahman movement in both Maharashtra and Tamil Nadu was not simply for the upward mobility of the Maratha or the Mali or the Vellalla or the Thevar, or the Gowda castes, but also to undermine the status of the Brahmans in these provinces. In feudal societies the aspirations of powerful groups of hitherto subjugated people can only be realized by overthrowing the existing nobility, or by significantly undermining its status.

In an open system of stratification upward mobility

does not mean that somebody else must lose status as a consequence. The fact that such a movement take place with relative ease is again because it is at the level of the individual who is not marked by differences but positioned according to the degree to which the quantifiable attribute (that resides within the person) has been expressed. Ideologically such an open system of stratification must assume that people are all equal and that mobility occurs to the extent that people can realize their potential.

Status and Hierarchy: Impurities in Open Systems of Stratification

In closed systems of stratification it is assumed, on the contrary, that people are inherently different, which is why the notion of the upstart, the parvenu, and the social climber have such pejorative connotations. But an open system of stratification can also be held back by status considerations. Such status considerations are frequently placed on a hierarchy, but this again is a demonstration of prejudice more than anything else. Status distinctions are derived from lifestyle differences. Even in a modern society where there is a relative development of open systems of stratification it is not as if the issue of difference does not occur at all. Difference manifests itself in these societies in considerations of status. While such status markers do not have the obvious tag of being determined by birth, the qualities demanded are such that they are difficult to attain within a single lifetime. The emphasis now is not so much on the extent of education but in the cultivation of certain dispositions, like taste in music, in the classics, and the like (Bourdieu 1984). Status is marked on the basis of a prejudicial combination of those factors that best reflect the attainments and attributes of the superior communities. As Erving Goffman perceptively pointed out, an attribute of status snobbery can also be a deliberate and idiosyncratic elaboration of a routine aspect of everyday life (Goffman 1961). Thus, for example, table manners become very important as status considerations. How one eats a sandwich or pours out tea can indicate the status enjoyed by a person.

By imparting to such routine activities a certain style that is not generally known or prevalent a status group can set itself apart as being superior to the rest. Here again it is not a question of gradations. It is hard to grade the styles of eating a sandwich or drinking tea. Either one has the style or lacks it. When dispositions, habits and manners are cultivated to distance oneself from others this is not done on a continuous hierarchical scale but one that first emphasizes difference. Given this logic of status distinctions it would be incorrect, and, indeed prejudicial, to talk in terms of 'high' and 'low' culture, or in terms of crude and 'pedigreed culture' (Bourdieu 1984: 56-63). In Bourdieu, for example, what should have really remained as 'distinctions' are suddenly converted into a gradational scale thus sublating the fact that the variations were based in the first instance on 'differences'. That these differences have now been made to stand in a graded order is not a natural property of the system but has been introduced from without. Academics too are therefore susceptible to such slippages into prejudice. The scope and frequency of such prejudices can be reduced by realizing that hierarchies do not arise naturally out of differences.

Talcott Parsons said in *The Social System* that to give value to anything is to hierarchize at the same time. The truth of this statement can be gauged in studies of stratification, particularly in the understanding of closed systems of stratification. When a hierarchy is imposed after giving value to a difference then this hierarchy is very different from that of an open system. In an open system the continuous hierarchy accepts variations in the quantum of a similar attribute among a given population. When status considerations are introduced in an open classificatory system there is a normative mismatch. This can be again exemplified quite starkly by looking again at America.

Race relations in America are governed by status considerations of the kind that should not have been permitted in an open system of stratification. This is the essence of what Gunnar Myrdal once called the 'American dilemma'. On the one hand Americans freely admit that all are equal. This is in line with the American claim of an open system of stratification and equal opportunity of social mobility for all. At the same time there are strong attitudes of intolerance towards the Blacks. They are seen as inferior in culture, taste, and custom, by the White population. The inability of America to resolve this dilemma was what Myrdal's influential work was all about (Myrdal 1962).

Just as caste prejudices exist in spite of public declarations to the contrary, racism lurks in America even though it has been officially disbanded. As long as racism separates the Whites from the Blacks the chances of moving up the colour hierarchy will be severely restricted. The lighter-skinned Blacks may take some pride in their complexion, but when it comes to the category of colour a Black is always a Black. At one point there was an attempt to quantify this by saying that a person would be legally Black if it could be proved that one-sixty-fourth of his ancestry was Black.

This 'one drop rule' was legally quashed in the 1970s but sentiments of this order are quite dominant among Americans. The melting pot has done a good job as far as the White population of America is concerned, but as for the rest the 'mosaic' and the 'salad bowl' still function as lively metaphors.

The criteria for stratification, whether in an open or in a closed system have to be socially signified by a number of tangible markers. Though colour and wealth can be considered as features that are easy to identify, they are nevertheless given greater salience through a range of symbolic practices that repeatedly and incessantly underscore the validity of the stratificatory system. It is also true that the less obvious the criteria of stratification the greater is the symbolic energy spent to make them come to life. Race differences being quite obvious did not require too many symbolic markers to semaphore the divergent statuses and positions within the hierarchy. While we must recall the validity of what was said earlier that not all natural differences are important for stratificatory systems, it is also true that should these differences be obvious to the senses there is less pressure to mark statuses with rituals, symbolic observances and beliefs. This is probably why it is possible to have a Black cook in a racist society but not a Harijan in a Brahman's kitchen. As castes are first differentiated, and then capriciously hierarchized on the basis of supposed natural substances that are not tangible to the senses, there is a greater stress on ritual and symbolic behaviour in this form of stratification. It is as if the abundance of details in caste distinctions is to make up for the lack of convincing tangible evidence of differences.

Likewise, pure differences in wealth need not create

barriers between people. The owner-cultivating Jats and Gujars of western Uttar Pradesh cannot be easily distinguished on the criterion of land owned by them. A rich farmer and a poor farmer lead identical lifestyles and consume practically the same things (Gupta 1997: 41-44). Only when status considerations overlay economic differences does the economic hierarchy begin to show up in a more pronounced form. This again reveals the scope for demonstrating difference through status considerations in what should have been a pure and open gradational hierarchy. Once wealth is used to seal off the non-wealthy's access to status goods, status markers stand in for wealth, and differences are created on what was once only a continuous gradation. The fact that status differences supervene upon open hierarchical systems probably tells us that human beings are fallible everywhere. In some places this particular weakness towards creating distance between themselves gets greater encouragement for display than in others. But the tendency to create distinctions and social distance seems to have the status of an anthropological truism.

The Scope of Protest: Beyond Descriptive Sociology

It should be quite clear that though the analytical distinctions exist between open and closed systems of stratification, and between hierarchy and difference, no one system of stratification exists in a pure form. Open systems of stratification are perjured by status distinctions, and closed systems of stratification enforce a hierarchy on what are logically equal and horizontal categories. There seems to be a universal sociological reluctance to differentiate between hierarchical order and horizontally differentiated utopias. But it is still important to stress these analytical distinctions for they help us to organize our perceptions of how mobility and protest are worked out on the ground. If one were to be unaware of these conceptual distinctions then open and closed systems of stratification would be simple descriptive categories that appear in historical succession. But a sociology of social stratification cannot be just a descriptive exercise. It should also provide us with heuristic tools to understand the trajectories of change in different social orders. This in turn should help us to grapple with the variations in ambitions, drives and discontent that exist in different societies.

Keeping this in mind it is worthwhile to examine the scope of protests in different systems of stratification. In an open system of stratification protests can take place on two counts. The first (and the more innocuous) variety of protest occurs when for some reason mobility is blocked within the system. This can happen due to a downturn in the business cycle, leading to retrenchment and recession. In such cases the protest of those who feel their mobility stifled is usually aimed at bad managers and at faulty business decisions. This kind of protest may be termed as 'economism'. Economism does not challenge the hierarchy but attacks those who, it is believed, have not played fair by the rules of the extant hierarchical system.

If the open class system is to be challenged at the core then there is no alternative but to step outside the one-dimensional and flat variations of the graded hierarchy and call in a multitude of differences to fuel an ideology of change. The worker is not just somebody who occupies a certain position in the power hierarchy and in the economic hierarchy, but is an occupant of a social position that has many more aspects to it than can be subsumed by a continuous hierarchy. The agitating workers will now draw upon the diversities in tradition between themselves and their superior classes. While on the continuous hierarchical scale they acquiesced to a lower ranking, once elements outside the hierarchy are brought in to flesh out and substantiate the fullness of their being, dissension is built into the continuous hierarchy. Protests of this sort will recall working class traditions, tales of bravery and of sacrifice, homilies and aphorisms of moral probity and virtue, to realize a community, even a fraternity, that is redolent with a multitude of specific characteristics. The bundling of these diacritical attributes gives this class the fullness that is necessary to imagine and then realize an alternative social order. To build a dialectic that does not return to its starting point in the continuous hierarchy, in endless rounds of regression, ammunition for protest must be sought by stepping outside the hierarchy and attaining the gravity of difference. The sliding scale of a continuous hierarchy is far too parlous for sustaining such ambitions.

Perhaps the distinctions Marxists draw between a class in itself and a class for itself can be understood in this light. When a class functions within the ideological framework of the continuous hierarchy then it may be said to function as a class in itself. When this same class steps out of the quantitative hierarchy and attempts to delegitimize it, it must necessarily ballast itself by a substantiation of differences. It is only by the consolidation of such attributes of differences that an alternative social order becomes a tangible goal worth striving for. Though building a substantial body of differences the ideology of change can be symbolically energized. A revolutionary movement to be successful, or with a fair chance of success, cannot afford to be unidimensional in character. To be enthused by a vision of an alternative social order, or even of an alternative form of hierarchical ranking (which is admittedly much less ambitious) requires a gathering of differences on a variety of fronts.

In protest movements (such as caste mobilization) in closed systems of stratification there seems to be no real alternative but to emphasize differences. The hierarchy in force in such systems of stratification is largely a matter of power and not so much of ideological acceptance. Mobility in closed systems of stratification was therefore always a major historical event. There was nothing routine about it as is the case with movements up or down a continuous hierarchy. Its relative infrequency, particularly in pre-modern times, is because it took so much to effect social mobility in closed systems of stratification. This has often given contemporary scholars the impression that there was relative peace in ancient and medieval times. This, however, is just an illusion of distance.

Gradational and Relational Approaches: Stratifying Industrial Societies

It is not as if the deficiencies of seeing social stratification only as a ranked and continuous hierarchy have not been noticed earlier. Long back Stanislaw Ossowski noted the difference between gradational and relational theories of stratification. In recent years both John Goldthorpe (1987) and Erik Olin Wright (1979, 1985) have used the relational scheme of stratification to understand modern classes in industrial societies. Before we posit the advantages of notion of differences it is fair to give a quick overview of what Goldthorpre and Wright meant by relational theories. Both Goldthorpe and Wright felt that gradational (or hierarchical) theories of stratification lacked explanatory and dynamic capabilities. These theories just presented a static and timeless social order. In place of such gradational perspectives both Goldthorpe and Wright, quite independent of each other, proposed a relational approach instead. This relational approach was influenced by Marxist scholarship and its left-wing credentials are quite obvious.

Goldthorpe distinguishes between service, intermediate and working class in what might seem as yet another ranked hierarchy. But he disputes such a reading and insists that each of these classes and their subdivisions are relational in character and reflect the tension between classes. The service class consists of high-grade professionals, followed by low-grade professionals and managers in small businesses. The intermediate class is made up of clerical and rank and file non-manual employees. In this category he also includes small proprietors, self-employed artisans and supervisors of manual workers. The working class is made up of skilled, semi-skilled and unskilled manual workers.

The fact that these classes and their constituents are presented in a vertical fashion gives credence to the allegation that this is yet another gradational scheme. To go by Goldthorpe's own assertions, the class element in his presentation is determined primarily by considerations of the market and the occupational situation. Thus a self-employed artisan would not be at the same level as an employed one. A closer look, however, tells us that there is a quantitative variable that is present in the distinctions Goldthrope makes between the three major classes. This factor quantifies the power one has over one's work process. The service sector has greater control over its own work process as well as of the other classes; and at the bottom are the manual workers who have no control at all. In between are the independent artisans who are higher than those employed in a factory. In a sense then Goldthorpe's classes are also gradational, as his hierarchy is determined to a large extent on the uniform variable of power and control over the work process. This does not preclude a relational dimension for grades and ranks within a hierarchy would make no sense on their own. To be rich has meaning only when there are poor people around.

A charitable reading of Goldthorpe would encourage a somewhat different conclusion. The relation between classes that Goldthorpe is drawing our attention to is not simply a logical relation but a real one in a rather concrete sense. Classes are related in Goldthorpe's scheme because some classes exercise authority over others in the work process. This is somewhat analogous to the argument that the rich and poor are not merely logical necessities, but that the rich exist because it is the poor who make them rich. But then do the rich and the poor, or, as in this case, those who control the work process versus those who do not, ever see themselves as embodying differences that are independent of each other. It is only then, as we found earlier, that a class in itself can become a class for itself. To realize that as a subjugated class one is in the grip of a power hierarchy certainly does not by itself create the conditions for class action—and class action is one of the principal concerns of Goldthorpe.

How well does Erik Olin Wright's class map figure in this connection? Wright proceeds on a more markedly Marxist path. The terms that he uses for the various classes, such as bourgeoise, petty bourgeoise and proletariat, clearly announces his theoretical position. He too makes a composite index of sorts using the variables of ownership or non-ownership of the means of production, and control or autonomy in the production process. We then have a class map with the bourgeoise on top, followed by small employees, who are in turn followed by managers and supervisors. After this category we enter the distinctly blue-collar domain with the semi-autonomous wage earners and finally the proletariat. Wright has somewhat amended this map in his later works by clearly postulating a graph based on the quantifiable axes of skills and organizational assets (Wright 1979, 1985).

In Wright we have a combination of hierarchy and difference. The two great polar opposites manning the extreme ends of his hierarchy are the bourgeoisie and the proletariat. The more capital a bourgeois controls the higher is that capitalist's status. On the other hand the more dependent a worker is on the bourgeoisie and the managerial class, the lower is that person's position in the class map. This situation is not unlike Goldthorpe's analysis though the distinction between bourgeoisie and the proletariat class is put in irreconciliable terms. Subsequent elaboration of the class map undoes this irreconciliability to a certain extent, for the two get bridged by the hierarchy of power and control over the production process.

In the final analysis the relational theories provide an alternative to pure hierarchical and gradational approaches to social stratification. For both Goldthorpe and Wright class is not just occupation, as it was with a host of scholars who followed the lead set by Lipset and Bendix in their classic study *Social Mobility in*

Industrial Society (1957). Yet Wright and Goldthorpe fall short because the relational aspects that they so steadfastly emphasize are ultimately compromised by gradational considerations. Nevertheless, both Goldthorpe and Wright succeeded in presenting a picture of stratification in modern industrial societies, and of the tensions that underlie the relationship between classes. In that sense their contributions are also superior to the earlier works by Lloyd Warner and his team which were primarily descriptive and static in character. But to be able to exploit more fully the potentialities of the relational approach it is necessary to consider it in the light of the distinctions between hierarchy and difference.

Marx and Weber: Relating Hierarchy to Difference

The relational approach can be strengthened if the concept of difference is consciously integrated. Differences are salient features of social stratification when logically incommensurable phenomena are forced into a hierarchy. The tension that both Wright and Goldthorpe would like us to appreciate can only be underlined once the potentialities for developing differences within different classes are gauged. The sources for substantiating these differences cannot come from the hierarchy of power and supervisory control. When working class movements react primarily to hierarchies of this sort they only end up, as Marx once put it, in fomenting petty bourgeois revolts. While Marxism would posit that little could be gained in a confrontation between managers and big capitalists, or between big capitalists and small capitalists, or between workers and management, such conflagrations occur more frequently than thoroughgoing social revolutions. These classes may initially face off against each other because of their divergent positions in the hierarchy, but to sustain the tempo of protest attributes from outside the hierarchy will have to be factored in to give body to the many dimensions of differences between combatants. Only this would provide a variety of nodes of symbolic activity essential to sustain the imaginings of an alternative order with an alternative hierarchy.

Though it is difficult to straitjacket either Marx or Weber in the difference versus hierarchy scheme that has been proposed here, it can nevertheless be said with some caution that Marx was on the side of difference and Weber tilted towards hierarchy. Weber's famous essay 'Class, Status and Party' (Weber 1946) delineated the hierarchies that exist in what he believed were the three dimensions of stratification. For Weber economic class was determined by life chances in the market-place. The marketplace created a hierarchy of success and this determined class action quite directly without the mediation of any external ideology. In fact, according to Weber, if class action were to step out its bounds, or area of competence, and become some kind of communal action then that would undermine the legitimacy of such an action.

Likewise Weber felt that status and power were also ranked in a hierarchy. Status was measured on the basis of consumption styles, and power was defined in terms of the extent to which one could control the actions of others. Weber continuously emphasized that these three axes of stratification are independent of each other, and should not be collapsed into one. This is the specific characteristic of the Weberian approach to stratification. But this specific notion gets further support from his belief that all disputes are best understood within their own designated hierarchies. Weber agrees that status, wealth and power are intermingled, but the fact remains that they also have their own independent zones of relevance—and this cannot be sublated.

Weber's view on stratification gains further salience because it was consciously positioned against what is popularly perceived to be the Marxist view. Weber's constant exhortation that economics, status and power dimensions be kept separate was a rebuttal of the Marxian emphasis to see the economic realm as determining, or at least as setting the limits for all others. Marx's understanding of the economic realm was quite different from that of Weber. For Marx the crucial feature of a society is its mode of production. The mode of production of each historical epoch can be grasped by taking into account the fundamental contradictions that exist at the economic, or production level. In feudal societies the basic contradiction wages between the lord and the serf, while in capitalist societies it is between the proletariat and the bourgeoisie (Marx and Engels 1962). Now, the distinction between the proletariat and the bourgeoisie is not the same as between a rich and a poor person. The proletariat and the bourgeoisie are irreconcilable categories and gain meaning by virtue of their contradictory relationship with each other. In Marx's own writings there is no hint of a hierarchy between these two classes. It is not as if one can have a gradation between the proletariat and the capitalist. One does not become less of capitalist and more of a proletariat. As Marx saw the relationship between other classes constrained by this basic dialectic between the capitalist and the proletariat one could say that Marx was a theoretician of difference.

The divergences in the political positions of Weber and Marx can also be understood in this light. As

Weber highlighted hierarchy, he was necessarily drawn towards a more conservative, and, what he believed was, responsible politics. Weber was consistently opposed to the politics of commitment for he felt that such kinds of upheavals brought about needless bloodshed in the name of a cause that could never be properly grasped. Weber felt that such passionate ideologies were misleading because they did not obey the autonomy that the different axes of stratification possessed with respect to one another. Marx on the other hand was a proponent of revolution and structural change, and it is, therefore, not at all surprising that he should emphasize difference and irreconciliability in his theory of class.

It remains for us now to take cues from the history of sociological theory and realize the crucial relationship that hierarchy and difference have with each other in different stratificatory systems. While hierarchy steadfastly attempts to establish order, differences constantly and tenaciously pose an active or potential threat to stability. If stratification were only about gradations and ranked order (as in Sorokin 1967), then it would only mean inequality, and nothing more. Likewise, if stratification were justly about differences then that could be subsumed under studies of social differentiation. Only in the sub-discipline of social stratification do hierarchy and differences come together in a complex of ties that tell us at once about order and about stability, as well as about mobility and social inertia.

3

Continuous Hierarchies and Discrete Castes

Contemporary scholarship on caste continues to be influenced by the concern of early European scholars who, in addition to being perplexed by this peculiar institution, also pondered over the possibility of India's entry into the modern age burdened as it was by the incubus of the caste system. The great nineteenth century Indologist Max Mueller, the scholar-missionary Abbe Dubois, or even the sociologist Max Weber, were not very certain if India would even succeed in modernizing itself as they felt that the caste system would continue to frustrate all attempts towards social and economic progress. Their understanding of the caste system was largely conditioned by Hindu sacerdotal texts which are heavily biased in favour of a Brahmanical point of view. Even British administrators, whenever in doubt about what is proper Hindu custom only consulted Brahmans. The belief that Brahmans alone can speak on behalf of the entire Hindu society continues to dominate even contemporary scholarship on caste. Inspite of this overwhelming analytical presence in favour of a Brahmanical perspective on caste, modern scholars have succeeded in bringing to light contrary empirical findings. They are willing to recognize that the institution of caste has not particularly blocked the development of democracy and adult franchise (Rudolph and Rudolph 1969). Nor has the caste system held up occupational mobility and economic innovations (Singer 1972). What is more, it has also been discovered that the caste system provides for social mobility by an almost deliberate relaxation of rules.

However, while all this has been empirically demonstrated, the lessons emerging from it rarely took wing to articulate an alternate view of the caste system. Without such an effort the empirical findings on the dynamic and malleable character of caste remain like so much sociological small change. They are useful for short spurts of scholarship, but unable to sustain an alternative analytical perspective. We are thus faced with a somewhat curious situation. While empirical studies have disproved the traditional Indological-cum-sociological view of the strict and irreconcilable dichotomy between caste and modern social institutions, or practice, the conceptual framework within which castes in India have been understood has received no major analytical reformulation. It is probably for this reason that studies which demonstrate the malleability of the caste structure and beliefs remain only at the level of case studies.

In other words, the belief that caste ideology over-values 'karma' (a species of other worldiness); or that the caste systems orders a hierarchy which universally legitimizes the position of each caste; or that the caste system looks down upon competition and conflict; or that the caste system differentiates on the principle of purity and pollution are all closely interlinked and govern our conceptual understanding of the caste system. A quick reflection will at once reveal how much at odds the conceptual view of the caste system is with the dynamics of contemporary Indian reality. Our primary purpose in this chapter is to suggest an alternative conceptual formulation on caste, which can fully integrate many of these empirical findings.

Objectives

In this chapter we shall examine Dumont's understanding of hierarchy and his application of the term to the caste system. In this connection it is important to take into account Dumont's assertion that the principle of encompassment, which defines a true hierarchy, is applicable to the caste system as well. It is only at the end of this presentation that an attempt will be made to evaluate the larger social and political consequences of our criticism of Dumont. This will take us to discuss more directly the question of caste and class, and to the prospects and limits of caste and class mobilization.

Without anticipating the arguments that follow it is well to mention that our primary purpose here is to demonstrate that castes cannot be looked at only in terms of hierarchies without first understanding them in terms of discrete categories. The fact that it has been acknowledged almost universally that castes can be hierarchically arranged with complete acquiescence across castes is, as we shall try to show, a reflection of our uncritical acceptance of the ideology of the privileged castes. If we are able to demonstrate the above then the logical corollary of our contentions should lead us to a position contrary to Dumont's view. What is more, it should allow us to formulate an analytical alternative perspective which can explain caste conflict, change and social mobility without having to put them aside as so many anomalies of the system. In no way should such an analysis suggest that caste in India is a peripheral, social phenomenon either.

The strategy we have adopted is to take a step back and review the dominant theoretical position on the caste system where Brahmans are presumed to be on the top of the hierarchy. The strength of this position is that it explains the existence of hierarchy and the notion of 'substances' and natural differences that differentiate one caste from another. On the basis of these, community endogamy and occupational specialization are easily taken care of. While this view fails to answer empirical objections of the kind already referred to, it is still not threatened. An alternative position can start stirring to life by pointing to flaws in the existing paradigm. But it can come of age only when a conceptual grid can be crafted that can give a better and empirically more consistent view of the caste system in its entirety.

With this in mind we found it advisable for our purpose to build our contentions step by step, in direct opposition to the prevalent conceptual/theoretical view of the caste system. It is for this reason that we have taken on the most advanced and sophisticated proponent of the social anthropological mainline view of the caste system, viz., the author of *Homo Hierarchicus*, Louis Dumont.

Why Louis Dumont?

Dumont is not only is the most systematic exponent of the dominant conceptual view of the caste system but he attained this distinction by undermining almost all the known conceptual views on the subject, either in terms of detail—in the case of those whose overall conclusions match his—or, in terms of conception and methodology in the case of those whose conclusions that could perhaps be extended to refute his, to wit, those of Senart and Bougle. When he refutes Bougle, Senart or even Ghurye and Karve (Dumont 1970b: 66), he takes them on, not so much for what they say, but more for what they imply. As we find ourselves in sympathy with these implications, it is to Dumont that we must necessarily pay greater attention.

Even critics of Dumont must accept his singular contribution to this subject. Right or wrong, Dumont's plea to undertake the macro level as the only legitimate level for Indian sociology has significantly altered the format of research on the caste system. Whereas the bare conclusions of Dumont sponsor a sense of *déjà vu*, the methods by which he arrives at them are both novel and significant. In addition, terms such as stratification and hierarchy receive major renovations. Logical definitions and logic itself exercise a pervasive sway in his treatment of the caste system. The fact that this chapter is addressed to logic and logical definitions is a measure of our indebtedness to Dumont.

It is true that before Dumont, Hegel had said that in order to understand caste, ideology should be considered as the primary level of reality. But Dumont after specifically acknowledging Hegel's chronological priority in this matter (Dumont 1970b: 80), transformed the discourse by introducing modern structuralism with its notion of binary opposition as the critical clavicle to his methodology and adroitly remarked that Marx before him had derived great advantage by distinguishing between the empirical and the logical levels in order to understand facts on the ground (ibid: 112). Indeed this is what led many Marxists to rigorously pursue the homologous relationship between caste and the Marxian notion of class. If Marxists could say with emphasis that the proletariat could only triumph once the bourgeoisie was vanquished, then by a homologous logic, it was possible to say, as Dumont in fact does, that unless the purity of the Brahman is itself radically devalued (ibid: 92) caste hierarchies were here to stay, and its logic would continue to constitute the primary level of social and political reality in India.

The Making of the 'True' Hierarchy

As Dumont is easily misunderstood it is best to outline his principal positions in his own words, as far as possible. For Dumont:

> A hierarchical relation is a relation between larger and smaller, or more precisely between that which encompasses and that which is encompassed. (Dumont 1970b: 24.)

With this definition of hierarchy Dumont proposes to shift the focal point of accounts that deals with the caste system.

> In place of the isolation and the separation of castes from one another, which we have found so prominent, we shall bring hierarchy to the forefront (ibid: 30).

But the principle of the system has yet to be ascertained. How should one go about it? In this regard, Dumont writes,

> It is enough to observe that actual men do not behave: they act with an idea in their heads, perhaps that of conforming to custom. (Ibid: 40.)

> Finally . . . the caste system is a state of mind, a state of mind which is expressed by the emergence,

in various situations, of groups of various orders
generally called 'castes'. (Ibid: 71.)

This state of mind provides the orientation towards the
whole

. . . which in the eyes of those who participate in
it legitimizes their respective positions . . . (Ibid: 149.)

Moreover to adopt a value is to introduce hierarchy,
and a certain consensus of value, a certain hierarchy
of ideas, things and people, is indispensable to
social life. (Ibid: 54.)

It is therefore only via ideology that one can grasp the
essence of castes and come to know the true principle
behind the caste system. The 'single true principle' is
'the opposition of the pure and the impure' (ibid: 81).

This opposition underlies the caste hierarchy, which
can be translated into the superiority of the pure over
the impure. This opposition underlies separation because
the pure and the impure must be kept separate. It also
underlies the division of labour because the pure and
impure occupations must likewise be kept separate
(ibid: 81).

This hierarchical principle, Dumont concludes, is
responsible for the 'linear order of castes from A to
Z . . .' (ibid: 96). Caste A and Z must exist empirically,
for the 'two poles are equally necessary, although
unequal'. (Ibid: 93.) For the sociologist, Dumont writes,

The decisive step is accomplished once a quality
like impurity is attributed in a permanent manner
to certain people. There to a great extent will be
found the clue to Indian complexity. (Dumont and
Pocock 1957: 16.)

This is so because Dumont believes that it 'is generally

agreed that the opposition is manifested in some macroscopic form in the contrast between the two extreme categories: Brahmans and Untouchables'. (Dumont 1970b: 84.)

The next step is to understand what makes this hierarchy a true hierarchy? A true hierarchy 'cannot give place to power as such, without contradicting its own principle'. (Ibid: 117.)

> . . . but in concrete, we have seen that power, devalued to the advantage of status at the overall level surreptitiously makes itself the equal of status at the interstitial levels. (Ibid: 197.)

And yet it is not the interstitial levels, or the median zone, which is important if one is to appreciate a true hierarchy. Dumont categorically states: 'For us . . . what happens at the extreme is essential.' (Ibid: 116.) In a true hierarchy 'that which encompasses is more important than that which is encompassed.' (Ibid.) 'For pure hierarchy to develop without hindrance it was also necessary that power should be absolutely inferior to status.' (Ibid: 114.)

The caste hierarchy however is not merely a linear order but is 'a series of successive dichotomies and inclusions.' (Ibid: 106.) For instance, the Shudra is opposed to the block of the first three castes, Vaishyas are opposed to the block of Brahman and Kshatriya, which finally divides into two (ibid, see also p.79). In this manner, Dumont demonstrates again the relationship between the encompassing and the encompassed.

The above, most briefly, are the essential methodological points that Dumont makes in connection with the understanding of what constitutes a pure hierarchy, and why the caste system should also be considered as such. Incidentally, the steps that Dumont takes in explicating his position will also serve as signposts in the development of our position in this chapter.

The influence of Dumont on subsequent studies of caste is important. In many instances the authors themselves may be unaware of their indebtedness to Dumont, so widely assimilated is his position. There have also been significant additions to and substantiations of Dumont's contribution. Though we do not have time to exhaustively review this literature, it is necessary to take into account the contributions of at least Murray Milner (1994) and Michael Moffat (1979).

Milner, in a vein reminiscent of Dumont argues, that status cannot be equated with power or wealth (1994: 147). Further, as status is inexpansible (i.e. if someone goes up then somebody else must come down), if a lower caste climbs up, the upper caste must come down (ibid: 57, 71, 112, 160). As the caste system according to Milner, centralizes ritual status (ibid: 58), the position of the Brahman is virtually unassailable. This conclusion leads Milner to undermine social mobility, and over-value inheritance and ascription (ibid: 205).

Milner obviously assumes, as Dumont did before him, that the caste system has been devised by Brahmans (ibid: 78) while the other castes simply have acquisced to their position in the hierarchy. The fact that a 'lower' caste may successfully demonstrate a 'superior' lifestyle and yet not be accepted by Brahmans and, conversely, that an 'upper' caste may not, and most often, does not carry intrinsic legitimacy with the subordinated castes, does not find any place in Milner's analysis. His notion of 'inexpansible' status is a clear indication of his position in this regard.

From a Dumontian perspective again, but this time very self-consciously, Michael Moffat argues that caste rules are so thoroughly internalized that lower castes replicate the hierarchy at subordinate levels as well. Dumont, it may be recalled, argued that castes are arranged in a hierarchical gradation such that the principal of hierarchy encompasses all. Moffat makes this aspect more explicit when he says that 'untouchables . . . participate willingly in what might be called their own oppression.' (Moffat 1979: 303.) Moffat believes that even at the level of the 'untouchables' hierarchy is clearly evident. The 'higher' members of the scheduled castes dominate the 'lower' just as 'upper' castes dominate them (ibid: 103-51). At the end, however, he gives the game away when he admits that when replication of the hierarchy at the 'lower' levels breaks down it is because 'of an exhaustion of material resources of low (sic) humans unable to pay others and of other humans willing to serve them.' (Ibid: 148.) In other words, caste domination is wrought by material resources and not by spiritual, ideological and ritual compliance. If it were the latter then the caste system is primarily ideology, and the acceptance of it purely voluntary. This is as Dumont argues consistently in *Homo Hierarchicus*. But if it is a question of material resources, as Moffat finally accedes, then economics and politics are no longer interstitial intrusions into the caste system, but the bulwarks of its very existence. If material resources make all the difference then 'lower' castes do not necessarily 'participate willingly in what might be called their own oppression' (ibid: 303) as Moffat would like to conclude.

Facts Against Theory

In this section we think it is worthwhile to mention certain facts which militate against Dumont's theory, and which are not comfortably positioned in Dumont's system.

In fairness to Dumont it should be acknowledged that he is on most such occasions aware of the existence of these facts, but has a curious style of marginalizing their impact. Either such unpleasant things 'often' happen and are dismissed in a paragraph (Dumont 1970b: 98, 224), or they happen in relatively distant regions where the caste system is 'fluid' (ibid: 214), or they are simply characterized as variants and anomalies (ibid: 96). In this case then it is not so much for factual errors as it is for theoretical solecisms (made apparent by the so-called 'anomalies' and 'variants' which are, nevertheless, still facts) that Dumont is being faulted.

But what are these unpleasant facts? If power enters only at the interstitial levels, then how can a king—the supreme embodiment of power, or the Kshatriya principle intervene directly to refashion a caste hierarchy (ibid: 214)? Or why is a vegetarian merchant below the meat-eating king (ibid: 114)? Or why do upper castes on occasions beat lower castes to 'uphold a symbol of subjection' even if it has nothing to do with pollution (ibid: 122)? Or why do 'untouchables' of Tanjore village believe that if a Brahman were to enter their village, pestilence and disease would strike it (ibid: 98)? Or why does a certain caste refuse to accept all types of food, both kachcha and pacca from other castes? Why are these cases 'absurd'—to use Dumont's adjective (ibid: 128)? Why do farmers 'pose' as puritans (ibid: 129)? Why is the Kshatriya model of Sanskritization 'shamefaced' (ibid: 130)? Try asking a proud and robust

Jat to emulate a Brahman and the absurdity of the verdict 'shamefaced' will become apparent. In short, the major problem is: why do people who believe in the caste system not follow the dictates of the true hierarchy? Or should the question be posed differently? Is there a true hierarchy at all in the sense in which Dumont has enunciated it with reference to the caste system? Is it possible that contrary to Dumont's belief of total allegiance to the pure hierarchy, castes indeed have very different notions of who they are and what positions they should occupy in that hierarchy. Indeed, there are probably several hierarchies as castes find it very difficult to agree on any one.

Redefinitions

Let us now undertake a little definitional exercise ourselves. A true hierarchy, according to us, is an unambiguous linear ranking on a single variable. Besides such criteria as wealth in cash, women, cattle, or land, authority can also be a valid criterion for a true and continuous hierarchy. For if one moves up or down, say, on the authority scale within a particular organization, one's authority would accordingly increase or decrease. To illustrate, a foreman on the shop floor is not a manager, but is nearer to the managerial level than the ordinary worker. More importantly, within that particular organization the relative positions of authority are undisputed and can only be challenged on the pain of transforming that organization.

Discrete classes on the other hand separate units into exclusive categories. One is either a Maharashtrian or not a Maharashtrian, a Brahman or not a Brahman. At the level of the mode of production in Marxism it would be similarly unwise to ask if one was less proletariat or more bourgeois. Such a question, quite clearly, would be rather absurd. Continuous hierarchies are built around a single criterion which is shared to a greater or lesser extent by all those who occupy that hierarchy. Other factors need not be adduced to it to justify the ranking. Discrete categories are different. Proletariats are not merely *not* bourgeoisie, but are defined around a singular characteristic, or described by a host of characteristics not shared by the bourgeoisie. A Bengali is simply not a non-Maharashtrian, or a Baniya is not simply a non-Brahman. Therefore, the criteria that separate discrete categories or classes are incommensurable and qualitative. A continuous hierarchy, on the other hand, is made up on the basis of a quantitative variation of a single attribute across levels or strata.

The above does not mean that systems can be distinguished solely on the basis of whether or not they subscribe to continuous hierarchies or discrete classes. Generally, most systems are amenable to either forms of differentiation, it is only a question of the level, or plane, at which one or the other form of differentiation becomes relevant. In a factory system, for instance, while it is possible to unproblematically hierarchize on the basis of salary, or even power, the manager is simply not one who is not a worker, nor is the worker a person who is simply not an accountant. In this case we have to deal with social classes, the diacritical marks of which cannot be understood on the basis of a continuous hierarchy. Similarly in the agrarian system the sharecropper is simply not a person who is not a labourer, or a landlord. These social classes are discrete and exclusive. The separation between them is achieved and strengthened by a host of cohort features.

Much has been made about ranking on the principle of purity and pollution with respect to the caste system. It has also been argued by Dumont and others that this is a matter of ideology to which all those within the caste system subscribe. But as a matter of fact there are some problems with this too.

Rules and Ideologies

Rules are, most nakedly, instruments of the power hierarchy. Ideology, on the other hand, tries to mask this nakedness, and may on occasions, even, at times, succeed it. The caste rule in this sense, which holds that subaltern castes must serve the privileged ones, is an expression of power. And caste ideology attempts to cloak it. But what caste ideology also does is that it separates castes from one another on an enduring basis. Naturally this principle is active in the case of other castes as well so that ultimately there is no single caste ideology, but multiple ideologies sharing some principles in common but articulated at variance with, and even in opposition to, one another. In effect, therefore, the rule of caste is only obeyed when it is accompanied by the rule of power. Therefore, contrary to what Dumont claims, it is the hierarchy of power and economics where we believe that hierarchy is naked. Ideology, on the other hand, introduces hierarchy 'shamefacedly' but only after effecting the separation between discrete categories of castes.

There are two additional points to be made with respect to purity and pollution. From the vantage point of Brahmanical ideology, Brahmans are the purest and the level of purity decreases till we come to the other extreme who have no purity at all. Here Dumont quite unexpectedly helps us when he calls them actually polluted. Obviously at some point purity has undergone a dialectical change and is now a different category altogether viz., pollution. What is not pure need not always be polluted. Dumont is fully aware of this for he says that purity and pollution are categories in opposition. But he very quickly negates this insight by claiming that castes A to Z demonstrate the two poles of this opposition, with obviously castes B, C, D, etc., coming in between—in an orderly and hierarchical fashion.

But if one were to set aside the hierarchy of purity and pollution, and look instead at the ideology of purity and pollution, then one would find matters to be quite different. Ideology separates castes into discrete entities in a most self-centred way. Castes rarely, if ever, accept their alleged biological fallibility and consequently reject the attribute of impurity which some other castes may impute on to them. If they do abide on the ground by the ranking of purity inflicted on them then it is because of the conjoint working of the principles of economics and or politics. Both economics and power are amenable to hierarchical ranking but are unfortunately excluded by Dumont in his working out of the 'true hierarchy'.

It is still too early for us to define caste as it is essential to first appreciate the discrete character of caste in its fullness. We might however mention here that the task of defining caste is not an easy one, as many hitherto unassailable characteristics of the caste system, such as: (a) a uniform hierarchical ideology; (b) occupational specialization; and (c) the concepts of purity and pollution as the principal instruments for separation ('repulsion') etc., dissolve under a more contemporary gaze.

One final clarification before we proceed any further.

The terms caste and jati will be used synonymously throughout. When we have to refer to whole caste groups like the Brahmans, Kshatriyas, Kaibarttas, Mochis or Panchals, we shall simply use the term 'caste group' whenever necessary.

One Ideology or Many

A careful reading of Louis Dumont's several works on the caste system confirms that for Dumont the ideology of the caste system is all pervasive without exception in Hindu India. For the Hindus, Dumont avers, belief in God is secondary to belief in caste (Dumont and Pocock 1957: 20). But Dumont does not stop here. He goes on to argue that there is only one elaborated ideology based on these principles, and for the elaboration of this ideology he depends primarily on the ancient Brahman lawgiver, Manu. From the highest to the lowest caste everybody subscribes to this elaborated ideology, duly accepting as just their position in the ranking. Dumont believes that this is in concinnity with the fact that in traditional societies there is only the idea of the collective man. It is therefore the duty of the Hindus, as they see it, to uphold this one supreme elaborated ideology. Some others who have also read Dumont may, of course, say that we are misinterpreting him, but then they would have to account for Dumont's complete omission of what subaltern castes think of their caste position and of the caste system as a whole.

If one were momentarily to suspend belief of the prevalent Brahmanical ideology then it would not be very difficult to accept that there can be many caste ideologies. All these ideologies however adhere to similar values, but express the lived-in situation differently and offer different guides to action. One should not, at this point, confuse values with ideologies. All caste ideologies value the need to separate caste groups from one another according to a mythical notion of biological differences. This is because they value the principle of endogamy very highly. And yet the manner in which these values are expressed can be vastly different, and also opposed to one another, To draw an analogy: the racist ideology of say, the National Socialist Party under Hitler shared certain values with the ante-bellum politics of those states which united to form the American confederacy in the nineteenth century. Yet the ideologies of the ante-bellum southern confederacies and of the Nazi party were different from each other. We might reasonably suppose that the segregationist policy in South Africa, and the ideology of 'the white man's burden' too, are quite distinctive in character. All these articulations are racist as they have certain dominant values in common, but around which different ideologies condense. Likewise, we believe that there can be different ideologies around certain common values which are shared by all who participate in the caste system. The fact that these ideological variations are limited to a defined geographical area, and occur nowhere else, and also because identical symbols are used and reused with different degrees of salience in diverse ideological articulations, often blind us to the fact that we are actually witnesses to not one ideology but to multiple ideologies. Ideologies translate pure values into empirical categories in order to provide definite guidelines on the ground (Schurmann 1971: 38-39). They purport to explain the unhappy (or happy) circumstances in which the members of different caste groups are placed, what compromises they must effect to either consolidate or improve their positions; or what correctives they must adopt against real or imaginary challenges to their existence; and finally to assert their dignity and pride as separate groups.

It is in this context then of shared values that caste constitutes a discourse of beliefs, which has practical consequences. It is in this sense then that in spite of being discrete entities castes can still talk and relate to one another. Neither Bougle nor Senart were self-consciously espousing the cause that castes are discrete entities in the sense that we are, yet there is much that we can learn from them. Dumont faults Bougle and Senart for not being more explicit of the fact that castes constitute a system . . . If it had been possible for Bougle or Senart to reply to Dumont they would have said that they were not anti-systemic because what made caste a distinctive system were the principles that were universally employed in separation, viz., hierarchy, occupation, and repulsion. Our view is, however, not identical to either Bougle's or Senart's. In spite of the fact that castes are discrete, they are related as in a discourse because each caste in spite of its own idiosyncratic articulation of the caste ideology nevertheless uses identical elements and positions itself with reference to a notion of hierarchy nodes of which appear and reappear in different ideological formulations. As Cox perceptively observed, the caste system is 'a number of cultural unities invidiously juxtaposed, and the greater the struggle for position the more secure the structure is as a whole.' (Cox 1970: 4.)

Generally, the varna system forms a reference point to which each caste ideological formulation addresses itself, though very often the varna system is skipped, and the gods of the Hindu pantheon are referred to instead. But both the primary and secondary symbols employed to differentiate one caste from the other occur in the context of a common reference particular enough to render this context non-referential in any other system of differentiation. The caste system is a system of condensed symbols, and like all symbols what is signified at one point makes sense within a referential context, and yet any particular signification does not limit the potentiality of the signifier. The signified, as the linguists tirelessly remind us, does not exhaust the signifier. In other words, symbols are capable of multiple interpretations and no single rendition should be taken as the ideal signification.

We shall leave this discussion here and take it up again towards the end of the next chapter when we try to attempt a definition of the caste system.

It is not possible for us to give a complete ethnographic account of how the discrete character of castes is maintained. We shall detail such ethnographic evidence as is readily available to us, but a more detailed ethnographic study should also bear out our contentions. However, there is not much use in asserting a position contrary to Dumont's if it does not yield some tangible benefits. We hope to demonstrate in the following pages that if one were to view castes as discrete classes or categories and follow our distinction between a caste rule that is imposed and caste ideologies that are believed in, many of the facts that Dumont marginalizes or ignores can be accounted for. Nor would it be necessary to be uncomfortable about the notion of politics and economics in order to understand the Indian caste system.

Discrete Ideologies Tales of Origin

If ideologies separate the population and, surreptitiously

at least, subvert or legitimize the rules of authority, then caste ideologies should also contain these elements. Further as castes separate to maintain a distinct notion of their original heritage, ontology becomes an important component of all discrete caste ideologies.

Like the Brahman who must go back to the original division in the *Purusasukta*, each caste has its own theory explaining its origins. Not always is the occupation aspect upper-most in these tales of genesis. But often in the origin tales of the so-called lower castes, the occupational aspect is mentioned, as in the tales of the Telis and the Kumhars, but without implying that such occupations are degrading in any manner. In occupational valuations, and in other aspects too, individual caste ideologies are markedly different from Brahmanical versions. We shall illustrate this difference by reproducing below the tales of origin of the lowly Chamars, the even lower Chandals, and of the upper caste Kayasthas, as related by members of these castes. Note how pervasive the difference is between the Brahmanical view of how these three castes and the views that these castes have of their own origins.

Caste I—The Chamars. The orthodox view regarding the origin of Chamars is as follows:

According to the *Puranas*, the Chamars are descended from a boatman and Chandal woman; but if we are to identify them with the Karavara, or leather worker, mentioned in the tenth chapter of Manu, the father of the caste was a Nishada and the mother a Vaideha (Risley 1891: Vol.1, 175).

The Chamars view their origin as follows:

Chamars trace their pedigree to Ravi or Rui Das, the disciple of Ramanada at the end of the fourteenth century . . . Another tradition current among them alleges that their original ancestor was the youngest of four Brahman brethren who went to bathe in a river and found a cow struggling in quicksand. They sent the youngest brother in to rescue the animal, but before he could get it out the cow died. He was compelled therefore by his brothers to remove the carcass, and after he had done this they turned him out of their caste and gave him the name of Chamar. (Ibid: 176.)

Caste II—The Chandals. The orthodox view is the following:

Manu brands them as the lowest of mankind; sprung from the illicit intercourse of a Sudra man with a Brahman woman, whose touch defiles the pure and who have no ancestral rites. (Ibid: 184.)

The Chandals themselves, however, view their origins differently. Thus, according to a tradition of the Dacca Chandals, they were formerly Brahmans, who became degraded by eating with Sudras . . . (Ibid.)

Whereas the orthodox view claims that the Chandals have no ancestral rites, 'the Chandal celebrates the Sraddha on the eleventh day as Brahmans do, and the Gayawal priests conduct the obsequies ceremonies without compunction.' (Ibid.)

Case III—The Kayasthas. 'The Kayasthas themselves reject the theory which gives them for an ancestor Karan, the son of a Vaisya father by a Sudra mother'. (Ibid: 438.)

But the Kayasthas of Bengal go 'so far as to argue that the five Kayasthas of the tradition were political officers in charge as Kshatriyas on a mission from

> Kannauj to the king of Bengal, and that the five
> Brahmans played quite a subordinate part in the
> transaction, if indeed they were anything more
> than the cooks of the five Kayasthas. (Ibid: 439.)

These examples could indeed be multiplied ad nauseum, but they would all point to one single fact. The elaboration of the pure hierarchy from the Brahman's point of view is not shared by other castes. The Vaniyans claim descent from the Vedic seer Jamadagan (Wagle 1998: 27). The Kammalan caste which consists of artisans of five occupational sections, such as the goldsmiths, braziers, carpenters, masons and blacksmiths, 'claim descent from Viswakarma, the architect of the gods, and equality with Brahmans.' (Hutton 1963: 12; see also Brouwer 1997: 71 and Kramrisch, 1975: 18.) The Bhangis, who are as low as the Chamars, also partake of the myth that they were originally Brahmans (Blunt 1969: 4; see also Fuchs 1949: 235-36, with reference to the Balahi creation myth). Some other artisans castes like the Barhai, Bhatt and Lohar have sub-castes that also claim descent from Brahmans. The Nhavis (or barbers) of Deccan consider themselves superior to Brahmans because they claim descendence from the serpent Shesha who encircled Shiva's neck and was told to assume a human form at the time of the thread ceremony of the god Brahma (Enthoven 1975: 128). In several instances, castes may try and overlook the vedic texts altogether and claim superiority by virtue of being *adi* or first, before it all began. Meradha Kammara and Jajjagara Kammara, blacksmiths by occupation, claim such an *adi* status (Brouwer 1997: 71). By doing so they aspire to superiority by virtue of being in the world even before Brahmans arrived. The nineteenth century leader of the Non-Brahman Movement in Maharashtra, Jyotiba Phule argued for a similar *adi* status for the non-Brahman castes. Phule developed the belief that non-Brahmans are descendants of Bali, a pre-Arya king, who was deceived by Vishnu, the Aryan god (Gore 1993: 180).

The Mochis of Bombay Presidency claim Rajput descent for according to them, one of their heroic and redoubtable ancestors made a pair of stockings (moju) out of a tiger's skin (ibid: 56). Tamil bangle makers, the Balijas, claim to have been born out of the sacrificial fire. Wealthy herdsmen in South India call themselves Pillai, thus adhering to the Vellala model and purposefully rejecting the Brahmanical one (Silversten 1963: 3), and so on and on it goes. As discrete ideologies there is no embarrassment in accepting these facts for what they are, without introducing the notion of Sanskritization, which in any case does not apply to all these cases.

As is already clear in these tales of origin it is not always the Brahmans who are the models. Even when the claim is to have originated from Brahmans there is no mention of the actual Brahman jati. This is significant for it shows that these castes do not want to be assimilated into some other known and existent jati through marriage. By asserting that they are descendants of Brahmans they are actually referring to a varna category, and in that sense making a claim to a discrete caste status, quite different from the various extant Brahman jatis.

Those jatis that do not have a martial past and yet claim Kshatriya status are as varied as the well-to-do Chandraseni Kayastha Prabhus of Maharashtra, the Shimpis (or tailors) also of Maharashtra, the poor Kharwars of Bihar, or the, Noniyas of north India. In all these castes the myth of Parasuram, the Brahman, who vowed to kill Kshatriyas so that Brahmans may have temporal power, is invoked to explain why their Kshatriya ancestors had to take to different occupations to escape Parasuram's wrath. In all these cases Brahmans are viewed with a measure of hostility.

Discrete Castes and Muddled Hierarchies

The existence of so many diverse and contrary tales of caste origin is not the only way by which discrete castes maintain their separateness. If one were to look at the customs and traditions followed by different castes one would be hard put to force them into any grading system on the basis of purity and pollution. For instance, in the case of kachcha and pacca food it is not always the upper castes who are very particular in this matter. According to Blunt's classification, there is no relationship between orthodox caste ranking and the severity of the cooking taboo. The Koiris and Kumharas are as rigid in their cooking taboos as the Brahmans, and belong to the same group in Blunt's classification. The Cheros and the Khatris also belong to one group and the Banjaras, Byars and Dangis are about as severe in maintaining the taboos relating to kachcha and pacca food as are the Kayasthas (Blunt 1969: 93). The Telis, or oil pressers of Orissa, not exactly upper castes in terms of traditional caste aristocracy, nevertheless, are very particular about matters of food. Sometimes they can be more orthodox than the Brahmans as this episode recorded by N.K. Bose reveals. At a ceremonial feast of the Telis somebody asked for water and used the words 'pani lao' whereupon the Parichha (the traditional spokesman of the Telis) lifted his hand and abstained from proceeding with his meals. He complained that the sacramental social feast was defiled by the Urdu words 'pani lao'. Everyone in the feast followed suit (Bose 1960: 15). Nesfield too pointed out that a scavenger by caste can be more punctilious about rules than Khatris and Kayasthas (Nesfield 1885: 104). Yalman has also observed in his study of castes in Sri Lanka that when a Hena washerwoman married a tom-tom beater they were both ostracized from their respective castes (Yalman 1969: 83).

Similarly it is difficult to say according to any one ideology who is regarded as an untouchable by whom. Though a Dhobi is higher than a Bhangi by orthodox valuations, sixteen castes will not touch a Dhobi but only eleven castes will avoid touching a Bhangi (Blunt 1969: 102). The low caste Kuricchan of Malabar plasters his house with cow dung if it is polluted by the entry of a Brahman (Hutton 1963: 78). The Kurmi will not take any food from a Brahman unless he happens to be his guru (Risley 1891: Vol. 71, 536). The Sonar sub-castes of the Panchals such as the Lohars, Kansars, Sutars and Patharwats will not take any food from Brahmans either as they believe they are superior to Brahmans. The Sonars, on the other hand, consider themselves to be superior to the other four sub-castes among the Panchals (Enthoven 1975: 158, 369). The Meghavals or Dheds are a highly depressed caste group because carrion carrying has been their traditional occupation, and yet they will not eat at the hands of the Kolis who are certainly superior to them by orthodox standards (ibid: 52). The Patidars of Gujarat earlier claimed Kshatriya (Rajput) status, but now claim Vaishya (Baniya) status, thus preferring a category which orthodoxy would hierarchize below the Kshatriya order (Shah and Shroff 1975: 662-3).

Such inconsistencies and muddles in the hierarchy

are also evident as we move from region to region. Consider, for instance, the following inconsistencies and hierarchical muddles in the cases of the Babhans, the Gareris, and the Goalas in different parts of East India. All these cases are reported by Risley (1891, Vol. 1):

(a) The Babhans: In south-eastern Bihar they (the Babhans) rank immediately below the Kayasthas, but in Shahabad, Saran, and north-western Provinces they appear to stand on much the same level as Rajputs. The fact that in Patna and Gaya the Amashtha or Karan Kayasthas will eat kachi food which has been cooked by a Babhan, while the other sub-castes of Kayasthas will not, may perhaps be a survival from the time when Bhabhans occupied a higher position than they do at the present day. (Ibid: 33.)

(b) The Gareris: . . . the Gareri is reckoned higher in rank than the Ahir, and equal to the Majroti and Krishnaut Goalas, with whom, as has been mentioned above, Gareris will eat both kachi and pakki food and will smoke the same hookah. It is not clear, however, that this intercourse is reciprocal, and that the Goalas will accept food on the same terms from a Gareri . . . In Bihar and Bengal this caste is generally reckoned a clean one from whose members Brahman can take water; but in Puraniya, says Buchnan, it is impure. (Ibid: 273.)

(c) The Goalas: In point of social standing the Goalas of Bihar rank with Kurmis, Amats, and the other castes from whose hands a Brahman can take water. In Bengal they occupy a lower position, and are counted as inferior, not only to the Nabashakha, but also to the cultivating division of the Kaibartta caste. The Orissa Goalas, on the other hand, affect

a high standard of ceremonial purity, and also look
down upon the Bihar and Bengal divisions of the
caste. (Ibid: 290.)

A similar problem arises in South India with reference
to the classification between right and left-hand castes.
As the right hand castes are considered to be superior to
left hand castes there are irreconcilable disputes between
castes on this subject. Arjun Appadurai correctly points
out that the division between right and left hand castes
is not based on 'some single, consistent, and substantive
property which underlies the diverse appearances of the
dual classification.' (Appadurai 1974: 216-27.) Thus,
this division too is both contentious and idiosyncratic
(ibid: 218; see also Beck 1970: 784).

The principle of segmentation and inclusion cannot
therefore be applied universally in the case of castes.
This situation is noticeably different among tribes.
Segmentalization in tribes follows a continuous hierarchy
because the distance of a clan or sub-clan from the
ancestor is clear and unambiguous. Characteristically,
there is no muddling in this hierarchy. We, therefore,
disagree with Dumont when he uses the segmental
principle of tribal organizations to explicate
encompassment in the caste system (see Dumont 1970b:
79). Instead of a single hierarchy we should be prepared
by now to see the caste system as being composed of
multiple and contending hierarchies (see also Cox 1970:
13).

The discrete character of jatis and the pride that the
members of each jati have in their own community are
denoted by multiple observances and beliefs. These
many marks of separation are not linked by any precise
convention and for this reason the notions of purity or
pollution are not always active in the many rituals and

symbols that separate jatis.

Occupational distinctions which have very little to do with any extended notion of purity and pollution are employed to maintain the separation between different jatis of the same caste group. Some years ago the Srivastavas broke away from the Kayasthas who were patwaris (keepers of village records) because the latter had earned a bad name for chicanery. The Srivastavas for this reason alone do not permit intermarriage nor observe commensality in matters of food with the patwari Kayasthas. This is especially true in the erstwhile Oudh region (Blunt 1969: 222). The Gacchua Teli and the Bhunja Teli no longer belong to the original caste of Telis, because the latter began to extract oil in a novel manner. The Gacchua Telis extract oil by crushing the seed between wooden rollers. The second, or Bhunja Teli, parch the seed and then extract oil (Risley 1891, Vol. 2, 306). In neither of the two processes is there any association with any polluting substance and yet these two castes were excommunicated from the larger Teli caste group.

Three new castes are emerging among the Mochis of western India on the basis of their newly-acquired occupations. The Chandlagaras make lac bangles, the Chitaras are painters, and the Rasanis are electroplaters (Enthoven 1975: 57). While the separation of these castes from the original Mochi caste group can perhaps be explained on the basis of the notion of purity and pollution as these castes no longer do any tanning or skinning, however, the internal differentiation between these three jatis is not based on any polluting factor (see also Ghurye 1969: 83). Further, the Chungira Chamars distinguish themselves from other Chamars because they smoke their pipe differently (Cox 1970: 12). The

Ekbaliya and Dobaliya sub-castes of Telis separate
themselves from each other on the basis of whether they
yoke just one bull to the plough or two. The Goriya
potters refuse to identify themselves with other potters
and they keep this distinction alive by only fashioning
white pots and never black ones. There are also
communities of weavers that were once excommunicated
because they used artificial dyes (ibid). There is yet
another case, this time between whole caste groups.
Kaibartta and Tiyar fishing communities consider
themselves superior to Malos, another fishing caste
group, because in the netting process, the Kaibarttas
and the Tiyars always pass the netting needle from the
above downwards, working from left to right; while the
Malos pass it from below upwards, forming meshes
from right to left. It is remarkable that the same
difference is adduced to the Bihar fishermen as a proof
of the degraded rank of the Bajpar (quoted in Risley
1891: Vol. 2, 66).

Differences in marriage rites, jewellery, dress and
other such factors also neutral to purity or pollution are
adhered to rigidly by different castes, not always to
show their superiority, but to emphasize their differences.
These differences need to be made and emphasized.
Ideologies thrive only when they are able to condense a
large number of discrete phenomena in a comprehensive
and total manner and it is through this process that
ideologies attain their diacritical marks. There are certain
features many castes share in common. The Nabashakhas
(originally nine but now a group of fourteen castes)
have their ceremonies performed by the so-called
'orthodox' Brahmans. Their distinctiveness, however,
does not become redundant because of this. The Baidyas,
the Kayasthas, the Tantis, the Goalas—all members of

the Nabashakhas—follow customs which also separate them comprehensively from one another. These differences are zealously guarded, and the so-called lower castes observe caste distinctions as rigidly as their social betters (O'Malley 1975: 37; see also Briggs 1920). The Mahanayaka Sudras, a depressed agricultural caste, agree that '(L)oyalty to one's own caste must be preserved even at the cost of life.' (Bose 1960: 82.) It would seem as if these caste distinctions are also a matter of aesthetic judgment. The leader of the Jatav movement in Uttar Pradesh said: 'We do not want to be absorbed into others (caste and religion) and thereby lose our identity . . .' (Lynch 1972: 218.) In this connection it ought to be remembered that the Jatavs belong to an ex-untouchable community. As Yalman once put it 'Caste is not just appellation but quality of blood.' (Yalman 1969: 87.)

Within caste groups too endogamous jatis are separated by divergent customs. The Mogers, traditionally fishermen, are divided into three endogamous jatis: the Aliyasantana who inherit through females, the Makalasantana who inherit through males, and the Raudesantana who allow their widows to remarry (Enthoven 1975: 60). The Maheshri Meghvals do not worship Mata but the Marwada, Gojra and Charanua Meghvals do. Further, the Marwada and Gojra Meghvals unlike the Charaina Meghvals revere the saint Ramdev Puri. Maheshri Meghvals do not have the chori or marriage altar, but the Marwada Meghvals do (ibid: 49). The Charania Meghval will not do any skinning and tanning while the others have no particular objection to performing these tasks (ibid: 59).

Jati differentiation through multiple rituals signifies not so much different social histories of the various jatis

as it does a natural history which separates jatis
irreconcilably on a biological plane. This is the pre-
eminent value to which all those who participate in the
caste system subscribe. It is for this reason that endogamy
is effective only at the jati level. The abundance of
rituals, through social and aesthetized codes, guarantees
that neither common social circumstances nor the absence
of any visible biological variation among jatis sublates
the rationale of endogamy.

The need to separate is accompanied by a certain
reverence and pride in one's own customs and traditions
which is not easily jettisoned just to fall in line with
orthodoxy. The Dosadhs, a depressed agrarian caste
group, insist on a high-caste Hindu status and in keeping
with this claim have Maithil and Kannauj Brahmans
officiate their ceremonies; yet they do not conform to
Brahmanical views all the way. The Dosadhs revere the
deity Rahu even though this deity is considered a demon
(daitya) by Brahmans (Risley 1891: Vol. 1, 255). Other
castes like the Bhats—a pseudo-Brahman caste—or the
Kanhaipuriya Rajputs revere distinctly tribal, even anti-
Brahman deities (Blunt 1969: 285). The items that enter
into the making of the discrete character of castes are
thus very varied in character, and some of them do not
even have a Brahmanical or textual pedigree, but are
revered nevertheless by individual castes. To quote
Guirand (1975: 25):

> The greater the imprecision of the convention, the
> more the value of the sign varies according to the
> different users.

The necessity of symbols allows for the variation in
salience given to different symbols and ritualized practices
at different points of time. A primary symbol may at

times become a secondary symbol, and vice versa. This is especially evident when castes enter politics, as we shall see a little later. Some symbols and practices may even be dropped if they come in the way of secular advancement of the members of a particular caste, or if they are seen by them to be unduly onerous. The so-called 'fallen Brahmans', who perform ceremonies for the depressed castes were forced, due to pecuniary pressure to flout the Brahmanical ban against performing such services. Quite expectedly, they believe that their current degradation resulted from a chance occurrence in the remote past. The Dogras of Palampur in Himachal Pradesh consider themselves to be Rajputs and yet have, by and large, given up the practice of asking Brahmans to perform their ceremonies. They believe the Brahmans are too expensive and greedy. The Telis of Orissa have long valued child marriage, but are now asking their caste members to fall in line with the Sarda Act which prohibits child and infant marriage (Bose 1960: 29). The many rituals and beliefs that have been dropped, or added on, to justify occupational change are too numerous to be recorded here. Even the expiatory rites which all caste Hindus had to religiously undergo if they interacted with aliens are now increasingly becoming a thing of the past.

4

Race and Caste: Divergent Logics of Mobilization

Why Caste is not Race

It might help in furthering an understanding of the caste system if it were to be compared with a cognate phenomenon, viz., race, and particularly, racism. In doing so we not only discover new dimensions in race, but it also deepens our conception of the discrete nature of castes. As caste and race function on divergent logics, their political expressions too are quite varied. Consequently it will be worthwhile to spend a little time to spell out why the politics of preference—reservations and affirmative action—are carried out so differently in India and America. Of course, India and America are vastly dissimilar countries, but through it all the contrast between race and class also becomes more apparent.

There are certain similarities between caste and race, particularly when we compare the bottom end of the caste system with segregationist racism which, till recently, was practised in some parts of the United States and South Africa. The manner in which untouchables were treated in India, and, sadly, still continue to be persecuted in some parts of the sub-continent even today, and the treatment meted out to Blacks under segregationist racist regimes do possess startling commonalities. There were designated seats and water fountains for Blacks so that they would not intrude upon White spaces, just as untouchables were not allowed to drink, eat or mingle with the upper castes. Just as colour-based segregationism is justified on the basis of the superiority of the White race over others, the caste system too is informed by the notion of natural substances on account of which some castes are deemed to be less pure than others. These are the reasons why it is possible to talk of a 'racial caste system'. (Wilson 1978: 35.)

In spite of these many similarities there are important differences too between race and class for which reason they should not be collapsed into a single analytical category. Of course, the most obvious difference is that racial attitudes are determined by what is phenotypically on the surface. Except in rare instances, it is hard to distinguish between castes in the same fashion through appearance or skin colour. The belief that caste status varies inversely with the breadth of the nose is clearly an untenable proposition.

Further, the separation between races is not governed by notions of purity and pollution. While it was quite common in antebellum South to employ Black cooks, the very idea of having an untouchable in the kitchen would horrify caste Hindus. Blacks were not just cooks, but occasionally even wet nurses. In fact if one takes a closer look at antebellum South, it is interesting to observe that segregationism as it later developed in nineteenth century United States was not quite as virulent even on slave plantations. Racial segregation was never a part of public policy as the White plantation owners never felt threatened by the Black slaves.

Instead of segregationism there was a 'paternalistic racial etiquette'. (Ibid: 38.) The distance between the races was so great, and the threat of Blacks encroaching upon White privileges so unthinkable, that it was not necessary to come up with a segregationist policy. Even the infamous lynchings that used to take place in antebellum South rarely involved Blacks. Between 1840 and 1860 only 10 per cent of those lynched were Blacks (ibid: 36). Alexis de Tocqueville too observed that racial prejudice was higher in those parts of United States where the institution of slavery did not exist (Tocqueville 1969: 343). A fully developed racial theory which put Blacks down as being naturally inferior gained currency and body once the abolitionist became active in America (Gutman 1976: 46). Even as late as 1887, there were significant sections of the conservative White economic elite that did not really feel the need for Jim Crow legislations (Van Woodward 1951: 211).

Racism differs from caste on yet another level. In the caste system one's identity gets stronger as the unit of attachment gets more and more localized till we come to the jati level. So, the category Brahman, or Kshatriya does not arouse a sense of loyalty as jati affiliations like Kanyakubja Brahman, or Chitpavan Brahman do. But in racist Southern America or South Africa it does not matter whether a person comes from Norway or Germany or France or Holland. The important point is that they are all categorized as White. Likewise, anybody from Nigeria, or Mozambique or Ghana would be considered Black in spite of their many cultural differences. In racism, therefore, the logic is just the reverse. It is only Black or White that matters and not the actual points of origin or provenance.

Discrete Categories versus Continuous Hierarchies

Caste, as we discussed earlier, should be understood first in terms of discrete categories. Hierarchy obviously comes in, but as castes resist being placed together in a continuum, there is not one hierarchy but several. No caste considers itself to be actually made up of base and impure substances, no untouchable community believes that it rightfully occupies such a lowly position. This is in spite of the fact that all castes, no matter where they may be placed in terms of the existing structures of power, believe strongly in impurity and purity, and in all the other basic beliefs that inform the caste system. The disagreement primarily lies in the elaboration and in the practice of social distance based on hierarchy. The untouchables have their own origin tales as do the many castes that call themselves the martial castes, as also do those that claim Brahman status. Through these disparate tales and clearly differentiated rituals castes constantly signal their differences with one another. Thus, even if members of a depressed caste were to claim Brahman status, it is not as if they want to merge with the more established Brahman castes. They would rather want to be known as Brahmans of a different kind with their own distinctive diacritics. Endogamy would be kept alive and any suggestion that they marry into other Brahman castes would be fiercely resisted.

In the caste system if one were to marry against the rules then a person is outcasted. It is not as if they are merely brought down a notch or two in the caste hierarchy; instead, they are actually thrown out. The various Indian law books such as the *Yagnavalkyasmriti* and the *Manusmriti* warn that from the union of inter-caste marriages monsters and lower-caste people are produced. Indeed, this is how these texts conjure the origins of polluting castes such as leather workers (Chamars) and scavengers. Predictably, none of those castes that are considered to be polluting accept the Brahmanical versions; instead, they counter these versions with their own origin tales.

The matter is quite different with race. As race is based on phenotypical criteria there can be no dispute about where one belongs in the race hierarchy. It is of course the case that those who are Black resent the injustices heaped on them, but on no account can they dare claim that they are really not Black but White. This is quite unlike the case of the untouchables who can argue that they are really not untouchables, but have been degraded to this status because of chicanery, deceit, or lost war. In other words, while the race hierarchy may be seen as unjust, the fact that there is only one hierarchy, and a common standard, is indisputable. In the caste system, as we have already demonstrated, there are multiple hierarchies in existence on account of the discrete nature of caste categories.

The children born out of inter-caste unions, in the strictest sense, fall outside the caste system as do their parents. Such unions cannot be really called marriages as Hinduism forbids inter-caste sexual relations. The children of mixed racial marriages, however, are not outcastes or thrown outside the race hierarchy. They are part of the race hierarchy and are positioned within it. As long as one is one-sixty-fourth Black, convention has it that one should be considered as Black. This is what led Gene Lees to comment in *Jazzletter*: 'Is Black blood so strong and white blood so weak, that an ounce of the former is capable of wiping out generations of the latter?' (In Russel, Wilson, Hall 1992: 79.)

The Race Continuum

Children of inter-racial marriages often see themselves as superior to those who are Blacks, and indeed this is also how White people look at them. Light-skinned Blacks in fact do much better than those who are dark, and the most successful ones are those who are 'light at the top'. (Ibid: 34, 38.) Therefore, between the White and the Black there is a continuous hierarchy of colour gradations. The quadroons are one-fourth mixed blood, the octoroons are one-eighth, and so forth. Harry Hutchinson found eight terms in Brazil distinguishing different shades of Black. They are (i) preto—all Black, (ii) cabro—lighter than preto, with less kinky hair, (iii) cabo verde, who have dark skin but straight hair, thin lips and nose, (iv) escuro—dark skin with Caucasoid features, (v) mulatto—yellowish skin colour, kinky and curly hair, (vi) pardo, which is characterized by an even lighter skin than mulatto, (vii) followed by light skin, who are reddish blond but with Negroid features, and finally (viii) moreno, who are almost like Caucasians (Hutchinson 1957: 120). In French West Indies, there are a range of colours starting all the way from *beke* (white) to *congo* (black). (See Wagley 1959.)

In America too these fine colour distinctions exist. In 1945 Charles H. Parrish discovered 145 terms such as half-white, yaller, high yellow, brown, red bone, chocolate, ink spot, and tar baby (see Russel, Wilson, Hall 1992: 60). In the early decades of the twentieth century, mulatto clubs existed in different parts of America where darker Blacks were not allowed. Some of the well-known mulatto clubs were the Bon Ton Society in Washington and the Blue Vein Society in Nashville. Admission to all these clubs were based on strict physical critieria. In the Blue Vein club the applicant was examined to see whether the fine criss-cross of veins were clearly visible around the wrist. In some clubs the aspirants had to pass a 'brown paper bag and comb test'. If their skin colour was lighter than the paper bag and the comb passed through the hair without resistance then the person could be considered for admission (ibid: 24-38). Fortunately, these clubs are no longer in existence today.

As race is the determinant factor to one's status in such a society, a large number of Blacks would like to look as Caucasoid as possible. This is how the colour continuum is consolidated in the race context. In spite of the resistance of Black nationalists, journals which have a preponderant Black readership like *Ebony*, *Essence*, and *Jet* feature advertisements that promise to cure Blacks of their 'hair problem'. (Ibid: 47.) Light skin is definitely preferred to black if one were to examine the marriage pattern of successful Black men. In a survey conducted by the famous sociologist Melville Herskovits it was found that of the successful Harlem couples, 56.5 per cent men married lighter-skinned women (ibid: 108). Though Black men prefer to marry White women more than Black women want to marry White men—76 per cent : 29 per cent respectively (ibid: 116)—what is indubitable is the desire to merge with the White population to the maximum extent possible. Successful Black men like Fredrick Douglas, Alex Haley, Quincey Jones, Sidney Poitier, James Earl Jones, O.J. Simpson, and Justice Clarence Thomas, all married White women. While all these super-successful Black men could boast of White trophy wives, those who were not quite at that level married mulattos and lighter-skinned Blacks. Franz Boas once held out the hope that if inter-racial marriages were encouraged this would probably be the best way of combating racism (Sanjek 1994: 104). In this sense, perhaps, successful Black men are showing the way.

Race and Caste: Contrasting Implications

This should help to underscore the point that unlike caste, mixed marriages in the race situation lead to a colour continuum which is in principle very different from the discrete character of caste categories. In the race situation we also have the phenomenon of 'passing' which exists even today. 'Passing' occurs when deracinated persons of Black descent successfully conceal their ancestry and *pass* off for Whites (ibid: 73). 'Passing' is an unacceptable option in the caste system. No matter how disprivileged a jati might be it would not like to pass off as any other existing jati. It would stake its claim to a higher status than what it currently enjoys, but would keep its distinctiveness alive through endogamy, rituals and origin tales.

The colour complex in race is ideologically driven by Whites from above, while in the caste system the notion of purity-pollution and of multiple hierarchies have multiple points of generation. The caste system is not driven purely by Brahmanical preferences or pretences. As we discussed in the previous chapter it is not as if the Brahman is always held up as a model in the caste system. In fact there are occasions when the Brahman is actually despised. This is not so in a racist society, though Blacks have had a major difficulty in working up a specific heritage of their own of which they can be proud and with which they can stand up against the Whites. This can be contrasted again with castes where each discrete caste has its own origin tales, ritual observances, rules, and deep pockets of pride in their traditional heritage no matter how misunderstood some castes may feel in the current power configuration.

Stephen Steinberg argues that Blacks have all the ingredients that make for a strong sense of cultural identity. They have a sense of peoplehood, common ancestry and multiplicity of social and religious institutions (Steinberg 1995: 9). Though this is probably true what still remains is that Blacks do not have an established sense of common cultural identity of which they can be proud. Slave culture hardly affords the right kind of support for building such a heritage (Gutman 1976: 309). The African heritage did not go very far either. It attracted a few intellectuals, but a majority of them were not enthused by it. In a 1991 survey, for instance, 72 per cent still preferred to be called Blacks rather than Afro-Americans (Russel, Wilson and Hall 1992: 71).

There are major political repercussions too on this account. It is worthwhile in this context to contrast Black politics with caste politics. Before we do so we need to acknowledge the fact that social mobility among the Blacks has been very significant in America, especially in the last thirty years. Successful Blacks have now begun to move in to White neighbourhoods. The number of racial inter-marriages has also gone up quite dramatically. From a mere 51,000 in 1960, inter-racial marriages have climbed up to 2,11,000 in 1980. Even in the 1970s much of this would have been practically unthinkable. Today one among ten college students is a Black which is up from 6.1 per cent two decades ago (Kilson 1983: 85). The largest expansion in Black employment figures has been in professional ranks (ibid), with the most startling changes in the rising compositions of Blacks in engineering and managerial jobs (ibid: 86). As Kilson notes: 'Upper strata blacks are employed increasingly not in ghetto but in national job markets in national (White) banks, insurance companies, retail firms, industries, and universities, and government agencies (ibid: 86-87).

It is important to acknowledge these figures for they tell how effectively Blacks have been able to make inroads into White establishments. If the Jews can now be 'white folks' (Sacks 1994; see also Sanjek 1994: 108), Blacks too can one day hope to enter the White mainstream. Yet their colour will always mark them out from Whites. Race will still be an important social marker, but perhaps racism will lose its sting.

The manner in which successful Blacks are able to consolidate themselves is an indication of the basic open-endedness of American class society. That Blacks are able to come up through sheer dint of hard work and merit clearly demonstrates that the significance of race is declining (Wilson 1978). To a large extent the Affirmative Action programme also helped. But Blacks have not come out in full-throated support of Affirmative Action programmes though undoubtedly the rise in the number of Black professionals was significantly aided by such legislative measures. On the whole, it would seem that Blacks are reluctant to accept that Affirmative Action has had anything to do with their upward mobility, and when these programmes are dismantled in different states of America (most dramatically in San Francisco), there has been no marked protest by Blacks. The inability of Blacks to ideologically succour themselves as a distinct and independently buoyant community has contributed to their pacifism on this score.

Politics of Preference: India and U.S.A.

In contrast to Black politics which is slowly becoming obsolete, caste politics shows no signs of ennui or decay. Partly, it is because India is still not a dynamic industrial society as America is, and this point cannot be overlooked. But it must also be said that the inability of Blacks to sustain an independent identity and heritage has contributed to the failure of Black politics. The quiescence with which they have accepted the dismantling of the Affirmative Action programme demonstrates this fact. This inability to work up opposition to the abandonment of Affirmative Action policies reveals, rather starkly, that the continuum of race within which Black identity must be factored has political implications. These are quite different from what happens when mobilizations are stoked by the logic of discrete castes with deep, compelling and independent heritages.

Most Indians do not realize that our country is not unique in having a reservation policy. In many modern nation-states, and not all of them are terribly democratic, there is some form of affirmative action or reservation policy. In Malaysia reservation exists for the Malay *bhoomiputra* (literally 'sons of the soil'); in Pakistan, for bringing a fairer representation among the various provinces; in Ireland for the Catholics; and in North America for Blacks and Native Indians. India is probably the first country in the world to devise reservation policies, but there are many others now that have their own form of preferential policy in place.

That some form of reservation or affirmative action exists in many countries should not blind us to the many differences that exist between them. It is true that communities as diverse from one another as the Malays, the Irish Catholics and the Mohawk Indians may all be targeted beneficiaries of reservations or affirmative action programmes, but the circumstances of their lives are quite different. The Malay *bhoomiputras* are the dominant political community in their own country but depend on preferential policy to combat the prosperous Malays of Chinese origin in the urban sectors (Means 1986: 95-118). In Pakistan, a kind of preferential employment exists so that different regions in the country feel represented (Horowitz 1985: 668). Originally, the policy was intended to accommodate the East Pakistani Bengalis, but it continued to remain in effect even after the formation of Bangladesh. The Catholics in Ireland may be persecuted, but they are certainly not lacking in skills and education necessary for being competitive in modern times.

The reservation policy as envisaged in the Indian Constitution, and Affirmative Action in the United States resemble each other to a remarkable extent. In both cases, the express intention is to rely on preferential policy to uplift those communities that have been historically disprivileged. The Scheduled Castes and Tribes in India and the Native Indians and Blacks in America have been victims of discrimination and prejudice for long periods of time. This prevented them from acquiring educational and cultural skills necessary for economic success in contemporary societies. Skills such as the ones they possessed not only confined them to the lowest rungs in the traditional order, but did not empower them either to forge ahead independently when the old economy and its accompanying social relations were dismantled.

Modernization and the Liberal Agenda

Modernization and industrialization did not however

inaugurate the awareness that historical disprivileges need to be corrected. That sensitivity came with the deepening of democratic practices and sentiments. Early liberal philosophy was only committed to the market and to the curbing of monarchical authority. In John Locke, for instance, property qualifications still remained the basis for exercising franchise, women were not recognized as being politically equal to men, and those who were not Anglican were not seen as full citizens and were accordingly prevented from occupying certain public offices. Liberty and equality had a much more restricted scope than what they enjoy today. When William Wilberforce and Lord Shaftesbury fought against slavery they met with serious opposition even in Britain. In nineteenth century England the Chartists had to struggle to give women the right to vote.

Democracy in practice today is thus vastly different from what it was even till as late as the early decades of this century. The racist 'separate but equal' clause operated in America, particularly in relation to educational institutions, till as recently as 1954. Under this clause Black children could be legally disallowed from attending schools meant for White children. Even after this provision was shot down in the justly famous Brown vs. Board of Education case in 1954, many southern states in America refused to implement it. Affirmative Action first made its appearance during Kennedy's presidency, and even then it was not powered by legislation but by executive decrees.

Preferential policies came up when it was recognized that liberty and equality do not necessarily mean the establishment of fraternity. If the triumvirate are to go together then there needs to be a self-conscious designing of political interventions such that those who have been historically disprivileged can actually in practice get a fair chance to compete as equals. Obviously such a programme recognizes unequal starting conditions for politically equal citizens which the forces of the market are generally blind to, and indeed would even exaggerate. Therefore, while such preferential policies do not disband the market, except in extreme 'socialist conditions' the attempt is to restrain the market in certain spheres so that eventually there can be a greater and fulsome market participation.

The introduction of preferential policies to uplift the historically disprivileged came about for different reasons in different countries. In America it was certainly a combination of factors that brought it about. The growing civil rights movement, the Democratic Party's striving for a political niche, and the ideological need felt by America to stand out as the leader of the free world in the Cold War era, together led to the establishment of Affirmative Action. Preferential policy in Canada had a different trajectory and inspirational source. The divide between Quebec and the rest of Canada prompted the politics of multiculturalism around which provisions for equal rights opportunity and minority representation found their ideological rationale.

Though the reasons, provocations and compulsions to introduce reservations or affirmative action differ from country to country, the Indian case still remains unique because preferential policies were introduced here along with the inauguration of democracy and the founding of the republic. What took about two hundred years to make a tentative appearance in the United States emerged fully articulated and theorized almost at the instant that India became a sovereign and democratic nation-state.

Questioning Quotas

The major differences between reservations in India and Affirmative Action in America crystallize around the question of quotas. All other divergences between these two forms of preferential policies flow from this basic distinction. In India, from the start, reservations have been operationalized on the principle of quotas. Thus, in proportion to their population, approximately 23 per cent of jobs and educational opportunities are reserved for the Scheduled Castes and the Scheduled Tribes. In America, on the other hand, Title VII, which is the main weapon of the Affirmative Action programme, makes explicit that the quota principle will not be entertained at any cost. Title VII went on to assert that Affirmative Action will not in any case mean the lowering of qualifications and the undermining of merit. It is interesting that on this issue there has been a near unanimity in American politics. The left and the right, as well as the Affirmative Action activists, have all concurred that *quota* is a bad five-letter word. Time and time again proponents of Affirmative Action go to great lengths to clarify that they do not support the quota system. In fact a 1988 survey found that about 50 per cent of Black respondents said that they were against Affirmative Action and would not like to benefit from it.

This in no way should suggest that racist attitudes have died in America. Though White males in America constitute only 43 per cent of the population they hold 95 per cent of the top executive jobs in the country. Black adult males have an unemployment rate that is five times higher than the national average. Even the judicial system is weighted against Blacks. Possession of crack invites much higher punishment than the possession of cocaine. One must possess 100 times more cocaine than crack to receive the same sentence. In spite of medical evidence that shows that the two are equally harmful this law is still in force. This is because Black drug users are addicted to crack whereas the White addicts consume cocaine. Though roughly 13 per cent of drug addicts in America are Blacks, which is roughly equal to their proportion of the American population, 74 per cent of those serving jail sentences for drug possession are Blacks. Add to this the startling fact that between 1982 and 1992 the Los Angeles Federal Court did not convict a single White person for possessing crack.

In spite of all this many Blacks still feel reluctant to take advantage of the Affirmative Action programme. American democracy from the very beginning has been strongly individualistic in character. The Horatio Alger story of rising from rags to riches, the tales of how the west was won by sheer individual persistence and determination, and accounts of how the early settlers refused to allow status considerations of the Old World to nestle in the colonies, are all parts of the popular lore that most Americans hold very dearly.

Contrast this individualistic spirit of the Americans with the Indian case. During the Constituent Assembly debates over the making of the Constitution, the Sub-Committee on Fundamental Rights held that 'it is difficult to expect that in a country like India where most persons are communally minded, those in authority will give equal treatment to those who do not belong to their community.' (Shiva Rao 1968a: 98.) In fact the Constituent Assembly proceedings are littered with instances of community considerations overriding those of the individuals. This is what prompted Alladi Iyengar and Rajkumari Amrit Kaur to remark during the debate on fundamental rights that the exceptions were constantly eating up the rule.

Part of the resentment to quotas in America can be traced to the time when a kind of reverse quota system was in operation against the Jewish community. Till about the 1930s many universities had an informal quota system that restricted the number of Jewish students in their campuses. Now that Jews have 'become white folks' (Sacks 1994: 83-84) the fact that such a practice was ever in place fills most Americans with revulsion. While this sentiment is genuine among most Americans, their opposition to quotas in the Affirmative Action programme is at a more fundamental level. In a series of surveys conducted in America by a variety of agencies all confirm the finding that Americans of different socio-economic categories are united in their opposition to quotas. Blacks too find the quota system distasteful and would not like affirmative action linked to it. The Gallup Poll of March 1991, the NBC Wall Street Journal Poll of March 1994, the L.A. Times Poll of January 1995, as well as the poll conducted by the National Conference of Christians and Jews in March 1994 all confirm this tendency. American law too does not allow exceptions of any kind on the question of equal treatment for all, unlike Indian law (see Sowell 1995: 105-06).

The fact that a constitutional amendment was easily made after the Champakam vs. State of Madras case of 1951 to accommodate caste-based admissions and preferences would be quite unthinkable in American jurisprudence. This is why whenever there is any sign of Affirmative Action infringing on individual rights the courts in America generally rule against Affirmative

Action. For example, the court upheld the petition that the regents of California University had filed against race-based quotas in the famous Steve Bakke case. Subsequently there have been whole slews of legal decisions that have stopped all considerations of quota in their tracks in America. These include landmark judgements such as City of Richmond vs. Croon in 1989, and Miller vs. Johnson in 1995.

India and America: Role of Individualism

In order to understand public policy and its implementation in America, it is important to pay attention to the emotive bonds that define what is it to be an American. This strategy holds equally for other nation-states too. Thus, to appreciate the complexities of, and the complicities behind, the reservation system in India it is necessary to have an idea of how this policy found its place in India's political and social firmament. Americans do not revere family wealth the way most Indians, or even Europeans, do. Many Americans even manufacture a 'rags-to-riches' story just to look good and be admired. For example, Sylvester Stallone had once invented a heart-wrenching penury-to-wealth fable of himself that so offended his upper-middle class parents that they had to publicly deny it.

The strong individualism that is dramatized in these rags-to-riches narratives, in many ways brings to the fore how Americans generally perceive themselves. In popular recall, America was made by intrepid colonizers who by their sheer grit and valour tamed the west. In America too, the early settlers made sure that foppish old European ways replete with Old-World status considerations were not allowed to gain ground. This vision of itself by America was further reinforced in the

Cold War days. Communism was demonized effectively for it was portrayed as being fundamentally antithetical to the foundational ethic of American individualism. As America is the land of the free and the brave it was duty-and honour-bound to resist communism and its collectivist ideology at home and abroad.

There are other ways too, in which this individualist tendency is manifested and indeed encouraged. In America role models do not last for more than a generation. In fact, parents are rarely idolized by their children, and each generation must find its own stars and templates. The drive to realize oneself and not to fall back on hand-me-down role models pressurizes Americans to find themselves and do their own thing, no matter in which walk of life they may be placed.

The workplace too is a site for self-expression, just as much as Hollywood studios and playing fields are. It is not at all surprising, that several leading figures in twentieth-century commerce and industry, from Henry Ford to Bill Gates, have come from America. Some of the most path-breaking films are still American productions. In the sports arena from basketball to boxing, America leads the way in innovative styles and superlative performances. Music is another industry that carries the imprint of American experimentation with a variety of *genres*—from blue grass, to jazz, to rock and roll. America's fashion industry too is very unlike its European counterpart. Whereas in France, for instance, fashion is created on the drawing board by eminent designers in haute couture fashion houses, distinctive styles in America emanate from the kind of gear young people wear when shuffling around in the mean streets of Chicago and New York. Quite like the marketing of jazz in the 1930s and 1940s, fashion innovations at the popular level are picked up by commercial houses, who then package and label them for a wider audience.

Seen against this background it is not at all surprising that quotas should have such a difficult time in America. Title VII that backs up the Affirmative Action programme in the United States does not just stop at quotas. It goes further to say that Affirmative Action should not dilute standards in order to be more representative. The thinking behind this is obviously that preferential policies in America are there to remove prejudices that exist among individuals who are intrinsically equal. Compromising on standards would then be seen as a patronizing act, made worse by the fact that individual brilliance may cease to be rewarded. What the Affirmative Action policy endorses is that, other things being equal an effort should be made to encourage Black and Native Indian employment and school enrolment. The fact that the University of California had introduced a quota system, which expressly went against this formulation, led to the eventual dismantling of Affirmative Action with the passage of proposition 209. Interestingly, proposition 209 was placed by the regents of the University of California at Berkeley, and piloted by a leading Black member of that committee.

Role of Community

It is tempting to see either the Indian or the American case as paradigmatic, and the other as the exception to the rule. There are, however, some striking similarities in the two instances. In both America and India, the targeted community is a clear minority. Blacks make up about 12 per cent of the American population, whereas the Scheduled Castes and Tribes constitute roughly 22

per cent of the population of India. Against this common
feature it is worthwhile to factor in the various differences
which can explain why quotas are so appealing in one
case, and anathemic in the other. We have already said
how individualism in America acts as a deterrent against
quotas. Yet to fully appreciate why this argument has
won the day it is necessary to take into account some of
the other specifics that separate these two countries.

Politics in India has always been acutely sensitive to
community pressures. In fact on occasions the debates
in the Constituent Assembly was so tilted in favour of
community representation rather than individual rights
that it prompted Alladi K. Ayyar to rebuke the members
with the remark: 'Is this a chapter on fundamental
rights or is it a chapter on discriminatory provisions?'
(Ibid: 221.) The fear, quite obviously, in the minds of
those like Alladi K. Ayyar, B.N. Rau, and Rajkumari
Amrit Kaur was that such undiluted concern for
community privileges would erode the status of the
individual, and make the community a perennial interest
group. Anticipating this eventuality, Ambedkar while
moving the draft Constitution on 23 November 1948
commented rather explicitly that it would be 'equally
wrong for minorities to perpetuate themselves.' (Shiva
Rao, 1968b: 766.)

In contrast to the United States, in India the individual
is not as important as the group. It is through group
membership and not category affiliation that the
reservation programme in India gets its impetus. One of
the major reasons is of course to be found in the
character of India's national movement. As the British
authorities kept attempting to divide Indians along
caste, religious and linguistic lines, it became all the
more important for the protagonists of the national

movement to rise above such fissures, present a united front, and not let community spokespersons be persuaded by colonial designs. This is what led to a heightened sensitivity among the nationalists to unite communities across lines drawn by caste prejudices and religious intolerance. This is why the establishment of quotas was never seriously opposed, even though some like Jawaharlal Nehru were very skeptical of it.

Obviously, it is not enough to say that communities dominate India while the individual occupies the centre-stage in America. Such a statement needs to be fleshed out in terms of the social milieu that makes such sentiments dominant in their respective settings. When India became independent in 1947 the democratic world had moved way ahead of what it used to be even as late as in the opening decades of this century. Thus India was striding two time scales. On the one hand it could not turn its back on the centuries of progress that liberal thought and practice had introduced in the modern world, and at the same time it did not have the necessary institutional depth to abide by individualistic norms so characteristic of liberalism. While liberal societies realized the importance of self-consciously boosting fraternity after approximately two hundred years of democracy, India launched into preferential policies right away with the stroke of the constitutional pen the moment it became a republic.

In America preferential policies were initiated during the Kennedy years, advanced, paradoxically, by Richard Nixon, and began to atrophy from around the mid-1980s. Somehow they do not seem to possess the necessary ideological thrust and for which reason they are alive, but sick: more kicked about than kicking. This is largely because America prides itself in being the home of the free in the sense that communities and religious affiliations can neither be used as a source of strength, nor the focus of abuse. The American Revolution, quite characteristically, brought disestablishment of churches in its wake. New York was the first state to be disestablished in 1777, followed by Virginia in 1785. Gradually the remaining states followed suit and in 1833, with the disestablishment of the Congregationalist church in Massachusetts, the process was complete in the entire country. In this entire series of spectacular reversals for the church it is true that the individual triumphed, but this was really possible because the Protestants amalgamated, for all practical purposes, as a single phalanx. As an overwhelming majority it set standards for the rest by depending, above all, on its unquestionable dominance in society. To understand how this denouement eventually occurred is not central to this paper. Suffice it to say that women and clerics took the sting out of an angry and wrathful Protestant religion and made it soft and forgiving (see Douglas 1977: 18, 94 ff.). At any rate, the White Anglo-Saxon Protestants (WASPs) put their distinctive stamp on the American way of life and controlled the social and cultural life in the New World. Other communities became 'ethnics' against the backdrop of WASP homogeniety, and indeed, hegemony. No wonder ethnics such as Italians, Greeks and even Jews, strove to shed their peculiarities and merge with the powerful and influential WASP majority. The effects of this tendency are clearly visible in America today, but the process began long ago. The interesting point in all this is how such a WASP majority was constituted by deliberately underplaying the doctrinal differences between discrete extant Protestant denominations such as the

Episcopalians, Methodists, Baptists, Congregationalists, and so forth. Perhaps, as Ann Douglas suggests, 'Ministers and Mothers' had a great deal to do with this (ibid).

In Europe and England, on the other hand, majority culture dominated largely because of religious intolerance and discrimination. In England, the home of democracy, non-Anglicans suffered from all kinds of disprivileges. It was only after the Tests and Establishment Act was disbanded in the 1880s that the Catholics became legally equal to Anglicans. The American route to majoritarianism was certainly more democratic in orientation but the fact still remains that minority consciousness was not on the agenda. When minority consciousness came about it was with reference to Blacks and Native Indians, but these communities were faced with a rather monolithic WASP majority whose social lifestyle and aesthetic preferences set the tone for the American way of life. Thus even while Hollywood was dominated by Jews, the films they produced were all about WASPs. It is only now—after Jews have become 'white folks'—that the likes of Woody Allen have made the portrayal of Jews quite acceptable in American films. Movie stars like Paul Newman can now openly talk about their Jewish heritage. Not just films, but in the academic world too, it paid to be a WASP, or, at least to be perceived as one. The famous sociologist Robert K. Merton did not reveal his Jewish identity till well after he had retired. All through these years he put up the front of a quintessential WASP. No one suspected his real identity for he played the role of the WASP to the hilt.

To Compensate or To Redress:
Emphasizing the Individual or the Community

In some ways it could well be said that India was ahead of other democracies because it did not allow majoritarianism to congeal. At any rate, from the beginning minority consciousness was dominant in the Indian political process. The concern with Scheduled Castes and Scheduled Tribes is a subset of this minority consciousness. These communities were considered vulnerable not just because they were fewer in number, but also because they were historically prevented from acquiring skills and qualities that could enable them to prosper independently. This is why reservations is not really about protecting cultures but about raising the status of hitherto disprivileged peoples so that they can compete as equals and indeed be able to fight more effectively for rights guaranteed in the Constitution.

In America the presumption behind Affirmative Action is somewhat different. Preferential policy in this case is to combat prejudice that disallows otherwise qualified Black people from occupying their rightful positions. This is why in America the principle of *compensation* animates Affirmative Action (see Cohen, Nagel and Scanlon 1977). In India, on the other hand, it is not so much compensation but the extirpation of the caste system that is emphasized. This is because it is believed that the caste system left to itself would routinely bar members of certain designated castes from acquiring competitive skills of the marketplace. Americans obviously tend to believe that there are qualified Blacks around and it is only prejudice that stands in the way. It is for this reason that Affirmative Action activists too would not allow for dilution of standards. However, in India the reservation system is based on the conception that basic skills have to be developed before the hitherto disprivileged stand a chance to compete on their own. This is probably why quotas are so important here. Compensation works best when it is individually handed out. Further compensation makes sense when the origins of discrimination are historically recent and in some ways today's advantaged sections can feel guilty of the deprivations their forebears had subjected other communities to in the not too distant past.

Compensation does not work in India because the origins of caste discrimination go too far back into the hoary past. Secondly, compensation is effective when the benefits are given out to those who can make full use of it as and when the situation presents itself. A compensation is never given out in advance but only after a case has been made out and the beneficiary is found to be worthy of receiving it. Compensations are generally graded depending upon a variety of circumstances, of which the claimants' qualifications count for a good bit. In India it is not the principle of compensation but that of extirpating the evils of the caste system that provided the initial ideological rationale for reservations. There is more redressal here (which is community based) than compensation. It is for this reason that the founding figures of the Indian Constitution were keen that reservations should not be allowed in perpetuity, but should be reviewed every so many years. But reservations were given to communities and that is why the quota system and the dilution of standards for accommodating Scheduled Castes and Tribes had to be entertained.

The next question is: why has the reservation system been allowed to last this long though the Constitution had clearly stated that there should be periodical reviews

of it? It is true that the lot of the Scheduled Castes and
Tribes has not changed enough for the reservation
system to be disbanded altogether. Nevertheless, the
fact is that there does not seem to be any political will
to curb the wanton use of quotas in India. In my view
the Scheduled Castes and Tribes by themselves are not
responsible for such a political sentiment. Quotas have
become politically sacrosanct because the prosperous
agricultural castes have used them to enhance their
prospects in urban India. Though the Constitution left
room for the so-called Backward Castes to receive some
form of preferential treatment, the wholesale adoption
of the quota system is just a willful political extension
of the reservation system as it was applied to the
Scheduled Castes and Tribes. Tamil Nadu was the first
to initiate this change following which, the Champakkam
case was filed against it in 1951. But by 1971 the
prosperous agrarian castes like the Vokkaligas of
Karnataka demanded and received the benefits of quota-
based reservation as they had Devraj Urs and Mrs
Indira Gandhi to back them up. Initially the Lingayats
were kept out in keeping with the Hanavur Commission
report. This was a political move as Devraj Urs wanted
to isolate the Lingayats and win over the Vokkaligas.
However, the Lingayats eventually were included once
Ramakrishna Hegde came to power in Karnataka (Parikh
1997: 172-75).

The acceptance in 1990 by V.P. Singh of the Mandal
Commission recommendations only nationalized what
was already happening in large parts of South India.
This fact is not always fully appreciated. With the
Yadavs, Kurmis and Koeris now becoming beneficiaries
of reservations for the Backward Castes, there is no
question now of holding back quotas, or even of revisiting

them. The Scheduled Castes and Tribes are therefore the indirect beneficiaries of the Mandal Commission and the Hanavur Commission and all that happened between these two events. Kaka Kalelkar's inability to designate Backward Castes on any firm set of criteria was considered as being too academic. The Rane Commission's espousal of economic criteria for backwardness had just no takers. Quotas instead came to rule the day. The outcome was an espousal of the equality of results more than the equality of opportunity. In other words, the end product became more important than the democratic process.

Even so, what has been achieved is a big step for a country in which till recently even the shadow of an untouchable was polluting. We may not yet fully appreciate the credo of the equality of individuals, but democracy in India has certainly brought about a developed understanding of equality between groups. This is why there is fierce, competitive rivalry between groups rather than between individuals. It is not as if the individual does not exist, but the tendency to refract the individual through a group rather than see it apart is indeed very strong. Unfortunately, with the extension of the quota system, and the entrenchment of the quota mentality, it will not be very easy to make the transition from equality between communities to equality between individuals. It is here that political statesmanship is critical as it helps society either skip through, or make a rapid exit from painful stages that come in between. A sociologist can only comment on the consequences of different political interventions. It is for the political system to ultimately make the difference.

Conclusion

The sense of belonging that the caste system engenders is on account of its discrete character. Each caste values its heritage as inviolable and does not want to merge with other castes, no matter how highly placed or privileged, the latter may be in the current context. Democracy today has made it possible for a caste to express its antagonism in a routine manner against hierarchies of the privileged communities. Such resentments do not have to wait for a cataclysmic upheaval, a war, or large-scale revolts. Democracy allows lower-class resentment to be voiced as a matter of right, and not because of some extraordinary privilege. Given the strong attachment to caste identities, politics in India has a greater predilection towards an expression of group equality than towards individual opportunities and dignity.

It is of course very likely that over the years caste identities might get eroded, because of the combined effects of increasing urbanization and economic mobility. This would bring about a greater number of inter-caste marriages which would make ascriptive identities more a matter of choice than just birth. In American censuses, self-identification is now becoming the norm as it is impossible to affix any one cultural identity on account of the high frequency of inter-cultural and inter-racial marriages. It, therefore, depends on what the respondent wants to believe is his or her cultural heritage. The same person's sibling, or parents, may give a completely different response regarding their cultural identity. A particular person may enter his or her identity as Scottish, but others in the same family may believe they have an Irish background. Both would be true, because neither of them would be expressing the whole truth, which in any case is too varied to remember or record.

The more potent form of identity in America is thus race rather than cultural heritage. But as race can be arranged unambiguously in the form of a continuous hierarchy it cannot provide the kind of symbolic energy that is required to sustain long-term political mobilization. This is truer still of contemporary American society. Over the past decades there has been a gradation of different races and of their accompanying economic status in the United States. Strong attachments cannot emerge from within a continuous hierarchy, especially when there is significant scope for vertical mobility within it. On the other hand, in the case of discrete communities like castes, there is no question of merging with someone else who is of another caste. The deep commitment that people have to their own caste explains why in the Indian case quotas possess such ideological resonance in caste mobilization. It is the entire community that seeks redressal. In America on the other hand, individuals can be separated from their community and compensated as racial ties are not full-bodied on account of their location in a continuous hierarchy.

5

Brahman, Baniya, Raja

Scholarship on the Indian caste system was initially predisposed towards a Brahmanical point of view. This, as we said earlier was on account of Indological studies and also because scholars were usually trained to rely more on the written word and on sacred texts.

Gerald Berreman's spirited attack of such a Brahmanical perspective is already well known (Berreman 1991). He was one of the first scholars to dramatically draw our attention to the Brahman-obsessive and dependent nature of caste studies. Since then there has been a renewal of interest in Hocart (1945) as can be seen in the works of Dirks (1987), Raheja (1988) and Quigley (1993) where the Kshatriya principle is elevated over the Brahmanical one. This has considerably opened up the field of caste studies. Even so the Baniya end is still woefully under-researched. This is indeed unfortunate for Hocart-inspired scholarship tends to replace purity with power without fully appreciating the discrete character of castes and the existence of multiple hierarchies.

But let us begin with Brahmans. The case at this level too appears highly contentious.

The Brahman as a Fiction

The discrete character of castes and of individual caste ideologies, as reflected in their tales of origin, make it possible for those belonging to the depressed and subaltern castes to not see themselves as intrinsically impure or despicable. They regard their current, rather unenviable, position as an outcome of Brahman chicanery, or of some chance misdeed of their ancestors (see Cohn 1975: 207). It is for this reason that they find it possible not only to believe in myths contrary to Brahman myths (see also Fuller 1992: 30) but are also capable of inviting Brahmans to perform their ceremonies even though this is contrary to superior caste injunctions. In case Brahmans as a whole steadfastly refuse to service a particular caste then the caste itself comes up with its own caste priests. That the Lingayats of Mysore learned to do this is often recorded. The Chamars too have their own Chamarwa Brahmans (Briggs 1920: 277), and according to Risley's report even Goalas have their own priests (Risley 1891: Vol. 1, 289). In Orissa when Brahmans boycotted Gauras (or Gopalas) because the latter refused to be their palanquin bearers, the Gauras got hold of an unlettered and unattached Brahman to perform religious services for them. This Brahman assiduously attended the government-sponsored Adult Education Centre to become more than functionally literate, and then trained himself to to the ritual needs of his Gaura clients. After three years the Brahmans broke their boycott (Bose 1960: 157).

Today, low castes such as Koeris, Bhars, Pasis and Dosadhs are served by Brahman priests. These priests are not given priestly status by the orthodox Brahmans, but are recognized as priests by the castes they serve, and therefore, it is eventually the caste itself that accords priestly status or otherwise in flagrant opposition, if necessary, to orthodoxy. The low-caste Mauliks of Bengal, like the powerful Lingayats of Mysore, also have their own priests and as a matter of fact revere them more than they do the so-called fallen Brahmans who occasionally serve them (Risley 1981: Vol. 2, 83). The Maheshri Marwada and Gojra Meghvals have their own jati priests too (Enthoven 1975: 50), and do not feel the absence of pure Brahmans. The Dravida Kazhagam went so far as to create its own ritual text from the Thirukkural and called it the Tamil Veda (Subramaniam 1974: 15). On the ground, the Brahman thus degenerates to a fiction, and his exaltation as a putative reality is dependent on other castes. Only orthodoxy, and the Brahmanical elaboration of the caste ideology can assert, as Dumont does when he writes, that 'Brahman could exist without Kshatra not conversely.' (Dumont 1970a: 63.)

To quote a very revealing passage from E.A.H. Blunt (1969: 37):

> Eggeling, for instance, has asserted that the cardinal principle which underlies the system of caste is the preservation of purity of religious belief and ceremonial usage. All that need be said here is that if the caste system was devised with the object of preserving 'the purity of belief and ceremonial usage', it has been a singular failure.

The Impure Priest

That the position of the Brahman is not quite unassailable was never seriously entertained in earlier studies. It was routinely assumed that Brahmans were always unquestionable primarily because they were ritual specialists (e.g. Singer 1972: 89; Heesterman 1985: 27). Purity of status and ritual functions were thus seen as being closely related. The Brahmans were also considered to be authorities on Hinduism, orthodoxy and orthopraxy. If scholars or administrators had any doubts about caste ranking or practices the problem was sorted out by asking for the Brahman's opinion on the subject (Cohn 1987: 245).

In 1985, Parry struck the first blow, in mainstream anthropology, on the hitherto unquestioned correlation between purity and ritual specialization. In his study of the funeral priests of Benaras, Parry asserts that Brahmans remove spiritual impurity by taking on the sins of the person for whom the ritual is being performed (Parry 1985: 89). This is why Brahmans often complain that the *dana* they receive during the course of a ritual is so 'difficult to digest' (Parry 1990: 621). As Fuller had earlier clarified, it is important to distinguish between a *dana* and *dakshina*. The *dakshina* is like a tip which may or may not be given (or taken) after the completion of the ritual, but the *dana* is an integral element of the ritual itself (Fuller 1984: 66) and the Brahman is obliged to take it along with the impurities or inauspiciousness (Raheja 1988: 33-34; also Parry 1986) it purveys. This is what allowed Declan Quigley to felicitously contrast the 'pure' Brahman against the 'impure' priest (Quigley 1993: 54-60). Raheja's field material also confirms this. The Brahmans of Pahansu village in Uttar Pradesh know the dangers of accepting *dana* and yet accept it from the Gujars who are the dominant caste of the village (Rajeha 1988: 34).

Attention now shifts to an examination of whether being a ritual specialist is what it is often cracked up to be. Contemplation along these lines leads one to observe that the first thing that a Brahman community does on achieving power and wealth is to give up being a ritual specialist. If performing rituals were the key to a Brahman's superiority, as scholars from Max Mueller to Weber to Heesterman to Dumont assert, then why should a prosperous Brahman give up that very activity that adds to the prestige and purity of the individual and the community. On the other hand, if the performance of ritual implies the ingestion of inauspiciousness, or impurity, of others, then being a priest is quite a risky profession.

Chris Fuller's detailed ethnography of a South Indian temple (1991) adds body and credibility to this line of thought. The Agami priests of Meenakshi temple are considered inferior by domestic priests who perform Vedic rituals. The domestic priests consider themselves to be better off for unlike the temple priests they do not have to serve devotees of all castes (Fuller 1991: 53-61). The further charge that domestic priests make is that the Adi Shaiva temple priests are originally from non-Brahman stock and hence are not quite up to the mark (ibid: 53). Needless to say the Agami priests dispute such an allegation. The Adi Shaivas go on to argue that they are superior to non-priestly Brahmans as well (ibid: 59).

Anthropology has certainly come a long way. Till not too long ago even a scholar of Milton Singer's stature had little inkling regarding the disputes over rank between temple and domestic priests (Singer 1972: 89,111). True, William Crooke and L.S.S. O'Malley had observed long ago that there exists a hierarchy among different categories of priests (Crooke 1906: 24; see also Fuller 1991: 51) but this observation was not substantiated nor integrated into anthropology in the way Parry's and Fuller's theories have been.

The Kshatriya Principle

If the Brahman's ritual function does not allow him the privilege of being undisputed at the top of the hierarchy, does this position then belong to some other caste, such as those who call themselves Kshatriya? This indeed would be the tenor of Nicholas Dirks (1987), Raheja (1988) and Quigley (1993). Though the original inspiration could have been Hocart (1945), but at least Dirks and Raheja seem to have been independently inspired by their respective field studies.

Nicholas Dirks superimposes anthropological theory on historical records to show the centrality of politics. According to Dirks '. . . politics plays a powerful role in the social organisation of caste and kinship, that politics is fundamental to the process of hierarchization and the formation of units of identity.' (Dirks 1987: 259.) This leads Dirks to conclude that the 'caste system as a whole was ordered in relation to the king.' (Ibid: 284.) In a temple ritual then, the first honour went to the king. The Brahman came next (ibid: 291).

Chris Fuller's study has a different focus but also arrives at a similar position. His detailed ethnographic expertise of South Indian temples leads him to conclude: 'At a temple the priest usually gives *prasada* to the person of the highest rank first . . . In the past, particularly at an important temple, the person was often a king. In most smaller temples, the person was and is a local magnate . . .' (Fuller 1992: 93.) These arguments are contrary to Dumont's view that the Brahman, without question, sits at the top of the caste hierarchy. Even the Indologist Madeleine Biardeau gives the king a far greater and critical religious role than what Dumont's 'pure' hierarchy would have allowed (Biardeau 1989: 14; see also Deliege 1992). All these observations are quite in line with Hocart's early assessment that the king was the main sacrificer (Hocart 1945: 35), and that it is the king who fixes the privileges of caste (ibid: 50). The king then is not a secular person. In Hindu kingship, ritual and political forms were closely intertwined (Dirks 1987: 5).

Such readings of the caste system leads one to conclude that power plays a dominant role in the elaboration of the caste hierarchy and it does not flit in and out of the interstices of the caste system, as Dumont had argued. The temple priest gives precedence to the king or local magnate, the king can raise or lower the ranks of castes, the king fixes caste privileges, the king is the supreme sacrificer, and it is in the institution of kingship that politics and ritual are intimately conjoined.

The power principle then makes the Brahman another *kamin*, a ritual specialist no doubt, but still a client of the Kshatriya patron. Therefore, whether we are in medieval India, or in Pahansu village where the Gujars are the dominant caste (Raheja 1988), or in Jaffna in Sri Lanka where the Vellalas have Brahmans and other artisans attached to them (Banks 1969: 71), the Kshatriya principle is dominant everywhere. This finally explains why a Brahman with wealth and power quickly relinquishes his priestly role with all its encumbrances (including the taking of *dana*), and aspires to be a patron and landlord himself.

If it is the Kshatriya principle that really determines hierarchy as it is realized, then it is not blind allegiance to ideology but the mechanics of power that set the ground rules for caste. Now it is all up to which caste can prove its dominance. If to be a Kshatriya power had to be proven then it would be difficult for subjugated castes to claim that status. It is much more convenient for subordinate castes to portray themselves as unrecognized Brahmans instead. No ostensible proof was required for this, nor would such an ambition (when expressed most guardedly) invite the wrath of the patron. As long as these castes do not claim Kshatriya status the patron, or the magnate, is not threatened. It does not really matter to the ruling family, or to the oligarchs, how many Brahman pretenders there are. What is critical, however, is that there should be no one else who challenges local power at the ground level.

This explains why Harijan castes in the past primarily claimed Brahman and not Kshatriya status. For 'lowly' Chamars to cast themselves as Kshatriyas and to affect a *rajasik* lifestyle would spell clear and imminent danger. But attempts on their part of belonging to a Brahman community might offend only other practising Brahmans, temple and domestic priests, which is not nearly as dangerous. For the Kshatriya patron only some Brahmans matter—those that perform rituals in their homes—so, what other Brahmans do in the privacy of their hamlets in none of his concern. A claim by a lower caste to being a Brahman is therefore less open to upper-caste retaliation than a claim to Kshatriya status. It is this non-aggressive aspect of Brahmanism that made the Brahman model more appealing in earlier lower-caste identity formations.

Today, the situation has changed. Local dominance by the village oligarch is no longer as oppressive as it used to be. Democratic politics and urbanization have made it easier for hitherto 'low' castes to move out and make any claim they wish to. Not surprisingly, therefore, the Jatavs of Uttar Pradesh who as traditional leather-workers were earlier called Chamars, today claim Kshatriya status and get away with it (Lynch 1972). In the past, when the authority of the local oligarch was paramount, Chamars would usually make the claim that they were once Brahmans brought down by chicanery and deceit.

The emphasis on the Kshatriya principle has a much greater impact on the understanding of the caste system than being and conveying a mere substitution of ritual by power. The power principle is primarily based on this-worldly achievement and demonstration of might. As it is no longer 'pure' ideology at work there is much greater conceptual room now to appreciate the contesting claims of different castes. Ultimately these contests can only be appreciated if the discrete nature of castes is fully understood. Each caste would like its own hierarchy to be realized but to do so it must have power at its bidding. This is what has allowed castes that were once low to claim undisputed Kshatriya status today. The transformation of Rajputs, Gujars and Jats from their early medieval Shudra positions to upper-caste Kshatriya status is clearly a case in point. Today if Jats or Rajputs are ever reminded of their Shudra past it would hardly carry with it a ring of credibility. The intervening years have given these castes a natural aura of 'Kshatriyaness'.

Baniyas, the Adis, and Others

The fact that power plays an important role in the realization of a caste hierarchy should not however sublate the fact that there could also be other caste identities that valorize neither ritual status nor power. The merchant castes, generically called Baniyas, sometimes fall into this category (see Timberg 1978). Doubtless there are many among them, such as the North Indian Khatris, who believe they are of Kshatriya extraction. Though the received literature on this subject is not nearly as extensive as it is on Brahmans and Kshatriyas, there is nevertheless enough material to entertain the view that a Baniya model is both logically possible and empirically available.

The Baniya castes occupy a very interesting position in the caste system. While they openly depend on the patronage of the Kshatriyas, they are sattvic, ascetic, and demonstratively pietistic in their social behaviour and relations (see Bayly 1983: 379). The orthodox Baniya lifestyles were very 'Brahmanic' (ibid: 381), to the extent that Marco Polo included them among the Brahmans (Mullick 1969: 49). In tradition, members of merchant castes would avoid staying in Mughal sarais (ibid: 386) so as not to be contaminated by Muslims. Any contact with Muslims was dangerous to the purity of the Baniya. The extent of this antipathy can be gauged from the manner in which the Ram Nagar Baniyas attempt to undermine the Suds (another Baniya caste) by referring to them as offsprings of a Baniya woman and a Muslim man (Hazelhurst 1968: 292). A Baniya's reputation rests on his honour. It is this that makes such a person a trustworthy merchant and banker. Richard Fox notes from his field study 'that a Baniya prefers honour to wealth. After all, money can be wiped out but honour cannot. If a merchant keeps his honour he can get a loan and make money again.' (Fox 1969: 146.)

Merchant communities do not always accept the Brahmanical assertion that as Baniyas they belong to the Vaishya varna and are therefore of an inferior status to Brahmans and Kshatriyas. Baniyas counter such attempts to downgrade them in a variety of ways. To begin with, Baniyas do not rely on the *Purusasukta* legend as Brahmans do. Even when it is referred to by them it is only to remind others that like the Brahmans and Kshatriyas they too came from the body of the primeval being. Seldom do they go any further along the Vedic trajectory which hierarchically places them below the Brahman and the Kshatriya (see also Das 1982: 86). In fact, it is often argued by the Baniyas that Lord Krishna evolved from the Vaishya and Kshatriya varnas (Gupta and Bhasker n.d.: 8-10). Or, for another variation on the same theme it is claimed that Brisavam, Lord Krishna's father-in-law, was a Vaishya (Mullick 1969: 49).

There are Vaishya and Baniya legends that also claim that the Baniyas were once kings of Ayodhya, Kausambi and Mathura (Gupta and Bhasker n.d.: 8). In fact the famous Gupta empire (c.4th century AD) is considered to be a Vaishya kingdom by these legends (ibid: 24). In other cases, the Baniyas trace their ancestry to Lord Shiva, no less (ibid). The Umar merchants in Fox's study Tejpur, trace their origin to *Om* in Hindu sacerdotal texts (Fox 1969: 242).

To take another instance, the Komatis of Andhra blame the gods for tricking the sublime Vaishyas 'in heaven to descend to earth and bring order to it.' (Gupta and Bhasker n.d.: 10.) There is deceit and chicanery too. King Ballal Sen of Bengal lowered the ranks of Baniyas because they refused to indulge him and bank roll his insatiable appetite for money (Mullick 1969: 38).

Baniyas not only claim equality with kings but also high spiritual status. Some of their origin tales portray them as incarnations of gods (see also ibid: 66), and others claim that they have produced sages such as the one who fatally cursed king Dasarath (Gupta and Bhasker n.d.: 18). The Subornobaniks (the Baniyas of Bengal) call themselves Aryan Vaishyas as they walked over the fire with Goddess Anayaka (ibid: 26; and Timberg 1978: 35). Subornobaniks also allege that other castes resent their fair Aryan complexion and therefore try to humiliate them and push them down the caste hierarchy (Mullick 1969: 41, 71; see also Cox 1970: 13).

It is not, however, as if Baniyas always want to be kings, though many of them have held this high office, nor do they want to be ascetics, though the *Baudhayan Sutra* and *Markanda Purana* clearly allow them to read the *Vedas*. They are proud of their traditional occupation and do not want to be merged with, or marry into, other castes—not even the mighty Kshatriyas (Gupta and Bhasker n.d.: 29).

If one were to fully appreciate the implications of looking at castes as discrete entities first and then try to realize their idiosyncratic hierarchies, there is no reason why there cannot be other axes besides the Brahman and the Kshatriya ones. Indeed, Jyotiba Phule, as was mentioned earlier, claimed an Adi status for the non-Brahmans of Maharashtra, and probably for the subcontinent as a whole (see Gore 1993: 180) and thereby expressed yet another axis. In tribal India too many communities call themselves Adis for the same reasons as Phule did.

It is difficult to close off the possibilities of other axes from coming into being, that is if they do not already exist. The depth and vivacity of these alternate rationales of caste hierarchy cannot be accommodated if a single hierarchy, either Kshatriya or Brahman-oriented, privileged above all.

In a recent study of the merchant castes, L.A. Babb was of the view that 'a purely Vaisya heritage is never quite acceptable, or at least not without some modulation.' (Babb 1998: 402.) The Maheshwari and

Khandelval Jains claim Rajput ancestry, while the Agravals stop a little short and only mention the kings in their caste genealogy without actually saying they are Kshatriyas (ibid: 394, 397, 401). The richness of Babb's essay, is heightened by a close study of a plethora of origin tales among the merchant castes. It is worth asking in this connection whether the recency of these documents have something to do with the pronounced inclinations towards asserting a Kshatriya past. It is unlikely that merchants in pre-modern times would have been so emphatic about their Kshatriyaness, particularly as they were generally patronized by the dominant castes and feudal overlords. Yet the fact that some Vaishyas/Baniyas were also peripatetic and moved from village to village perhaps gave them a greater degree of independence than possessed by the other castes who were physically rooted in a localized economy. This is an issue we will never fully know about given the level of contemporary research on the subject.

Nevertheless, to return to Babb, while the Khandelval Jains do claim a Rajput ancestry they have since severed ties with Hinduism, and Brahmanism in particular. In becoming Jains, the Khandelvals turned their backs in disgust from Hindu rituals and tradition (ibid: 395-97). Their rejection of the Kshatriya lifestyle too is very significant. As a matter of fact all but two of the merchant communities examined by Babb reject the Kshatriya model. A difference however needs to be established between having a Kshatriya past and claiming a Kshatriya present. This distinction is very important particularly in light of the fact that merchant castes very self-consciously abhor the Kshatriya lifestyle which includes meat eating and performing animal sacrifices.

The Agravals however make no claim to a Kshatriya

past. This is at least the way it appears in the most popular origin tale of this community as put forward by the famous nineteenth century poet, Bharatendu Harischandra, who was an Agraval himself. This version is also promoted by, the Agroha Vikas Trust and is by far the most widely accepted (ibid: 398). The origin of the Agravals is consistently Vaishya in this rendition, and here again the abhorrence of the Kshatriya lifestyle clearly comes through.

The case of the Vahivanca Barots is very illustrative in this connection. The Vahivanca Barots are traditional genealogists who were employed by the landed aristocracy of Rajputs in erstwhile feudal north Gujarat. In the past the Barots claimed a Kshatriya past for themselves, obviously influenced by their wealthy patrons. Today in Gujarat the business model dominates, and in large parts of this region the Baniya is considered superior to the Kshatriya. The Vahivanca Barots too have changed their allegiance and now call themselves Baniyas. The Patidar castes who earlier employed these Barots to manufacture Kshatriya genealogy for themselves are now in an ambigious situation. They do not want their genealogies brought up because they no longer want to be known as Kshatriyas. The Patidars too would like to be known as Baniyas but in earlier days they had the Vahivanca Barots manufacture their genealogies as Kshatriyas (see Shah and Shroff 1975: 63). This demonstrates the viability of the Baniya model and with it the possibility of other models emerging in the future. Obviously the traditional varna order is neither universally sacrosanct or unviolable.

Besides the Brahman and Kshatriya axes, therefore, one could also add the Baniya axis. Unfortunately, the Baniya side has not received adequate attention in conceptual works on the caste system. Yet, even from the sources presented here it is clear that the Vaishyas are proud of who they are and uphold a lifestyle that is not quite congruent with the Brahman or the Kshatriya mould.

A Summation

In the preceding sections we attempted to make the following points:

1. Any notion of hierarchy is arbitrary and is valid from the perspective of certain individual castes. To state that pure hierarchy is the one that is universally believed in or one which legitimizes the position of those who participate in the caste system, is misleading.

2. The separation between castes is not only on matters which connote the opposition between purity and pollution. Distinctions and diacritical notches which are not even remotely suggestive of purity and pollution are observed as strictly. Obversely, distinctions relating to purity and pollution do not systematically affect caste status. The cultivating Amot caste solemnize their Goraiya festival with the sacrifice of a pig and yet Brahmans take water from them (Risley 1891: Vol. 1, 18). Further, it is only after we accept castes as discrete are we in a position to understand why castes equally pure refrain from merging their identities. The Nabashakha group of castes provides us with a telling example of this phenomenon. This also explain why inconsistencies in caste behaviour do not trouble the Hindus, as Srinivas noted while studying the Coorgs.

We are now in a position to quickly review the implications of the above on some major issues that dominate studies of the caste system.

The Jajmani System

The jajmani system, in theory, establishes, and indeed orders, religious protocol for the exchange of services between different castes specializing in different occupations and economic activities. But in fact the jajmani system is a sporadic empirical reality. Even Dumont concedes this, but he is soon compelled to add that economic services and religious prestations are mingled together and 'this takes place within the prescribed order, the religious order.' (Dumont 1970b.) But this is possible only if each caste follows its hereditary occupation which has been sanctified in the sacred texts. But surprisingly the sacred texts do not mention a larger number of jatis in existence today, and if it had been the job of sacred texts to clearly identify jatis with occupations then this was done very carelessly.

To begin with, let us examine the agricultural castes which are so numerous and are constantly increasing in number every day. In the prime sacerdotal text, the *Manusmriti*, no prominence is given to '. . . either landowning or agricultural castes or the corresponding occupations, though a large part of the population must then, as now, have consisted of cultivators, and their importance in the social system must have been great' (Blunt 1969: 232.) Further, castes that declare different origins, like the Kurmis who claim Kshatriya status, others like Bhumihars and Tagas who call themselves Brahman, are also . . . traditionally landholders (ibid). The number of those castes whose caste names are clearly non-agricultural but who are moving into agriculture is constantly being enhanced (ibid: 251-52; Bose 1975: 192-93, 198; with reference to untouchables see Desai 1976: 162). Even Brahmans, as Bougle found, are not only ploughmen, but soldiers, tradesmen and

cooks (Bougle 1958: 19). The suggestion that a caste
which follows an occupation which is not hereditary
nor sanctioned in the texts is either degraded or
excommunicated must necessarily be rejected. Even
Brahmans such as Tewaris, Ojhas, Upadhyayas or Jhas
have engaged in agriculture without losing caste (see
Risley 1891: Vol. 1, 29). As one Brahman is reported to
have confessed to Abbe Dubois: 'To fill one's belly one
must play several parts.' (Bougle 1958: 19.) In fact,
ascetic orders such as the Bairagis and Gosains played
an important economic role in protecting the movement
of goods and money through different regions in medieval
India (Bayly 1983: 183). If this is true for the Brahmans
it should be equally true for the other castes as well.
Ultimately the castes that cling to their traditional
occupations the most are those 'which deal most with
trade questions . . . the Bhangi, the Nai, the Bhishti, the
Darzi' (Blunt 1969: 245), the drummer, the washerman,
etc, (Dumont and Pocock, 1958: 47-48). Not surprisingly
when any attempt is made to elucidate the jajmani
system the authors invariably deal with these castes
alone.

The jajmani system is, in other words, an idealization
which in fact works out in a somewhat pure form only
in a small minority of cases. This further strengthens
our view that castes achieve their separation not primarily
by the criterion of occupation as supposedly
recommended in the texts, but in fact distinguish
themselves from each other hyper-symbolically by a
cluster of characteristics, the more important of which
need not be recommended by the ideology of the true
hierarchy. If certain members of a caste believe that they
can forsake their traditional occupations because they
do not regard them as prestigious then they promptly

abandon them at the earliest opportunity. The development of the cultivating caste of Helos from among the erstwhile caste of Kaibarttas is a case in point. At other times, as with the various Brahmans who turned to agriculture, it is a question of economic advantage. But even after these castes change their occupations they do not merge their caste identities with those who from earlier times were performing that economic activity.

Sanskritization

The concept of Sanskritization imperfectly understands the incongruence between deemed occupation and actual occupation. Any move on the part of lower castes to appropriate lifestyles that were not traditionally theirs is interpreted as if these lower castes are ashamed of their identity. In some cases this might be true, but in fact when subaltern castes claim elevated caste status it is a phenomenon often independent of Sanskritization. Sanskritization is a reassertion in an extraverted form of what was till then an introverted expression of the caste's overall rejection of the position given to it by hierarchical rules as governed by the twin principles of economics and politics. But only in rare cases, if ever at all, do these castes want to give up their identity. They are successful when they have access to the axes of economics and politics (Lynch 1968), as in the case of the Jatavs of Agra, or the Izhavas of Kerala, or the distiller caste groups of Orissa and Tamil Nadu. The importance of the economic factor cannot be overemphasized for very often the claims of well-to-do sections of a depressed jati are accepted by the powerful and dominant castes, while the identical claims of their indigent jati brethren do not win such acceptance. The prosperous Noniyas, for instance, were accepted by the privileged castes as Chauhans but the poorer Noniyas were not accorded a similar status. These poorer Noniyas nevertheless did not abandon their claim that they were really Chauhans. Sanskritization seen thus is an extraversion of long standing, deeply felt, and believed in judgement of their caste status which was hitherto privy only to members of that caste.

If Sanskritization does not give this rejection of imposed caste status adequate salience, Dumont seems to ignore it almost completely. For Dumont the true hierarchy is paramount and castes have no business to believe otherwise. Dumont realized the difficulties his true hierarchy would face, so he introduced power and economics surreptitiously at the interstitial levels. But if castes are seen as discrete classes there is no need to make this concession. And in any case mobility and transfer of occupation for economic and political purposes occur both at the lowest level as also at the highest, and not only at the interstitial level or in the median zones. It is worthwhile to recall the case of the proud landowning Brahmans we mentioned earlier in this paper, as also the case of the so-called untouchables claiming Brahman status.

If jatis can independently and idiosyncratically set up objects of veneration then by equal facility they can also set up independent models for emulation, or Sanskritization. These objects of veneration and ritual practices are not always recommended by Brahmans but are devoutly adhered to, nevertheless, by both privileged and powerful jatis, as well as by the subaltern ones. Likewise, non-Brahmanical models of Sanskritization carry as much commitment as the Brahmanical model. It is not as if jatis choose the non-Brahmanical mode shamefacedly as a second-best choice (Dumont 1970b: 30). The Brahmanical lifestyle and symbols do not excite universal favour among many jatis. As a matter of fact the Kshatriya, or Rajput, or Jat model contains an inbuilt hostility to Brahmans which is in line with the sentiments of these caste groups. This hostility is sans envy, as the Rajput Ikshwaku clan myth or even the myth of Parasuram demonstrates. The pride and the generic swagger that are built into the 'I-am-a-Rajput' syndrome (Hitchcock 1975: 10) cannot be undermined. Further, the Patidar's transference of loyalty from the Kshatriya model to the Vaishya (or Baniya) model (Shah and Shroff 1975: 41) demonstrates an alternate preference, viz., the devaluation of the Kshatriya lifestyle and their concomitant over-valuation of the Baniya one.

Caste and Politics

If castes are discrete classes (or categories) and if hierarchy is never universally acknowledged then alternative hierarchical rankings are not only believed in introvertedly but can also be asserted by political power. This does not happen only where castes are fluid, or in remote regions (Dumont 1970a: 214). But in point of fact, it happens all over.

O'Malley describes the plight of some high-caste subjects of one of Orissa's erstwhile feudatory states in pre-independence India who refused to accept the decision of their ruler in a caste case, and were then outcasted by him as a consequence. No priest, barber or washerman could render them any service, with the result that 'they had long beards matted with dirt, their hair hung in long strands and was filthy in the extreme, and their clothes were beyond description for uncleanness.' (Hutton 1963: 95-96.)

Ballal Sen in the eleventh century, is said to have divided the Kshatriyas into four castes according to locality, and not on the basis of purity and pollution, nor under the instance of Brahmans (Risley 1891: Vol. 1, 440). In his observations he also raised the positions of some castes and degraded others (Hutton 1963: 94). Cox even drew our attention to the Raja of Cochin raising castes of lower rank to Nayar status (Cox 1970: 8). The Mysore king Vira Bukka Raya decided to place Jains with the other right hand castes (Appadurai 1974: 226).

The principle that caste is ultimately a matter for the secular or political authority is carried so far that landlords, at any rate in eastern India, are apt to interfere in purely caste matters. So clearly has the principle that the secular power is the final arbiter of caste been accepted in the past, that the Mughal rulers of Bengal and their British successors have in turn found themselves in the position of judges of such matters (Hutton 1963: 96). Significantly, in keeping with our understanding of castes as discrete categories intra-caste matters are solved primarily at the level of the caste panchayat. The village panchayat, except in the hill regions, did not exist in pre-modern India, a fact that Dumont observes but fails to draw the proper conclusions from.

In modern politics too the principle of encompassment as detailed by Dumont is conspicuously absent. The principle of discrete castes is however upheld in a variety of situations. In Bihar, for instance, there has been no pattern at all in the political alignment of castes. In caste atrocities in Bishrampur the main issue was sharecroppers' rights over cultivated land, and the Kurmis were the main attackers. But the Kurmis were aided by a variety of upper-caste landlords to attack not only the Harijans, but also the Yadavs who are closer to them and traditionally considered to be of the same rank. But in Belchi their attack was on Brahmans, the kingpins of the true hierarchy (Dhar, et.al., 1982: 110). In Gujarat the Bareyas and Kolis who are of the same rank often unite with the Rajputs to oppose one of their own kind, the newly-ascendant Patidar caste (Shah 1982: 139). In Marathwada the Mahars were attacked by the powerful castes, but the Mangs, who are traditionally supposed to be lower than the Mahars, were left untouched. Neither did the Mangs stand by the Mahars according to the principle of encompassment (Gupta 1979: 12).

Rather than encompassment what one finds is deliberate and conscious linking between different jatis depending upon the exigencies of the situation. The so-called caste associations, like the Kshatriya Sabha or the Kayastha Samaj, also have members belonging to a variety of jatis and who independently decide, uninfluenced by the principle of encompassment, to participate in one organization or another. This is not only true of the so-called upper-caste organizations, but as Bose found, it is also true of the Teli (oil pressers) association. Many members of this association in Orissa had nothing to do with oil pressing in Orissa or elsewhere (Bose 1960: 79).

It is true that 'to adopt a value is to introduce hierarchy . . .' (Dumont 1970b: 54), but it should also be noted that hierarchy is a consequence of adopting a value and can therefore on occasions be shamefaced without disowning the symbols of separation. The Dhanuks, the Kurmis, and the Avadhis independently and internally position each other differently on a hierarchical scale, and yet they came together, in 1932, from Oudh to Bihar to form the Kurmi Association. Likewise, in the peasant movement in Oudh (1919-92) where peasants from various caste groups came together, caste separation was strictly maintained without any overt antagonism or signification of inequality among them. The Ahirs fed the Ahirs, the Kurmis fed the Kurmis, the Pasis fed the Pasis, and yet they all united as equals on the political front, and that too, under the leadership of the low caste—Madari Pasi (Siddiqi 1978: 117).

Though hierarchy is consequent to separation, the former can, as we have seen, on occasions be suspended. Castes widely separated by orthodox hierarchization can unite irrespective of the vaunted principle of encompassment. While hierarchy becomes shamefaced and introverted on these occasions the discrete character of castes is still upheld. The Telis of Orissa upheld sub-caste endogamy, and thus separation, while welcoming all Teli sub-castes as equals (Bose 1960: 11). As John Harriss observed in Tamil Nadu, the village people interpreted the notion of equality as meaning 'the removal of hierarchical distinctions' and did not find the principle of egalitarianism incompatible with the persistence of a strong caste identity so long as separation remained important (Harriss 1980: 58). Hierarchical notions in such cases become introverted and are forced to be shamefaced. Equally, as we illustrated with the Belchi and Bishrampur incident, when two caste groups are politically opposed, then hierarchy becomes strident. The opposed groups see each other as inferior irrespective of the classical hierarchy. That such a group itself is composed of discrete jatis widely separated from one another, further violates the orthodox hierarchy. Finally, in keeping with our contention that castes are, first and foremost, discrete entities, any unity between jatis is time bound and specific. These same jatis may on another occasion find themselves in opposition.

Caste, Class and Social Class

In our understanding, class in Marxism refers to the essentially antagonistic classes like the bourgeoisie and the proletariat in the capitalist mode of production. To understand and appreciate the analytical uses of the mode of production and the two classes in opposition is not to claim that the former is all, and that it also informs us of the division of labour in society. Or, to be more specific, the mode of production does not immediately tell us of the exact positioning, distribution and proliferation of social classes in a given society. The caste system on the other hand, in its idealized form refers to the division of labour in society and is thus far from resembling the fundamental classes in Marxism. Moreover in Marxism, the mode of production is an unconscious structure which constrains without prejudice different social classes. The caste ideology is not only a believed-in and conscious structure, but there are almost as many believed-in ideologies as there are castes in India. In a system of classes when a worker becomes an accountant he leaves his former social class and becomes a member of another social class. Significantly, a change of occupation does not automatically entail a change of caste. The proud landowning Brahmans remain Brahmans, nor do the traditional agrarian castes like the Dhanuks and Dosadhs cease to become so when they change their occupation. The Jatavs remained Jatavs though they moved upwards economically. The Mahars remained Mahars even after many of them refused to follow their traditional occupation. This, more than anything else, is the difference between caste and social class.

Following from this we may come to another conclusion. As castes and occupations do not coincide, so quite naturally there is no identity between the secular status of social classes and the caste identity of members who occupy these social classes. Blunt (1969: 251-52), Ghanshyam Shah (1982: 139), I.P. Desai (1976: 162-63, and Bose (1975: 192-93, 198) among many others, give ample documentation of this phenomenon which is widespread among all castes. In this situation to believe that caste ideology can be activated for economic or class war is fallacious. Caste ideology essentially separates castes, and consequently also separates social classes over and above the fundamental classes of Marxism. If caste divisions unambiguously overlap with social class distinctions then some benefit might accrue in using caste ideology. But if caste ideologies merely separate caste, then the reliance on caste ideology even the traditionally lower-caste ones, will give only limited gains and will, be counter-productive in the long run. All castes, high and low, secrete, propound and consolidate ideologies which separate them from their fellow-beings in other castes.

Defining Caste

Looking back at all that we have been through thus far, we may, at this stage, attempt a definition of caste. History has liquidated many characteristics of the caste system and has offered us, without any conscious phenomenological effort, an 'imaginative variation of facts'. Hereditary occupational specialization is not active any more, the principles of purity and pollution do not invariably intervene to hierarchize, the notion of the encompassing and the encompassed can no longer summon the liegemen. Only the principle of endogamy remains to ensure biological separation between different jatis. But as the biological separation can fall on no significant biological characteristics, jatis are forced to hypersymbolize their discrete character through a multiplicity of rituals.

Though the caste system is also a form of differentiation, it cannot be subsumed under a system of *fundamentum divisionis*. For this reason caste cannot be seen as an extreme form of class, race or estates and here Dumont is correct. And yet it is not within us to come up with an analytical definition of caste; the best we can do is to offer a definition that is traditionally known as a definition *per genus et differentiam*.

We will define the caste system as a form of differentiation wherein the constituent units of the system justify endogamy on the basis of putative biological differences which are semaphored by the ritualization of multiple social practices. The above definition according to us takes care of some of the crucial features of the caste system.

The phrase, 'ritualization of multiple social practices', however needs further explication. By rituals we mean all those social practices that are valorized and upheld irrespective of Weber's 'means-ends' rationality. For instance, to follow an occupation, and pursue it in a certain mode, regardless of the means-ends rationality would also be considered by us to be a form of ritual activity. It is for this reason that we have not considered hereditary occupations per se to be an essential aspect of the caste system for it would have led to some misunderstanding. In any case, hereditary occupational specialization is not universal within the caste system, as has been argued earlier, nor is it a peculiarity of the caste system alone.

The caste system also exhibits two further characteristics which cannot be seen as its essence but may be understood as its properties. These properties are hierarchy and hypersymbolism.

(a) *Hierarchy:* The discrete character of jatis is maintained by the enhanced valuation that members of a jati place on their own customs, ritualized practices, and geneaological heritage. This should, and does imply a value-loaded scale which places different jatis at different positions in the hierarchy. But this hierarchical placement by virtue of being value loaded, is extremely idiosyncratic. Consequently, different and conflicting hierarchies exist at subjective levels. There are perhaps, as we have said earlier, as many hierarchies as there are jatis. But very often in practice we find more than one hierarchical order in effect. Any hierarchical order in effect is not the essence of the caste system, nor the inevitable consequence of it, but an expression of political or politico-economic power. Logically, an alternative hierarchy can also effectively come into existence with a change in the political and economic strength of certain castes—a reshuffling, that is, of jatis on the secular plane. It is true, as Bougle said that Hindus are obsessed with the right to be organized hierarchically (Bougle 1991: 25), yet it needs to be recorded that it is not as if there is a consensus on the hierarchy (see also Alfred Nandy's observation in Rowe 1968: 205).

(b) *Hypersymbolism:* Our definition tells us that the discrete character of jatis is maintained through a multiplicity of ritualized practices. These rituals are not to be lightly taken as they indicate to us the substantive and emotive content of jatis. The number of rituals and beliefs, and the plethora of diacritical marks that particularize individual jatis, do not follow any single rule. Neither are they restricted to the number necessary to differentiate one jati from another. Many of these rituals and beliefs are historical accretions and effects of past associations and contingent conditions. Members of a jati do not only value what separates them from other jatis. They also value those symbols and beliefs that are fairly widespread and held in common by a number of castes, leading to what we have called hypersymbolism.

The multiplicity of rituals in the caste system does not convey fresh information with every instance. Hypersymbolism and the consequent redundancy of rituals, on the other hand, heighten values characteristic of the caste system to invoke a passionate sense of belonging to one's caste. Contemporary semiology can legitimately stake its claim to clarify this domain. According to the semiologist (Pierre Guirand 1975: 13):

> The greater the redundancy, the more the communication is significant, closed, socialised and codified: the lower the redundancy, the greater the information and the more open, individualised and decodified the communication.

Where would we place the question of purity and pollution? Historical evidence tells us that untouchability is a later addition in the history of the Indian caste system. Till about the second century AD certain castes, like the Ayogava, Paulkasas, and the Nishads, were despised, but were not considered to be untouchables. Untouchability is, therefore, a historical cohort of the caste system, but not its essence. The notion of purity and pollution, as Dumont correctly observed, is integrally linked with the institution of untouchability. But like untouchability, the notion of purity and pollution is also an historical accretion. Over time this notion freed itself from its specific and original task of separating untouchables from the others and began to be operative at different planes of the caste system, thus providing additional gusto to the property of hypersymbolism. But it is in keeping with its character of being an historical accretion that the notion of purity and pollution does not subsume hypersymbolism: for, as we have been at considerable pains to point out earlier, purity and pollution are not universally involved to effect the diacritical marks separating different jatis.

Consolidating the Gains

At this point we may begin to round off our discussion by referring to Veena Das's insightful work, *Structure and Cognition* (1982). She was probably the first to take serious note of Dumont's understanding of hierarchy and provided a substantial theoretical and ethno-historical criticism of it by going back to the *Puranas* (ibid: 67-69). According to Das, jatis can be understood on the basis of the relations between three separate poles, i.e., the Brahman, the king, and the sannyasin (ibid: 68). Thus while she shifts attention from the over-concern with Brahmans to two other categories, viz., the king and the sannyasin, there is still no clear logical reason why it should stop at three. According to us each jati attains its distinctions on a variety of axes and the condensation principle whereby the manifold are encapsulated in one category is, for this reason, comprehensively and perpetually active. This, according to us, is the essence of jati distinctions. To give some examples as to why, neither singly nor collectively, the three poles mentioned by Das are sufficient to understand the discrete character of castes, let us quickly remember the vibrancy of the Baniya model. In addition, sample the following two cases. The Bhats—a pseudo-Brahman caste—in addition to worshipping Mahavir, also worship Bare Bir, a deified ancestor and Birtiya who is considered by them to be the protector of cattle (Blunt 1969: 285), and is obviously a non-Vedic deity. The Kanhaypuria Rajput worships such deities like the Mahisa Rakshasa or Bhainasura, the buffalo demon. The Dais clan among these Rajuts worship Mathote, a tribal goddess (ibid).

Probably, the three poles sufficed for Das as she was dealing only in the context of the *Dharamaranya Purana*. This difference between Das and ourselves could also arise because we believe that the content she gives to structural categories in her analysis of *Dharamaranya Purana* is exhausted within that context, and cannot be extrapolated outside it. In the previous chapter and in this one, we have rather promiscuously sought instances and evidence from folklores of ex-untouchables to those of Brahman, Rajput, merchant castes and so forth. If the *Dharmaranya Purana* provides the possibility of three axes, a wider search of ethnographic evidence warns us from constricting the possible variations in advance. As castes are discrete in character, a diversity of templates is possible, and perhaps many others might emerge under changed circumstances in the future. This is at least the lesson we have learnt from Lévi-Strauss's structuralism.

But apart from our partial, even minor, disagreement with Das, considering our present preoccupation, we are in full agreement with her when she says that the difference between jatis is not to be seen as one of degree but of quality (Das 1982: 69). From her case material Das is also able to show that fission in jatis take place not only because a particular section of the jati has performed an impure act, but because of a disagreement over a particular issue which is more often than not political in character. But her more interesting comment is that even after the cause for the disagreement has been removed or forgotten, they are (recall the condensation principle) translated into separate diacritical marks of each group (Das 1982: 70).

The arguments put forward in this chapter also build on the findings of recent sociologists like J.P. Parry (1985, 1990), C.J. Fuller (1991), and Nicholas Dirks (1987), to mention just a few. They have enlarged the scope of discussion by pointing out the many variations in what is generally assumed as a monolithic caste system. From Parry and Fuller we learn of the dissensions and ranking within Brahmans. Dirks argues strongly for a Kshatriya-centred (as opposed to a Brahmanical) understanding of the caste system. In his view, power subsumes ritual status which is why the king in traditional India played a crucial role in upholding dharma. Armed with such knowledge it becomes much easier to mount an attack on the widely prevalent Brahmanical view of caste. We are now certain that purity is not unambiguously connected to ritual, we also know that the Kshatriya principle is not to be overlooked. Further, caste is not just a matter of degree, but of quality as well (ibid: 69). Quite clearly we are on the threshold of a more comprehensive optic of the caste system. But before we announce the departure, our strengths and weaknesses need to be audited.

On the positive side we are aware that ritual status cannot unproblematically assume superiority. We are also reasonably convinced that power plays a significant role in the maintenance of caste order. Nor can we doubt the fact that the hierarchy of purity is often challenged. On the other hand, what analytical ground have we won to be able to integrate all this? Is the Kshatriya now at the apex of the caste hierarchy? Clearly that too would be an unwarranted leap for it takes for granted acquiescence of other castes, just as the Brahmanical version does. If there are multiple axes then are the multiple hierarchies on these axes part of a common discourse? Or do they have entirely different thresholds of validation? Can a sannyasin claim superiority over a Kshatriya or a domestic priest? On what bases can all these questions be answered without shifting terrain constantly? In insisting upon separating continuous hierarchies from discrete classes apropos the caste system, we believe we have been able to accommodate facts without evasions and embarrassment. It is no longer necessary to surreptitiously bring in politics and economics as Dumont does as neither politics nor economics militate against the existence of a system composed of discrete categories. For if one were to conceptualize jatis as discrete entities, and see their difference as one of quality rather than degree, then this would account for the facility with which castes who occupy a very low position in the varna hierarchy, like the Shudras, find it possible to assume political power and claim Kshatriya status. Likewise, Baniyas can claim to be superior to Kshatriyas, and Kshatriyas can claim superiority over Brahmans, and so on. All these combinations are possible and in fact exist. But to allow them the status of legitimate facts it is necessary to accept at the analytical level that castes exist first as discrete categories. Hierarchies come later: for which reason there are so many hierarchies, so many models of emulation, and considerable tension between different evaluations of status and power.

6

Caste and Politics
The Presumption of Numbers

The Limits of Caste Arithmetic

It is commonplace in the analysis of caste politics to give in to the presumption of numbers. Thus it is often argued that political outcomes can be determined to a fair degree by the caste composition of electoral constituencies. This falls quite in line with the overall assumption that Hindus are generally bound by their caste loyalties, so why should politics be any different? There are periods when the domination of politics by caste seems like a near truism (as during the 1996 elections), but then again there are times when caste does not seem to play that influential a role. Even so, in many considered works on the subject of caste and politics it is assumed that political fortunes depend primarily on the caste composition of individual constituencies (Frankel 1989: 823, 100-01; 1990: 512-13).

There are indeed several problems with such a perspective. A scrutiny of election results reveals quite easily that political parties are rarely able to hold on to their seats over successive elections. A Bharatiya Janata Party (BJP) stronghold today might well be stormed by the Congress or by the Samajwadi Party (SP) in the next election. This is also true of parties that are supposedly based on caste loyalties in a more overt fashion. The Samajwadi Party is said to be the vehicle of the newly-emergent peasant castes such as the Ahirs or Yadavs, yet it is not easy to predict its electoral fortunes. All this should not have been the case if caste and political preference were so closely tied together. For example, in Kodarma, Chhapra and Bettiah constituencies in Bihar the Janata Dal (out of which the Rashtriya Janata Dal, or RJD, was born) won in 1991 only to lose to the BJP in both the 1996 and 1998 elections. Likewise, the BJP won in 1991 in Jaunpur, Saidpur, Ghatimpur and Ghazipur constituencies in U.P. but lost them in 1998 to the Janata Dal.

Similarly, in Maharashtra the Shiv Sena (SS) won from Amravati in 1991 but lost this seat to the Republican Party of India (RPI) in 1996. In 1998 the same seat was won by the Congress. In Bhid, again in Maharashtra, the BJP won in 1991 and 1996 but lost to the Congress in 1998. These illustrations demonstrate that electoral outcomes in India cannot be predetermined, and therefore the role of caste in politics should also be cautiously understated.

In this paper examples will be drawn from Maharashtra, Bihar and Uttar Pradesh in order to estimate the extent to which caste influenced electoral verdicts in the last three elections. As the Indian political situation has changed considerably over the past five decades it would be more pertinent to focus on recent elections. It is for this reason the parliamentary elections of 1991, 1996 and 1998 have been taken into account.

In these years the Mandal Commission recommendations helped consolidate the politics of the so-called Backward Castes. The Bahujan Samaj Party (BSP) and the caste support to Mulayam Singh Yadav and Laloo Yadav have also been much written about during this period.

It needs to be admitted at the outset that it is difficult to match population by caste and election results. This is for two reasons. In the first place the last caste census was published as far back as in 1931. Secondly, caste enumeration is provided districtwise and these districts do not always coincide with parliamentary electoral constituencies. Nevertheless, with the help of Singh's painstaking efforts (Singh 1996), an attempt has been made to match one with the other. The result is an approximation, no doubt, but a close approximation (see *Census of India, 1931*: Part II tables, for Bombay, for United Provinces, and for Bihar and Orissa). For obvious reasons attempts to superimpose census areas over the smaller state legislative assembly constituencies would be victim of much greater inaccuracies. At the level of parliamentary constituencies it is worth taking the risk. There is a fair chance that census information can be a reliable indication of a parliamentary constituency's caste profile. The examination of the relationship between caste numbers and electoral results not only help us add another dimension to our understanding of caste and politics, but can also be useful scaffolding for revisiting conceptual discussions on the caste system. Let us now turn to the cases that we have selected for our study.

Maharashtra

The situation in Maharashtra is certainly not conducive to advancing the conception of caste-based politics. This is primarily because Marathas constitute such an overwhelming proportion of the population of this province that the other castes are all reduced to some kind of a minority status. The Marathas alone constitute about 31 per cent of the population. In the Konkan region of Maharashtra they account for nearly 40 per cent of the population. After that there is a huge drop. The second-most numerous caste in Maharashtra is that of the Mahars who make up 4.7 per cent of the population. Brahmans come next with a mere 3.9 per cent of the population. The other castes are usually below 1 per cent, (Lele 1990: 117-18). The political contest in this state over the last three elections has really been between the Congress and the BJP-SS alliance. Occasionally the Republican Party of India (RPI) appears but without any consistency. In fact, barring a few constituencies, there is hardly any consistency whatsoever in the electoral profile of Maharashtra. Bombay North Central was won by SS in 1996, by RPI in 1998 and by the Congress in 1991. The latest RPI victory is, in all likelihood, an outcome of its alliance with the Congress. It is interesting to note that the RPI won in Akola, Amravati and Chimur as well, but only in 1998 when it came to an electoral understanding with the Congress.

Maharashtra is really a two-party state. It is either the Congress or the BJP-SS that has won see-saw battles in the last three elections. In general, a high Maratha presence can be correlated somewhat with the Congress. This would be particularly true of south-west Maharashtra constituencies such as Khed, Baramati, Karad, Sangli, Icchalkaranji and Kolhapur. In all these areas the Congress won consistently between 1991 and 1998. In Kopargaon and Sholapur which belong to the same region and have the same caste profile, the Congress has yielded occasionally to the BJP. Ramtak and Bhandara tell a somewhat different story. Though these constituencies are somewhat atypical, as the Marathas constitute less than 30 per cent of the total population, they nevertheless voted for the Congress in the last three elections, just as Maratha-dominated areas mentioned above did. So the easy identification between the Congress and the Marathas does not always hold. Marathas are known to reject the Congress just as much as the other castes are known to vote it to power.

TABLE: 1

High Maratha Presence (Over 30%) and Electoral Results

Constituency	1998	1996	1991
Bombay South	Congress	BJP	Congress
Bombay South Central	Shiv Sena	Shiv Sena	Shiv Sena
Ahmednagar	Shiv Sena	Congress	Congress
Kopargaon	Congress	BJP	Congress

Source: Singh (1996); *Lok Sabha Election Results, 1998* (Mimeo); and *Census of India, 1931*, Bombay (Part II Tables).

The situation is the same with the BJP-SS alliance. This combine does particularly well in parts of urban Bombay. Bombay South Central, Bombay North West, and Bombay North have been strongholds of the BJP-SS alliance from the 1991 election onwards. These constituencies share roughly the same caste profile as Bombay North Central and Bombay North East, but in these areas the Congress fared better during this period. In general, the BJP-SS and the Congress share the electoral booty in and around Bombay. In areas with the same caste profile political allegiances have changed, and at the same time different caste combinations have often brought about the same political results.

If we introduce the Muslim factor into the picture there is nevertheless no significant change. Take Bombay for instance. A relatively high Muslim population of between 15-20 per cent in Bombay South Central could not prevent the BJP-SS from winning successive elections between 1991-98. Aurangabad which also has a Muslim population between 15-20 per cent returned Shiv Sena candidates in 1996 and 1991.

The picture however would be incomplete if the presence of the Scheduled Castes are not taken into account. In constituencies around Marathwada where the SC population is quite high the Congress seems to do better than the BJP-SS alliance. In Latur, Nanded, and Osmanabad the Congress is, by and large, better placed than its rivals. In all these constituencies the SC population is quite high. They constitute roughly 20-25 per cent of the population. Akola is the only other place in Maharashtra that has such a high proportion of Scheduled Castes. But it does not conform to the pattern just suggested. In 1991 and 1996 the BJP or the BJP-SS alliance won the elections. In 1998, however, the RPI won at the hustings, but this, as we said earlier, was probably because of Congress support.

It is quite apparent that caste loyalties are quite fickle when it comes to electoral choices. Obviously there is a lot more than just caste that matters. But Maharashtra may well be made out to be a special case as the Marathas numerically preponderate over all other castes by a long way in the entire state. In practically every region of Maharashtra the elites are drawn from this caste (Lele 1981: 56-57). With the kind of overwhelming majority the Maratha caste enjoys it can probably afford the indulgence of internal differentiation.

At least this could be a possible explanation. As the Marathas are not threatened by any other caste there is little compulsion for the Marathas to consolidate and present a united front to the outside world. But in Bihar and Uttar Pradesh no single caste numerically predominates like the Marathas do in Maharashtra. In which case, the facts from U.P. and Bihar should help to fill out the picture a little more comprehensively.

TABLE: 2

Strong Scheduled Caste Presence (Over 20%) and Election Results in Maharashtra

Constituency	1998	1996	1991
Latur	Congress	Congress	Congress
Nanded	Congress	Congress	Congress
Osmanabad	Congress	Shiv Sena	Congress
Akola	RPI	BJP	Shiv Sena

Source: Singh (1996); *Lok Sabha Election Results, 1998* (Mimeo), Behera (1999: 15).

Uttar Pradesh

The facts that the census figures present about U.P. are indeed very striking. In only a handful of districts do castes such as the Brahmans, Rajputs, Ahirs or Kurmis barely make it to between 15-20 per cent of the population. In Kanpur and Gonda Brahmans constitute between 15-20 per cent of the population, in Robertsganj and nowhere else are Kurmis somewhere between 15-20 per cent of the population; in Saidpur, Azamgarh and Jaunpur Ahirs are between 15-20 per cent of the population; and, finally, Rajputs are roughly 15-20 per cent of the population of Garhwal, Tehri Garhwal and

Nainital. In only nine out of a total of sixty-three districts do the so-called upper castes and dominant agrarian castes have some kind of a presence. In the famous Jat districts of Muzaffarnagar, Meerut, Agra and Saharanpur Jats hardly make it to being even 10 per cent of the population. In Muzaffarnagar, which is widely acclaimed to be a Jat lair, only 8.44 per cent of the population belong to that community. The same trend holds for districts such as Bijnor, Bulandshahr, Agra, and Meerut, and yet they are famously associated with the Jat leader Chaudhari Charan Singh (see *Census of India, 1931, United Provinces:* Part II tables). Obviously, the identification of certain dominant agrarian castes with a region cannot be based on numbers alone. Why then is it believed that Jats, or Ahirs, or Kurmis control the politics of certain constituencies? The answer surely does not rest on numbers alone.

Interestingly, only the Scheduled Castes constitute above 25 per cent, and in some cases even above 30 per cent, of the population in practically every district of U.P. Yet, there is no area in U.P. that is known to be controlled by Scheduled Castes. If numbers and caste loyalties were all that important, then surely the SCs should be ruling U.P. In Muzaffarnagar the Jats number only about 8.5 per cent of the population, but are able to contain the SCs who make up over 20 per cent of the population. One answer to this conundrum could easily be that the dominant landowning Jats terrorize the SCs into submission and do not let them either organize politically, and, perhaps even disallow them from casting their votes. Such an explanation sounds very compelling once caste populations are factored into the analysis.

It is, therefore, not just numbers, but something more that makes for the power of certain castes over other castes. In contemporary times, however, an explanation that rests on sheer power appears a little less convincing than what it would have in the past. This is because SCs are now increasingly able to free themselves from rural subordination. More and more rural SCs are looking outside the village for employment; and if within the village, then not as agricultural labourers. To a great extent this situation has arisen because there are not enough jobs in the villages. The Green Revolution and sub-division of holdings have converted most farms either into family plots or capitalist enterprises. Lack of agricultural jobs in the villages has had at least one salutary effect. Now that SCs are relatively free of Jat, Gujar, Ahir or Rajput domination they have greater political manoeuvrability.

This loosening of ties with the landed castes has not always led to successful urbanization of SCs. In a large number of cases they continue to live in the village and work in neighbouring cities and townships. Even so, the fact that they are no longer dependent on the agricultural sector for jobs, the way they used to be in the past, has enabled and emboldened them to join alternative political formations. It is not at all surprising that it is only in the last ten-fifteen years that politics of the Bahujan Samaj Party (BSP) is becoming credible in U.P. As long as the SCs were fettered as agricultural labourers without any opportunities outside the village, a party like the BSP could hardly be expected to be an active political option for them.

In Maharashtra something quite similar happened that allowed the SCs, particularly the Mahars, to become politically active. The literacy rate and urbanization of the Mahar community is the highest among the Scheduled Castes of Maharashtra. This process of secular literacy and employment was also aided by the formation of a Mahar regiment in the British Indian Army. From such stirrings the Republican Party of India under B.R. Ambedkar was born. Scheduled Castes in U.P. have not yet undergone the same kind of cultural upliftment as the Mahars of Maharashtra have accomplished. Even so, the general secularization of economic opportunities outside the village have certainly played an important role in consolidating the BSP in U.P. The Harijans (or the Chamars) of U.P. are the most advanced of all the SCs in U.P. and it would be safe to surmise that many of them play a leading role in the SC politics of their respective constituencies.

TABLE: 3

The BSP's Progress in U.P. Lok Sabha Elections

Years	Percentage of Votes
1985	2.6
1989	9.5
1991	11.9
1996	20.6
1996	22.0

Judging from the figures of caste population and electoral outcome it appears that the BJP and the Congress tend to do well when the Brahman population is higher than average, i.e., around 10-15 per cent. This seems to hold in constituencies like Garhwal, Tehri Garhwal, Nainital, Almora, Amethi and Sultanpur. But before we set off to draw conclusions from this we ought to note that Sultanpur and Akbarpur share roughly the same kind of caste profile, but with vastly different electoral outcomes. In both these constituencies Brahmans and Ahirs comprise 10-15 per cent of the population, Rajputs and Kurmis roughly 5-10 per cent of the population, and the Scheduled Castes over 25 per cent of the population. Yet in Sultanpur the BJP has consistently won the last three elections while in Akbarpur the BSP won in 1996 and 1998. So an explanation based on caste numbers does not do too well beyond a point.

TABLE: 4

Higher Than Average Brahman Population and Election Results

Constituency	Brahman %	1998	1996	1991
Garhwal	5-10	BJP	Congress	Congress
Tehri-Garhwal	5-10	BJP	BJP	Congress
Nainital	5-10	BJP	Congress	Congress
Almora	5-10	BJP	BJP	Congress
Amethi	10-15	BJP	Congress	-
Sultanpur	10-15	BJP	BJP	BJP
Akbarpur	10-15	BJP	BJP	JD

Source: Singh (1996); Census of India, 1931, United Province of Agra and Oudh (Part II Tables); Unpublished Lok Sabha Elections Results, 1998.

The BJP prospers in a variety of caste configurations. It has also been successful in areas where the population of the more affluent and powerful castes is quite low. For instance, the BJP won in Kheri, Hardoi, and Shahabad where Ahirs, Brahmans and Rajputs each comprise between 5-10 per cent of the population while the SCs make for more than 25 per cent of the population. The BJP has also done well in areas such as Etah and Bareilly in the last three elections. Ahirs make up about 11.7 per cent of the population in Etah, and in Bareilly the Kurmis are approximately 10.2 per cent of the population. The same could be said about Gorakhpur as well. The trend is expressed more strongly in Saidpur. The population of Ahirs is quite high here. It stands at between 15-20 per cent of the population.

Elsewhere, however, when castes such as Ahirs and Kurmis are between 15-20 per cent of the population the Samajwadi Party (SP) of Mulayam Singh Yadav appears to fare well. This is certainly true of Azamgarh, Jaunpur, and Ghazipur. However, it is not as if the SP or JD have these constituencies in their pockets. The BJP, and even the BSP, have done equally well in these same areas too. Judging from constituencies where the JD or SP have won it is quite clear that no straight correlation can be drawn between these victories and caste numbers.

It would be worthwhile to reiterate in this connection that with the same kind of caste composition a variety of electoral results are possible. Take for instance the case of Moradabad, Kheri, Hardoi, Shahabad, and Misrich. In these constituencies Ahir, Brahman, Kurmi, Rajput and SC proportions are roughly the same. Yet the election outcomes differ widely between constituencies, and within the same constituency over different elections.

The relationship between the Bahujan Samaj Party and Scheduled Caste population figures too is rather tenuous. As we have noted earlier SCs dominate the population of U.P. in terms of sheer numbers. The SCs on an average make up about 21 per cent of the population of U.P. In several constituencies they comprise more than 25 per cent of the population. Yet the BSP does not always do well in places where the proportion of SCs is very high. For example, the BSP has failed to make a significant impact in constituencies such as Unnao, Rae Bareilly, Amethi, Sultanpur, Faizabad, Bansgaon and Chail, where the SC population is quite high, viz., above 25 per cent. In Misrich, however, BSP victory could be linked to the fact that the SCs constitute more than 25 per cent of the population there. But Misrich is also a reserved constituency, so it is hard to be sure if caste numbers alone made the difference. On the other hand, Bahraich has a lower than average percentage of SC population and yet the BSP won the last elections there. Interestingly, the BJP had won the Bahraich seat both in 1991 and 1996.

Neither can we relate literacy among the SCs with BSP's success at the polls. Though in 1998 the BSP, actually won only four seats in Uttar Pradesh, it won the second-largest number of votes in as many as fourteen constituencies. If we take all these eighteen constituencies together we find that we cannot correlate BSP's positive performance with either SC population or literacy. With lower than average population and literacy rate the BSP won in Pilibhit and Bahraich. But in Saharanpur and Mathura the literacy rate among the SC is higher than the average for U.P. and the BSP stood second in both these places. This conclusion, like the other ones, are only approximations as we do not have literacy or caste population figures constituency-wise. In the case of electoral constituencies like Misrich, Akbarpur, Hathras and Khurja I have not been able to make an assessment of SC population ratio or literacy rate with any degree of satisfaction. In such cases only a field study can help.

When mapping the areas where the BSP is quite strong it is interesting to note that they seem to be clustered in four strips that are geographically quite

TABLE: 5

BJP Strongholds and Caste Composition of Constituencies

Constituencies	Castes and their Percentages					
	Ahirs	Brahmans	Rajputs	Kurmis	Scheduled Castes
Kheri	5-10	5-10	5-10	5-10	Over 25
Hardoi	—do—	—do—	—do—	—do—	—do—
Shahabad	—do—	—do—	—do—	—do—	—do—
Etah	10-15	—do—	—do—	—do—	15-20
Bareilly	5-10	—do—	—do—	—do—	—do—
Gorakhpur	10-15	10-15	—do—	10-15	—do—
Saidpur	15-20	5-10	—do—	5-10	Over 25

Source: Singh (1996); *Census of India, 1931, United Province of Agra and Oudh* (Part II Tables).

TABLE: 6

Ahir Population Percentage and Janata Dal (JD)/Samajwadi Party (SP)

Constituency	Percentage of Ahirs	Elections Results		
		1998	1996	1991
Azamgarh	15-20	BSP	SP	JD
Jaunpur	15-20	SP	BJP	JD
Ghazipur	15-20	SP	BJP	Other

Source: Singh (1996); *Census of India, 1931, United Province of Agra and Oudh* (Part II tables); Unpublished Lok Sabha Elections of 1998.

TABLE: 7

Caste Composition and Election Outcome

Constituency	Caste Composition					Elections			
	Abirs	Brahmans	Rajputs	Kurmis	SCs	1998	1996	1991	
Moradabad	5%-10%	5-10%	5-10%	5-10%	15-20%	SP	SP	JD	
Kheri	—do—	—do—	—do—	—do—	15-20%	BJP	SP	BJP	
Hardoi	—do—	—do—	—do—	—do—	Over 25%	BJP	SP	BJP	
Shahabad	—do—	—do—	—do—	—do—	—do—	BSP	BJP	BJP	
Misrich	—do—	—do—	—do—	—do—	—do—	BJP	BJP	—	

Source: Singh (1996); *Census of India, 1931, United Province of Agra and Oudh* (Part II Tables);
Unpublished Lok Sabha Elections Results of 1998.

TABLE: 8

Scheduled Caste Population Percentage, Literacy Rate and BSP Performance in Some Constituencies of Uttar Pradesh

Constituency	Literacy			Population			BSP Position in 1998 Elections
	High	Average	Low	High	Average	Low	
Pilibhit			*			*	2nd Position
Sitapur			*	*			2nd Position
Bahraich			*			*	1st Position
Ghosi		*		*			2nd Position
Azamgarh		*			*		1st Position
Fatehpur		*			*		2nd Position
Jalaun	*			*			2nd Position
Mathura	*					*	2nd Position

Source: Unpublished Lok Sabha Elections Results of 1998; Behera (1999:18-19).

TABLE: 9

Low (below 10%) Ahir Population and Election Results (table shows other caste percentages as well)

Constituency	Muslims	SCs	STs	Ahir	Brahmans	Rajputs	1998	1996	1991
Jamshedpur	5-10	10-15	20-25	5-10	5-10	Below 5	BJP	BJP	JD
Khunti	5-10	10-15	20-25	Below 5	Below 5	Below 5	BJP	BJP	BJP
Purnea	20-25	15-20	10-15	5-10	Below 5	Below 5	BJP	Samata	—
Rajmahal	20-25	10-15	20-25	5-10	Below 5	Below 5	BJP	Congress	Others
Dumka	10-15	10-15	20-25	5-10	Below 5	Below 5	BJP	JMM	Others
Godda	10-15	10-15	15-20	5-10	Below 5	Below 5	BJP	BJP	Others
Singhbhum	5-10	10-15	20-25	Below 5	Below 5	Below 5	Congress	BJP	JD
Ranchi	10-15	10-15	20-25	Below 5	Below 5	Below 5	BJP	BJP	BJP

Source: Singh (1996), Census of India, 1931, Bihar and Orissa (Part II Tables); Unpublished Lok Sabha Election Results, 1998.

disparate. The first is the North Central region comprising Pilibhit, Shahabad, Sitapur and Misrich. The next is the eastern strip of U.P. where Salempur, Ghosi, Azamgarh, Lalganj and Saidpur are situated. The third area of BSP influence is in south east U.P. in constituencies like Banda, Fatehpur, Bilhaur and Jalaun. Finally, BSP presence is also quite significant in constituencies such as Mathura, Hathras and Khurja in south-western U.P. There is nothing in terms of either population or literacy that unites these four zones of BSP prominence. Nevertheless, the fact that the BSP is strong in four lots of contiguous constituencies would encourage the interpretation that it draws political strength from the synergies of proximity. Collectively, across constituencies, numbers help to shore up SC confidence, which enables them to support the BSP somewhat consistently. This fact also points to the relative weakness in the organizational capacities of the Scheduled Castes and that of the BSP. What they lack in terms of organizational resources and capacities they make up by geographical aggregation.

Bihar

In Bihar the Congress does not feature in any significant way in the last three Lok Sabha elections. The fight in Bihar is really between the Janata Dal, or its 1998 incarnation the Rashtriya Janata Dal (RJD), and the BJP. The RJD certainly got the better of the BJP in the last parliamentary elections of 1998. The relationship between caste and politics is a little clearer here than it is in either U.P. or Maharashtra. But in this case too there is no constituency where a dominant agrarian caste like the Yadavs or Ahirs enjoy a numerical majority. In a handful of constituencies such as Madhepura,

Chhapra, Arrah, Khagriya, Patna and Navadah the Yadavs are between 15-20 per cent of the population. Nowhere in Bihar do the Yadavs make up anything more than that in terms of their share in numbers. In Bihar too, quite against the general impression, caste arithmetic cannot explain too much.

Nevertheless, certain patterns can be dimly discerned. In Ranchi, Kodarma, Jamshedpur and Giridih there is a high concentration of Muslims, SCs and STs. The Yadav proportions are quite low in these areas. In Giridih and Kodarma Yadavs make up about 10-15 per cent of the population, while in Ranchi they are below 5 per cent. In all these three constituencies the BJP is quite strong. In Ranchi it has won every time in the last three elections, while in Kodarma, Jamshedpur and Giridih it has won two out of three times. From this the following conclusion can be drawn. When the number of Yadavs is not very high, but the proportions of SCs, STs and Muslims together make for about 50 per cent of the population, the chances are that the JD or RJD of Laloo Prasad Yadav will face a stiff challenge from the BJP. This conclusion can be extended to other constituencies like Khunti, Purnea, Rajmahal, Dumka, Godda and Singhbhum. They all seem to fit this pattern. Low Yadav population, i.e., between 5-10 per cent of the total population, generally leads to BJP victory. In some instances such a caste configuration has also helped the Congress and the Jharkhand Mukti Morcha (JMM).

Even as we come to this conclusion we cannot ignore the instances of places like Kishanganj and Araria where the Yadavs constitute only between 5-10 per cent of the population and are yet strongholds of the JD or RJD. It is not easy to explain this in terms of population figures for in Araria the Muslims, STs and SCs constitute well above 50 per cent of the population and yet the JD won both in 1991 and 1996. The BJP however wrested this seat in 1998. In Kishanganj, on the other hand, with a Yadav population between 5-10 per cent the JD and RJD have won all the three elections of 1991, 1996 and 1998. To add another wrinkle on this, it is quite likely that the JD or RJD does well in spite of low Yadav numbers because this shortfall is made up by the high proportion of Muslims. As it may be reasonably assumed that Muslims would not vote for the BJP, it is very likely that they voted for the JD or RJD instead. This may account for why the JD or RJD did well inspite of low Yadav numbers. This combination however did not work in Rajmahal and Purnea where the BJP has done much better than its other competitors.

I would still like to consider Rajmahal and Purnea anomalous cases that need further investigations. Generally a high proportion of Muslims tends to offset low Yadav numbers to keep out the BJP. Sometimes it is the Congress and on other occasions it is the JD or RJD that win in these constituencies. This explains to a great extent why Laloo Yadav's RJD is demonstrably 'secular' at least on its position on Muslim minorities.

If one takes into account where the JD/RJD has won with between 10-15 per cent Yadav population it is difficult to explain how the castes lined up. The same holds true in constituencies where the JD/RJD has had mixed results. With 10-15 per cent Yadav population the JD/RJD has done well in places like Gopalganj, Hajipur, Vaishali, Muzaffarpur, and Jhanjharpur. However, in constituencies like Ballia, Motihari, or Bettiah where the Yadavs are again between 10-15 per cent of the population, the JD/RJD has had mixed results. As this is the case in most instances it is hard to interpret electoral results through the optic of caste numbers.

TABLE:10

Yadav Population Between 10%-15% in Some Constituencies and Mixed Election Results

Constituencies	1998	1996	1991
Gopalganj	Samata	JD	JD
Hajipur	—	—	—
Vaishali	RJD	JD	JD
Muzaffarpur	RJD	JD	JD
Jhanjharpur	RJD	JD	JD
Ballia	RJD	CPI	Others
Motihari	RJD	BJP	Others
Bettiah	BJP	BJP	JD
Madhuban	Congress	CPI	Others

Source: Singh (1996); *Census of India, 1931* (Part II Tables); Unpublished Lok Sabha Election Results, 1998.

The major correlation in the Bihar scenario is between a middle-sized representation of Yadavs and JD or RJD victory. Except for constituencies like Jehanabad, Sitamarhi and Navadah, the RJD/JD has won in the last three elections in those areas where the Yadavs constitute between 15-20 per cent of the population. This is true of Madhepura, Chhapra, Arrah, Monghyr, Patna, Barka and Khagriya. While the correlation between Yadavs constituting between 15-20 per cent of the population and JD/RJD victories is quite impressive, this still does not explain how the JD/RJD won. It cannot be assumed that the Rajputs, Bhumihars, or Koeris would vote for an ostensible Yadav party out of sheer caste compulsions. There is a great degree of hostility and rivalry between these castes, particularly in rural Bihar. Therefore, in terms of pure caste arithmetic, JD or RJD need help from other quarters to add to the Yadav numbers This is of course assuming that the Yadavs vote *en bloc* for the JD/RJD.

TABLE: 11

Ahir Population Between 15%-20% and JD/RJD Performance

| | | Elections | |
Constituencies	1998	1996	1991
Madhopur	RJD	JD	JD
Arrah	SAP	JD	JD
Monghyr	RJD	JD	Others
Barka	Samata	JD	JD
Khagriya	Samata	JD	JD
Patna	—	JD	—
Navadah	RJP	BJP	Others
Chhapra	RJD	BJP	JD
Jehanabad	RJD	CPI	Others

Source: Singh (1996); *Census of India, 1931, Bihar and Orissa;* Unpublished Lok Sabha Election Results of 1998.

The connection between Yadav numbers and JD/RJD victory is thus not a clear one at all. To begin with, as mentioned earlier, nowhere do the Yadavs dominate in terms of sheer numerical strength. At best they constitute approximately 15-20 per cent of the population. If one takes into account the Kurmis, the other agrarian caste, the picture does not get any clearer. The Kurmis are to be found largely in Patna and in South Bihar constituencies such as Hazaribagh, and in the Chhota Nagpur areas. In Patna the JD/RJD does well, but this is also a Yadav area. In Hazaribagh, Ranchi and Singhbhum where there is some Kurmi presence, the JD/ RJD position is perhaps the weakest in the state of Bihar.

Caste Arithmetic or Caste Chemistry

In all the cases studied in this paper there was no clear indication of caste arithmetic determining electoral results. That we are accustomed to talk in terms of Jat or Yadav strongholds cannot be attributed to sheer caste numbers. In fact the population of Yadavs, or Gujars, or Jats or Kurmis, falls way short of numerically preponderating any electoral constituency. The fact however remains that politicians calculate on caste lines, and candidates too are chosen on this basis. This only means that the choices before the electorates are sought to be placed in caste terms, but it is not as if the votes are always cast according to this logic.

It is quite understandable why politicians should attempt a caste calculus. Most of them would obviously like members of their caste and people they can trust and depend upon to carry the mantle for them. From the electorate's point of view however the matter is quite different. Voters can only vote for whoever is actually contesting. The point then is to ask why certain castes figure more prominently as candidates than other castes. Concurrently, one must also ask why the SCs do not do as well as they should though they have a fair population representation in many constitutencies.

To explain why we easily equate caste numbers with politics has probably to do with the organizational capacities of castes. The poorer SCs and STs may have numbers on their side but lack organizational capacity. Politics is not only about numbers it is also about ability to exercise power in a concerted and organized fashion. It is here that economic capacity and relative financial security play a significant role in the matter. This was recognized even by Mahender Singh Tikait, the Jat leader of the Bharatiya Kisan Union. After a trip to the poor districts of Bihar he said that he quite understood why the poverty-ridden peasants there could not agitate for their demands the way the Jats and Gujars of west U.P. could. To quote Tikait:

> We spent forty days agitating in Bhopa, but the wretched kisans of Palamau, Kalahandi or Giridih are so poor that there is no way they can put up such a resistance for so long. I really feel sorry for them and [am] grateful to God that we were comparatively better off. (Gupta 1997: 94.)

To be able to participate in a sustained political fashion it is not numbers alone that matter, The ability to be organizationally effective demands a certain degree of economic security which poorer castes are, more often than not, unable to muster (see also Bose 1992: 379).

The fact that caste numbers and election results do not go hand in hand should caution those who are quick to succumb to the temptations of caste arithmetic. Every time an election is round the corner it is readily assumed that as caste loyalties dominate both the candidates and the public, it is really a question of fine-tuning the numbers game. Whoever does a better job in calculations of this sort wins the day.

This species of reasoning not only ignores the fact that no caste has the adequate numbers to win an election on its own, it does not in fact understand the caste system itself: neither its characteristics nor its logic. It is not as if all agrarian castes come together spontaneously and unproblematically because the Brahmanical ranking places them close to one another. To begin with, it must be remembered that one of the important features of the Hindu system of stratification is the profound mutual repulsion that exists between different castes (Bougle 1992). This is true for all castes, even those that appear to be close or contiguous to the outside observer. The Jats and Gujars of U.P., for example, are constantly undermining each other, though on the face of it 'they should, as owner-cultivators, be natural allies. Such examples abound everywhere— between the Srivastavas and Patwari Kayasthas of U.P., or between the Meecho and Helo Kaibarttas of Bengal, or between the Mangs, Matangs, Chamars and Mahars of Marathwada.

Inter-caste solidarities, therefore, cannot emerge full-blown from the logic of the caste system itself. If one were to add to it the fact that no caste can on its own swing an election unambiguously in its favour it is easy to understand why caste-based predictions have invariably come to grief. In states like Maharashtra where the Marathas can claim overall numerical supremacy votes are fragmented between different parties such as the Congress, BJP and the Shiv Sena.

It needs to be underlined in this connection that one's loyalty is not towards an untidy and amorphous category called Kshatriya, Shudra, or Brahman. A caste Hindu's affiliation is strongest to his or her jati. The various Brahman jatis, for example, quarrel ceaselessly among themselves to establish who is superior to whom. In the meantime, the Saraswat Brahmans and the Chitpavan Brahmans keep mutual repulsion alive between them (as indeed they must, for such is the logic on which the caste system operates).

A brief examination of the two most talked about caste alliances in recent times, viz., the AJGAR in U.P. and KHAM in Gujarat coalitions can be quite instructive. The AJGAR has Ahir, Jats, Gujars and Rajputs, while the KHAM is composed of Kshatriya, Harijan, Adivasi and Muslim. Such a front can hardly emerge from within the logic of the caste system. For Kshatriyas and Harijans to align together is unthinkable by any tenet of caste ideology. The fact that Muslims are a partner in this alliance denies the relevance of the Hindu hierarchy altogether. Where in the caste system or in caste ideology can one find a justification for an alliance between Kshatriyas and Muslims? Or between Jats and Gujars? In western U.P. the rivalry between the Jats and Gujars is intense. They accuse each other of cowardice, of moral impropriety and worse. They have physically clashed against each other on several occasions as well. Or, how is it possible that in Gujarat the peasant Kolis can team up with Bareyas and Rajputs to oppose the newly-ascendant agrarian Patidar caste? Further, how can the Kurmis in Bishrampur have made common cause with the other castes to attack the Yadavs who are also peasants like them?

Caste alliances thus appear to emanate from secular and political factors and do not spring full blown from primordial loyalties. The All India Kurmi Sabha (which stretches from U.P. to Bihar) is made up of disparate castes such as the Ayodhyas, Dhanuks, Mahatos, Koeris and Kurmis. These castes not only do not intermarry but in many cases there might even be problems of inter-dining as well. In the Oudh peasant movement of the 1920s the Kurmis, Pasis, and Muslims came together against landlordism, but throughout their struggle they ate in separate kitchens (Siddiqi 1978: 117). What brings about such horizontal solidarity between castes then is the extent to which their secular interests coincide, which in turn depends on their structural locations in the society.

Peasant castes often come together against non-peasant castes. Sometimes as with the Gujarat example, one section of the peasant community aligns with the enemy's enemy in order to assert its economic aspirations. And as secular and political interests vary, caste alliances too undergo significant changes. This explains why Madhavsinh Solanki in Gujarat was voted out after he powered his way to the top with KHAM support. It is not as if the KHAM coalition or its members—the Kshatriyas, Harijans, Adivasis and Muslims—have disappeared. This alliance could no longer sustain a shift in secular interests, which is why what seemed like a good idea some time back does not resonate any longer. Likewise, Mulayam Singh Yadav lost a chunk of his Backward Caste base when many of his supporters joined the Hindu wave that climaxed in 1992 with the Babri Masjid episode.

The popular assumption that caste loyalties contribute to caste alliances, which in turn determine voting behaviour, is clearly in error. If anything, alliances are a shorthand way of signaling a coalescence of secular interests. What needs to be appreciated is that these interests must really be powerful enough for castes to overcome their natural repulsion towards each other and form united fronts. It is therefore caste chemistry and not caste arithmetic that one should pay attention to.

The fact that SCs, inspite of their numerical strength do not have a proportional strength in the electoral system indicates quite strongly that they are held back by their weak organizational abilities. In rural India it is still very difficult for poor SCs or STs to politically form independent blocs without arousing the wrath of the more affluent communities. For this reason the political ambitions of the SCs rarely get off the ground. That the BSP's influence is also to be found in certain narrow geographical strips of U.P. may also be on account of the fact that in these regions the SCs have somehow been able to wrest some initiative for themselves. Unfortunately, without further empirical research it is hard to say why this should be the case; the gross figures, whether of population, literacy rate or urbanization, provide us with no substantial leads.

More research also needs to be done to ascertain why certain areas are considered to be Jat, or Gujar or Yadav terrain when numerically none of these castes can even remotely claim majority status in the political scene. In some cases, such as for the Jats, or Gujars, or Koeris, their proportions rarely rise above 10% of the population. We also need to know more as to why in certain constituencies in Bihar RJD candidates tend to get elected even when the Yadavs constitute about only 20 per cent of the population. Obviously, other castes are also voting for them. Assuming that there is a strong relationship between Yadavs and RJD, the point to enquire into is: why then are members of other castes also voting in the same direction? These questions can be asked and answers to them will resonate once we realize that in caste arithmetic numbers just do not add up.

7

Caste, Infrastructure and Superstructure

On the Uses of History

Once it is accepted that castes are discrete in character, it is easier to appreciate how there can be multiple interpretations of what is usually regarded as a monolithic ideological formulation. These several interpretations depend upon the circumstances at hand and the living contexts of each caste. To look at the caste system as pure ideology to which all Hindus acquiesce to is also to position it outside the play of history. All that matters then in terms of history is when the caste system came into being and began to exercise its unchallenged authority over society. The specific historical conditions that account for its growth, transformation and contemporary status are kept out of purview.

This attitude is in fact one that is encouraged by virtuosos of different religious groups and communities as well. To believe that a certain religion is pure emanation or unmediated voice of God, certainly helps to win unquestioning allegiance to it. At best the chronological starting point, the moment when this revelation was made known, can be accepted in terms of background information. But no more. Any search into the origins, transformations and adjustments that Christianity, Sikhism, Islam, Hinduism and so forth have had to undergo takes away at one stroke the charisma of religions. It is therefore not surprising that certain Sikh scholars should be attacked by believers of the Sikh faith for merely suggesting that this religion grew gradually over time and did not emerge full blown and finished from the very start. Or, at any rate, what passed for Sikhism in the eighteenth and nineteenth centuries is quite different from Sikhism today.

An understanding of the caste system is also held back by a general reluctance of sociologists and anthropologists towards the use of historical material. It is not as if an anthropologist would become a historian if this were to happen, or that history and anthropology do not have disciplinary specifics, but if one were to operate keeping in mind the limits of one's naivete (see Gluckman 1964), useful insights can be gathered from the cross-fertilization of disciplines.

In the case of caste, in particular, a historical sensitivity is important to correct the widespread impression that caste is somehow a peculiar ideological construction that the Hindu mind spontaneously conjured. If history can explain how the ideology of caste was wrought, elucidate the various stages it went through, as well as the actual confrontation between classes and communities that contributed to its making, then surely we are richer as a consequence. Further, if the ideology and practice of the caste system underwent modifications over time, as we will try to show it did, then there is no reason why it should not do so in future as well. These transformations can only be understood in terms of social pressures and cannot be gauged by looking at the ideological level alone.

Karl Mannheim put this idea across very well when he pointed out that the sociology of knowledge has as its raison d'être the investigation of social and historical forces responsible for the rise and transformations of different knowledge and belief systems. Paying attention to the ideological formulations alone would not take sociology very far, as in pre-modern societies it was the job of the traditional intelligentsia to systematize knowledge in order to save it from being undermined by social forces contrary to it. As in the past only the traditional intelligentsia had the means and the opportunity to produce such systematically formulated knowledge systems, an exclusive concern with such products will obviously bypass the lively social forces that such knowledges did their best to conceal. This is what preserves the illusion that in tradition 'thought remains eternally the same.' (Mannheim 1960: 6.)

This should make evident that sociology and anthropology can fine-tune their perspectives by being exposed to the historical conditions of social thought and practice. This should also heighten their awareness of possible sources of conflict and social change in contemporary times as well. History is not a placid recounting of things past, but a careful selection of what human societies have been through in order to clarify and give direction to concerns of today. History, as Croce argued long ago, has always been an obsession with the present.

A sociology of knowledge that seeks the historical conditions responsible for the emergence, growth and transformation of ideology and beliefs cannot accept that social practices come secondary to thought. To yield methodological advantage to the position that ideology is the primary level of reality and that all practices and social action must conform to it would be accepting the viewpoint of the traditional intelligentsia. That would defeat the purpose of sociology. That a large number of European Indologists functioned with just such a framework does not make it acceptable. Interestingly, much of eighteenth century German philosophy, from Herder to Fichte to Ranke, was all about crystallizing the specific cultural traits peculiarly characteristic of certain Geists. It is not surprising then that the German scholar Max Mueller, who for long pioneered Indology in Europe, should have also quested for a Hindu mind that would typify the Hindu Geist. Instead of furthering such conceptions of ideology and culture, it is the job of sociologists to take such contributions as data bases for sociological investigations.

Is Ideology Primary Reality?

The question whether castes or classes constitute the primary level of reality of Indian society has been asked so often that it needs to be attended to at various levels. If caste loyalties are discrete in character then it is necessary to show how the idea of an unchallenged continuous hierarchy could attain such social currency in the first place. Culturologists have long claimed that the ideological level is the primary level. In the earlier chapter we noted in detail Dumont's contribution to his point of view (see also Berreman's critique in Berreman 1971). As is to be expected of a scholar of Dumont's repute *Homo Hierarchicus* is not without historical assertions as well. Yet Dumont is fundamentally closer to a culturological perspective as he very quickly short shrifts history with the rather sudden conclusion that the caste system was perfected around 8000 BC (Dumont 1988: 37; see also 53, 67) and has remained essentially the same ever since. For some finessing of ideological detail Dumont returns repeatedly to Hindu texts principally to *Manusmriti*. It is as if caste practices in everyday life, and at various levels, are unquestioningly preordained by what Brahmanical texts have had to say.

According to this perspective castes constitute the primary reality of Indian society. All other identities and categories must therefore be subservient to caste. This view was also articulated by Weber and Hegel and by several other Indian and European scholars (O'Malley, 1975: 16). But it was with Dumont that this conscious model was cleansed of all impurities, delinked from all traces of economics and politics, and ballasted by facts and logic, characteristic of contemporary scholarship, to exercise a tremendous influence over sociological and anthropological studies of the caste system. The generic characteristic of this approach which Dumont amplifies is the belief that the caste system conditions material reality in its own image and is, therefore, an irreducible and immutable given. The suggestion then is that as the caste system is independent of material conditions and political power, it can only be overcome by a willful conscious abnegation of the principle of hierarchy beginning with a radical devaluation of the status of the Brahman, i.e., by 'caste action'.

A sociological approach, on the contrary, seeks to unearth the material and historical roots of the caste system, and in particular searches for those peculiar features of India's material history which were responsible for the genesis of the caste system and which contributed to its development. Marxist notions of base and superstructure, or infrastructure and superstructure, position the sociological approach quite centrally. Yet there are certain conclusions that are associated with Marxism that need to be carefully avoided. It should not be assumed that the ideology of caste is a creation of Brahmans alone, or that it is thrust on others, either against their will, or while the lower castes are in the ideological thraldom of upper castes, to justify economic exploitation.

While the Brahmans have indeed played an important role in the codification of the caste system, as can be gleaned from the various extant sacerdotal texts, it is not as if they were the sole motivators. Further, subscription to the notions of purity and impurity go much deeper and are not confined to the upper castes alone. This is one of the major conclusions of our earlier chapters on discrete castes and on various models of the caste system. Secondly, while upper castes strain to justify economic exploitation on caste grounds it is not as if this is blindly accepted by lower castes. If that had been the case then there would not have been caste dynamism, mobility and transformation in any form or degree in Indian history. The fact is that dominant castes exercise their power by forcing subaltern groups to accept their vision of caste hierarchy as the working principle in everyday life and conduct. That most castes abide by such norms does not mean that they intrinsically believe in them as well. It is the threat of force, and the actual use of force by the superior propertied castes that keep the lower castes in line. Yet, because the belief in hierarchy and purity and pollution runs right through the caste system, no matter who comes to power next, a new hierarchy is sought to be enforced in place of the earlier one. The caste system is certainly no myth, but the caste system rests on the basis of the myth of natural superiority which each caste would like to express in its own way, and to its advantage.

This position is not contrary to the basic Marxist approach which seeks to locate ideological articulations and political expressions in relation to concrete social practices and struggles for dominance. In this sense Marxism is the same as much of sociology but with the difference that Marxists would like to look at historical progression in terms of the tensions between determinate economic classes, and also condition contemporary analyses by framing them within the context of class struggle. This is what separates Marxism from other approaches in sociology and anthropology, for it is not Marxism alone that links ideology with material reality.

It is, however, not as if there is unanimity among Marxists on this issue. Maurice Godelier (1972, 1977, 1978), most significantly believes that the caste system exists at the level of the infrastructure, and not of that of the superstructure. Inspite of the use of terms like infrastructure and superstructure, Godelier's view gives credence to the culturological belief that castes constitute a primary reality. It also strengthens their argument that it is primarily by 'caste action' and not 'class action' (as classes do not constitute the infrastructure of caste societies) that one can overcome casteism. Indeed the latter conclusion has also been drawn by Omvedt (1978) and several others (see Atyachar Virodhi Samiti, 1979). If caste is infrastructure, then following from this major premise it is quite legitimate to argue for 'caste action' before all else. This is why Godelier surprisingly—given his Marxian orientation—appreciatively quotes Dumont, who very clearly rejects Marxism and denies its relevance for the study of Indian society. Whereas Dumont states that it is the cultural model, or the intellectual construct, that is most enduring (Douglas 1972: 19), and that one cannot go beyond the constraining logic of the purity/pollution opposition, 'until the purity of the Brahman is itself radically devalued' (Dumont, 1972: 92), certain Marxists argue that caste is infrastructure and that unless this stage is overcome the logic of a class analysis cannot be brought to bear on Indian reality (Godelier 1972: 1, 96-97, 275-276; Omvedt, 1978). Dumont quite clearly said: 'The road to their [caste] abolition is likely to lie in caste actions, and that only the content of a caste action indicates whether it initiates for or against caste . . .' (Dumont, 1972: 270).

The bulk of contemporary sociological literature, with the probable exception of Ghurye (1969), considers an investigation into the social origins of caste to be a non-issue, prone to clumsy ethnologist-type historical conjectures and not worthy of serious sociological study. True, some of the works by early Indologists were suspectible to the fault of grand theorization on shallow empirical foundations, but by devaluing them and often ignoring them sociologists and anthropologists have severed their ties with history. The result of this is that it has become difficult for sociologists and anthropologists to evaluate Brahmanical versions of the caste system from their disciplinary fields. This has helped to create a wider climate of acceptance for the views of those who trace the origins of the caste system to the Hindu mind, and also for the views of Dumont who believes that 'caste is a state of mind, a state of mind which is expressed by the emergence, in various situations, of groups of various orders generally called "castes".' The direct outcome of this approach is the belief that the Hindu mind is guided solely by a caste perspective and is perpetually bound by it (Dumont 1988: 34). The peculiarities of the Hindu mind are thus placed in the forefront, relegating the role of economic exploitation, classes and power in Indian society to, at best, a secondary position. Therefore, if a more just, egalitarian and progressive order is to be brought about, caste sentiment, or belief in the caste system, will first of all have to be erased from the minds of Indians. All material progress will have to wait till this ideological war is over. Caste is then the key factor which explains not only our present backwardness but also holds up our future progress. Such a position denies that traditional elements are malleable and often amenable to modernization. Scholars such as Singer (1972) and Rudolph and Rudolph (1961) certainly argued that such indeed was the case with India.

The King and the Priest in Ancient India

From extant information it appears that in Vedic India the distinction between a priest and a king, or a Brahman and a Kshatriya, never fully developed. The *Rig Veda* rarely mentions the Brahmans and the *Purusasukta* legend of the varna origins from the primeval being is a much later addition. Further the Brahman-Kshatriya combine worked in tandem, and both Brahmans and Kshatriya were engaged in clearing jungles, making land arable, etc. (Pusalker 1951: 314.) Apte also believes that the *Shukla Yajur Veda*, or the *White Yajur Veda*, gives the impression that the status of the Kshatriyas in general, and the king in particular had gone up in relation to the Brahmans (Apte, 1951b 431). In the *Satapatha Brahman* we find that the priest is made to serve the king and legitimize his supremacy.

'The priest makes the nobility superior to the people. And hence people here serve the Kshatriya, placed above them.' (Chattopadhyaya, 1977: 231.) Moreover, as late as in the Upanishadic period, we find in the *Chandayoga Upanishad* that King Pravahana instructed Brahman Gautam in the new doctrine of transmigration (Mehendale 1951: 469), revealing that the distinction between the warrior and priest had not yet developed. After all the *Chandayoga Upanishad* had declared that 'a performance accompanied by knowledge produces a better result than a performance without knowledge.' (Shastri n.d: 9). Thus one could be considered a legitimate interpreter of the Vedic texts and a spiritual leader on the basis of performance rather than on the basis of ascription alone. In the *Brihadaranakya Upanishad*, the King Ajatshatru exposes the superficial knowledge of the pretentious Brahman, Gargi. According to the ancient law-giver, Gautama, both the king and the Brahman are jointly responsible for upholding the social order. Note that the king is not responsible solely for the temporal order (see also Ghoshal, 1930: 6), R.S. Sharma, mentions that the *Pancavimsa Brahmana* records the conflict between Sudas and his priest Vashishta (Sharma, 1975: 10). Marglin also notes, after studying the *Dharmashastra*, that there is nothing in it to suggest that 'priesthood does not share in the power of royalty.' (Marglin, 1977: 249.) The Sunga kings were after all Brahmans who fully enjoyed and wielded state power. The above hopefully demonstrates that the distinction between power and ritual was not absolute during the Vedic age, and that the king was not always deprived, as Dumont says, of sacerdotal function.

Moreover, when Dumont asserted that the caste system was perfected eight centuries before Christ

(Dumont 1988: 37), he probably overlooked the *Upanishads*, which belongs to that period. The *Upanishads*, strictly speaking is not the work of Brahmans but of Kshatriyas. In the *Upanishads*, as Jawaharlal Nehru (1960) has recorded, '. . . the Vedas are referred to with respect but also in a spirit of gentle irony. The Vedic gods no longer satisfy and the ritual of the priests is made fun of.' The Upanishadic period is one of Kshatriya ascendance and the 'secret knowledge' (literally *Upanishad*) that these texts propounded triumphantly proclaimed that 'this knowledge has never yet come to Brahmans, and, therefore in all the worlds has the rule belonged to the Kshatriya only.' (*Chandayoga Upanishad* V. 36, quoted in Chattopadhyaya, 1978: 101.) Therefore the perfection of the caste system, with the Brahman on top, some eight centuries before Christ, i.e., in the Upanishadic period, is rather doubtful.

Looked at from another perspective, the pure hierarchy also suggests complete obeisance to the authority of the *Vedas* and the Brahman, for after all the pure hierarchy for Dumont, is a 'state of mind'. Such a position can again be held if one were to disregard the historical evidence that exists on the ideological and political struggles that occurred, both in the Vedic period and after, between the protagonists and the antagonists of Brahmanism.

The most noteworthy opponent of Brahmanism was the school of Brahaspati, variously known as *Vitanda* or *Vada* depending on whether or not one accepted the ideas propagated by this school. This school denied the supremacy of the *Vedas* and declared itself against the mere mouthing of Vedic hymns. 'The Manduka hymn is a panegyric of frogs who are described as raising their voices together at the commencement of rains like

Brahman pupils repeating the lessons of their teachers.'
(Shastri, n.d.: 8.) Shastri also notes that 'traces of an
opposition to the religion of the *Vedas* appear in the
Vadas and in later works. In *Aitreya Aranyaka* we find
the line 'Why should we repeat the *Veda* or offer any
kind of sacrifice?'

This tendency of opposition to the *Vedas* and to the
pretensions of the Brahmans cannot be dismissed as the
views of a group on the fringe. In the *Arthashastra*, the
Lokayata school which most fully articulated anti-
Vedism, was commanded rather highly as a science of
logic (Chattopadhyaya, 1978: 251). Moreover, the spread
of the later Lokayata schools, from which Buddhism
borrowed extensively, was significant enough for
Brahmans to launch a concerted attack on them through
the six Vedangas. The later *Manusmriti*, composed
before the Gupta period, was clearly hostile to the
logicians of the Lokayata and advocated strong legal
measures against those logicians who were transgressors
of caste discipline (Chattopadhyaya, 1978: 26). This
political aspect of caste ideology is so evident at every
step in the development of the caste system that it
cannot be thought of as making its presence felt only
'surreptitiously'. The protracted political and military
struggle between Brahmanism and Buddhism, the rise of
the Lokayata, of Tantricism and the Nastikas are a few
other illustrations along the same lines. The fact that
opposition to Brahmanism continued to exist long after
Brahaspati and Lokayata, and also Buddhism, is testified
to amongst other things by Madhava. Madhava,
incidentally was sponsored by the political and state
apparatus of the Vijayanagar empire.

The role of power in the development of the caste
cannot thus be underestimated, nor can it be said that

the distinction between power and ritual was complete from the very beginning. Till the Smriti period it is clear that the priestly authors did not detail out the duties of the king (Ghosal 1930: 6). It was in the *Manusmriti*, for example, that the role of king was demarcated from that of the Brahman (Thapar, 1978: 143). 'The Brahman came into his own in the post-Gupta period, when Buddhism began to decline and the Brahman's religious authority was backed by both an economic base and by his indispensability for the legitimation of power.' (Thapar, 1975: 32.) The large number of land grants made to Brahmans (Brahmadeya lands) during the Gupta period, coupled with the delegation of juridical authority over those lands to the Brahmans contributed to their ascendance. Around this time it was important for a usurper of state power as well as for petty oligarchs to claim noble descent which necessitated the manufacturing of false genealogies. Those Brahmans who loyally supported these claims and aided in fabricating such genealogies were the ones who were rewarded by the political authority with land and patronage. They were thus playing the role of status legitimizers to their political overlords, and were therefore intimately tied with politics and power without which their own status and were threatened.

Not all Brahmans *qua* Brahmans were granted superior status. In the earlier *Jatakas* the Brahman's status was inferior to that of the nobility (Nanjudayya and Anantha Krishna Iyer, 1928: 131) Brahmans were generally considered to be of inferior status 'until they became priests to some of the kings of Northern India.' (Thapar, 1975: 30-31.) This clearly indicates that proclaimed high ritual status had to be backed by political and economic power to be socially realized.

This is why not all Brahmans were of equal status either. For instance, the Kura Pancala Brahmans of Magadha were referred to as the 'so-called Brahmans' (Thapar, 1975: 30) in the *Jatakas*. Those Brahmans who could not get the patronage of rulers oɪ wealthy landlords were reduced to taking up other skills, even such 'lowly' ones as carpentry.

Pure Hierarchy and Untouchability

We also find that the presence of the Brahmans did not always entail the presence of the untouchables at the other pole; it was well after the Vedic period, after even the period of the Mauryan empire, that the notion of untouchability came into being. In the *Satapatha Brahman*, the chief or noble is advised to eat from the same vessel as the vis, or commoner (Sharma 1975: 12). In the *Rig Veda*, there was no mention of untouchables either. The later Vedic texts such as the *Vajaseaneyi Samhita*, *Taittrya Brahmana*, *Brihadaranakaya Upanishad*, *Chandayoga Upanishad*, considered certain communities like the Chandalas and Paulkasas as objects of abhorrence, but not as untouchables (Jha, 1975: 15). It was only around second century AD that the stratum of untouchables and the notion of untouchability became evident, for instance in the *Apastamba Dharmasutra* (Jha, 1975: 15).

There were, however, certain Buddhist sources around this period onwards which alluded to certain communities as untouchables. But Vedic or Hindu literature and archaeological references to that period are quite free of this categorization. The explanation for this, according to Romila Thapar, is that as Buddhism flourished in the urban centres, and as the audience of these texts were inhabitants of these urban settlements, all those who entered urban areas sporadically to render services and then returned to the non-urban hinterland were considered untouchables by Buddhists (Thapar 1984: 107-08). But in rural areas where Vedism reigned, and where these communities were settled, they were not given this lowly status, and this is reflected in Hindu texts. Strangely enough, Dumont notes the absence of any reference to untouchables in Vedic texts but dismisses its significance. His assertion that in the Vedic age the pure hierarchy contrived to conceal the factual accretion of a fifth category (Dumont 1988: 68), the untouchables, is contrary to the evidence that we have just presented.

As already mentioned, Dumont's contention that politics did not enter at the two ends of the hierarchy, but only 'surreptitiously' made an appearance at the interstitial levels is untrue as far as the ascendance of the Brahmans is concerned (ibid: 75, 235). It is not true of the other end of the pole, i.e, the untouchables, either. Politics has constantly surfaced at this extremity too, as witnessed by the large number of uprisings that have occurred in ancient India wherever the untouchables had revolted against their degradation. The history of Tantrism itself is a clear indication of this phenomenon. 'Tantrism in this more original form, had really been intimately associated with those castes and professions that were despised for many centuries.' (Chattopadhyaya, 1978: 327.) Chattopadhyaya also points out that supreme importance was attached in the Tantra to the members of the lowest castes, performing the most degrading and defiling occupations. 'Being thus associated with the despised castes, Tantrism, as is to be expected, was not respecter of caste distinction and caste superiority.' (Chattopadhyaya, 1978: 331.) This disrespect was also expressed by frequent revolts against the caste system. All men and women were deemed to be equal in the Tantras. The adoration of the human body in the Tantras, and the doctrine which proclaims that the human body is a microcosm of the universe, devalued the Vedic insistence on the profanity of the body, especially with reference to the body of such despised members of the low castes as Doms, Chandalas, Hadis, etc.

The Renouncer

But what about the renouncer? In the first chapter a lengthy section was devoted to this issue and we can only add very little to what was said earlier. To return to Dumont once again we find the argument: 'It may be doubted whether the caste system could have existed and endured independently of its contradictory, renunciation.' (Dumont 1988: 186.) What is the significance of bringing the renouncer? The significance lies, according to Dumont, in the fact that the renouncer by giving up his place in society, by eschewing power, and by adopting a superior lifestyle (as an ascetic and vegetarian) one commands higher ritual status, and the Brahman therefore is compelled to emulate him. The renouncer is thus intrinsic to the perfect hierarchy. In this connection Romila Thapar's essay 'Renunciation: The Making of a Counter-Culture' (1978: 63-105), is important. Thapar distinguishes between an ascetic and a renouncer who returns to society, as preceptor and mentor for those within it. She then notes that some renouncers denounced the *Vedas*; that the Shaiva monastics, notably the Kapalikas and the Pasupatas, were regarded with contempt by the *Puranas*. But the

Kalamukhas (another Shaivite sect) were treated more sympathetically by orthodox Brahmans as they did not question Brahmanical superiority. So, contrary to Dumont, not all renouncers were considered worthy of emulation by Brahmans; only some were, and these like the Kalamukhas were also advisers to kings and were thus not averse to power either. Both the Brahmans and the established order frowned at Tantricism, which, incidentally, was probably an undercurrent of one of the main strands in the ethos of renouncers since earliest times. Finally, the appearance of most renouncers, Tantrics and otherwise, as an organized section of society occurs historically at periods of change. During periods when there is a growth of urban centres and the development and expansion of the agrarian economy, there emerge within society not only religious but socio-economic situations which give impetus to and provide suitable conditions for the emergence and sustenance of such groups. Also the rise of a Tantric culture and the appeal of Tantric renouncers 'may be said to reflect the rise of the substratum culture coinciding with the social elevation of relatively obscure families and castes . . . The substratum culture was opposed to the orthodox tradition, an opposition which came to be symbolically expressed in tantric ritual; much of which is a reversal of Brahman values.' (Ibid.) Renunciation became highly salient socially only at particular points in history. It is not as if it was always strengthening its opposite, i.e., the orthodox caste hierarchy as Dumont argued. Further, not only is the separation of the political, economic and the ritual levels undemonstrable via the renouncer, but, on the other hand, the social relevance of the renouncer itself lies in the economics and politics of the time.

Economic Power and Caste

The narration of such historical facts which are indeed considered 'small change' in the ledgers of historical study places in considerable jeopardy Dumont's contention of the caste system being the primary level of reality. That the ideology of caste is constantly manipulated is quite different from arguing that caste exercises its pristine influence on social reality. The pre-eminent status attained by the Brahman and the debasement of the untouchable cannot be considered as pre-given outcomes of the Hindu state of mind but, rather, resulted from a long historical process. The most salient feature of this historical process was the constant rivalry between various communities for political and economic power which was reflected in their varying and conflicting perception of Brahmanism and of the *Vedas*.

There was never a universal acceptance of either Brahmanism or the *Vedas* in ancient India, let alone in the later periods. This alone can explain the great degree of mobility of groups in Indian history and also the manufacturing of fictitious genealogies for those who claimed higher status (Thapar, 1978: 353; Kosambi, 1975: 33). It also helps one to comprehend why, after the growth of feudalism, landed property was the most tangible basis of social and political status (Yadav, 1976: 45). From this perspective there is also little cause for disbelieving, as Dumont does, the empirical reality, recorded by McKim Marriot, that, it is to the landlord and not to the Brahman that maximum services are rendered in village India. The ideology of the 'pure hierarchy' then has been constantly contravened, and even the Brahman's authority in spiritual matters has been frequently challenged, as discussed a little earlier.

Further, powerful monarchs and land-owning communities in ancient and medieval India were not always of Kshatriya origin. Several powerful warrior kings from Chandragupta Maurya to Shivaji as well as 'those who became landholders by force of royal pleasure could hide their low origins by paying enough priestly Brahmans to support their claim.' (Kosambi 1975: 33.)

Moreover, superior ritual status did not always entail superior economic and political power. Only in the Vedic age, as we shall see in the next chapter, can it be said that the two coincided as the warrior-priest ruling class amalgam working in collaboration to clear virgin land and to subjugate tribes which were a threat to the Vedic Aryans who were quite primitive themselves. The amalgam came apart in the years to follow. The growth of large empires, the emergence of a developed state structure, with a standing army and large royal bureaucracy, necessitated greater preoccupation with administrative and political control. The list of duties of the king as prescribed in the *Arthashastra*, along with the multifarious activities for the officials of the bureaucracy detailed therein testify to this. This explicitly compartmentalized and segregated the activities of the warrior/king from the poet/priest. Operative political and social control was exerted exclusively by the non-priestly warrior class. But Brahmans continued to exercise their influence through clever manipulation of religion and rituals, and were also generously endowed with land, such as with the Brahmadaya lands. Hence, those Brahmans who did not own land, or were impoverished, were not dominant in terms of the operative exercise of political ritual and power. Yadav draws our attention to *Kathokosa Prakarama* of Jinesvara Suri to show that landed property in this age emerged as the most 'tangible basis of social and political status.' (Yadav 1976: 45.) We find here that 'the ruling landed aristocracy composed of two strata—paramount rulers and the different grades of the feudal elite, actually enjoyed higher status in society and emerged as a chief socio-economic class.' (Ibid.)

The priests, however, were given superior ritual status, as in all other pre-capitalist societies because they were the ideological fountainhead on which the myth of 'natural superiority' endeavoured to legitimize exploitation. But this ritual superiority does not necessarily subsume actual dominance in secular affairs. For instance, the rise of the Lingayat community of Mysore to dominance was challenged by Brahmanical orthodoxy, as a result of which the Lingayats employed their own non-Brahman priest to perform identical functions (Manor 1977: 177)—a measure that 'high' caste Brahmans could do nothing to prevent.

Similarly, it should be remembered that social and political power emanated not from wealth alone but also from the role of the individual and of his community in the system of production. Several merchants were wealthy even during Mauryan times, but they were not able to elevate themselves above the nobility and their fortunes depended upon the fate of their immediate patrons (Habib 1971: 33, 55-56). It was only after the middle of the nineteenth century, when first gradually and then increasingly, the feudal apparatus in India lost its stranglehold (without of course relenting completely) that the merchant-turned capitalists could become a dominant power in the state structure.

Conclusion

Once it is acknowledged that a 'state of mind' was unable to produce the caste system in its developed empirical form, some eight centuries before Christ, the primacy of the Brahmanical model is immediately devalued. Subsequently one has to make two further concessions. If the Brahmanical model developed through history, then as history itself is impregnated with contrary economic and political tendencies, the Brahmanical model of the caste system cannot be radically separated from these tendencies in its evolution. Secondly, if this model has ingested these contradictions and yet has pretensions of being a unitary system, then it must assert its universality by concealing the ground forces of these contradictions. It is precisely in order to fulfil this function that the rationale behind the caste system approaches the status of a myth, which according to Lévi-Strauss, bridges the unhappy contradictions on which society rests (Lévi-Strauss, 1966: 16; Gluckmann, 1974: 80).

8

From Varna to Jati: A Historical Excursus

In spite of the fact that it is hard to piece together a history of the caste system it is still worthwhile to get a sense of its past before we submerge ourselves in the present. The preceding sections, if anything, indicate that such a task raises more questions than it resolves. In the following pages we will make yet another attempt to add to our understanding of varna. We shall begin by placing varna in the history of the period in which it was first manifest, i.e., in the Vedic age, and then trace its fate through history. Our objective is to explain the possible social and material factors responsible for the varna scheme of stratification. It is our intention, therefore, to relate varna and jati to their respective epochs and to the modes of production to which these two forms of stratification correspond.

The four-fold varna scheme does not readily operate on the ground and because of this, it is often dismissed as a fiction. Varna categorizes Hindus into four orders—Brahman, Kshatriya, Vaishyas and Shudras. The reality, however, is that there are thousands of jatis, and not just four varnas. It is at the level of jatis that caste injunctions on marriage, occupation and social relations are conducted. There is no such jati as Brahman or Vaishya, but a large number of jatis claim to belong to different sections of the varna system. Thus we have jatis like Kanyakubja Brahmans, Saraswat Brahmans, Rarhi Brahman, Sarjupari Brahmans, and so forth. Though they are all Brahmans it is not as if they intermarry, nor is it that all these claims are uniformly accepted, as we have already discovered. In this connection it is necessary to underscore the fact that though varna categories may not operate with the kind of practical import as jatis do, notions of hierarchy and ascriptive status (based on putative 'natural differences') are clearly spelt out in this four-fold schema. Jatis draw their ideological rationale of purity-pollution, endogamy, commensality, and so forth, from the varna model.

To view varna as fiction has the dangerous consequence of positing that the jatis existed in their current form from the very start. This would then conform to the 'state of mind' theory that militates against an examination of an ideology over time in different socio-economic formations. If we wish to examine the hypothesis that the varna system was reflective of a material order and not merely fiction, we must consider the possibility of drastic epochal changes, so drastic that the varna scheme which corresponded to an earlier epoch might have been completely out of step in a later epoch, i.e., when the jatis were in the forefront. This would run counter to the proposition that Indian society has been stagnant and has remained unchanged from ancient to medieval times. Because the possibility of such epochal changes was not entertained in the past, the varna system was rendered incomprehensible and mystical.

Our primary focus then will be to relate the varna and the jati systems to different modes of production viz., the Asiatic and the feudal. This chapter does not claim to be exhaustive, nor does it pretend to bring to light fresh material, though there is some reinterpretation of data. It merely presents a preliminary framework by systematically arranging facts most pertinent to varna, jati and the socio-economic formations in which they found expression. It is hoped that this attempt will, at the very least, dispel some of the misconceptions surrounding the concept of caste. By drawing on the Asiatic and feudal modes of production we believe we can take advantage of very useful heuristic devices to plumb the depths of a social order whose origins are buried deep in antiquity.

The Asiatic Mode of Production

In order to understand the varna system as a viable historical category, we are forced concurrently to delve into another controversy—that of the Asiatic mode of production. In doing so we must take into account the latest contributions, much of which significantly re-articulated some of Marx's earlier positions on the subject. Marx found the concept of the Asiatic mode of production useful in understanding Asiatic societies, particularly India. According to Marx, the Asiatic mode of production is quite compatible with the fact that the all-embracing unity which stands above small common bodies may appear as higher or sole proprietor. It therefore follows that the surplus product (which, incidentally, is legally determined in terms of the real appropriation through labour) belongs to this highest unity which ultimately appears as a person. This surplus labour is rendered 'both as tribute and as common labour for the glory of unity.' (Marx 1965: 69-70.) As Maurice Godelier elaborates later, 'the exploitation of man by man assumes within the Asiatic mode of production, a form which Marx called "general slavery", distinct in essence from Graeco-Latin slavery as it does not exclude the personal liberty of the individual, is not a relationship of dependence vis-à-vis one another, and is achieved by the *direct* exploitation of one community by another.' (Godelier 1965a: 34-35; see also Marx 1965: 5, emphasis added.) In other words general exploitation of the people directly by the superior community, or the state, is the crucial feature of the Asiatic mode of production. This direct and general exploitation of one community by another precludes any relationship of dependence at the lower levels.

The Asiatic mode of production is not necessarily tied to a powerful state, as Marx himself had shown (Marx 1965: 70; see also Godelier 1965: 101), nor to a hydraulic society, as Habib has also argued (n.d: 61). It should be mentioned in this connection that Marx's characterization of the Asiatic mode of production does not in any way assume that the exploited community in these societies is an undifferentiated peasant mass (Hindess and Hirst 1975: 196-198). Stratification and differentiation among the exploited, as we shall see, in no way militates against the concept of the Asiatic mode of production, nor does it contradict the principles of general exploitation.

Even so, the status of the Asiatic mode of production, as a determinate historical category, is still extremely precarious. Several Indian historians have substantially revised and improved upon much of Marx's writings on Asia without arriving at a consensus on whether indeed any epoch in Indian history can be characterized by the Asiatic mode of production. This, in turn, compounds the difficulty in accounting for the sources of contradiction and change in the Asiatic mode of production, without which it falls short of being a true and demonstrable analytical category. Therefore, if the Asiatic mode of production is not to remain a purely hypothetical concept as it has been for some time now, any investigation into it would involve the two-fold task of identifying the era of the Asiatic mode of production and locating its dynamic potential. We shall touch upon these two areas with what little evidence we have from the Indian situation. Our treatment ought not to be regarded as definitive, but we hope to shed some light on these two very complex and important issues.

The Emerging Varna Order

The first sacred book of the Aryans the *Rig Veda*, was composed around 1500-1400 BC in the region between Kabul and Ganges. It is from the perusal of this and the three later *Vedas* that historians have been able to reconstruct the socio-economic conditions of that society until approximately 500 BC, when the Vedic age is said to have ended. The varna system came into being only after the Aryans settled in the vast Indo-Gangetic plains. It is not at all clear if the Vedic people were of a different racial stock, but they certainly belonged to a distinct linguistic family.

Though there is no proven Aryan skull form, according to Kosambi, 'certain tribes among the whole Indo-European group were conscious of being Aryans in some ethnic sense. For example, Darius of Persia proclaimed in his grave inscription (486 BC) that he was parsu, *parachaya puthra, Arya Arya Cithre*, i.e., a Persian son of a Persian, an Aryan of Aryan descent.' (Kosambi 1975: 173.)

The expansion of the Aryans and the early Vedic period did not occur by conquest alone. Some adventurous Brahmans and Kshatriyas from different Aryan kingdoms helped to clear jungles and made the land arable (Chanana 1960: 24; Kosambi 1975: 123). They also set up new hermitages. The close cooperation between the Brahmans (priests) and the Kshatriyas (warriors) made this possible and they consolidated their superior status in tandem. Brahman missionaries who accompanied Kshatriyas introduced the essentials of Aryan culture and tradition to the masses, converted the principal figures to Vedism and paved the way for social and cultural contact by allowing high-born Aryans to marry non-Aryans (Pusalker 1951: 314).

The primitive economy of the early Vedic period did not allow the Aryans to maintain a profound distance from the indigenous and subjugated communities in day-to-day activities. Even the Brahmans and the Kshatriyas worked on land and did other manual jobs essential in this phase of Aryan expansion. Therefore, for the conquering Aryans, the religious conversion of the non-Aryans into the Vedic folds was the most effective guarantee of their superiority. The ascetic Brahmanical, or the priestly side of Aryan expansion, was used to full advantage during this period by the Aryans. The esoteric sacred Vedic texts and religious rites were emphasized to bring about a peaceful acquiescence of non-Aryans to Aryan supremacy.

Varna System and Generalized Exploitation

The four strata of the varna scheme did not emerge full blown from the very inception of the Aryan settlement in India. It is true that in the *Rig Veda* the main division is between the Arya and the Dasa varnas. But the

Aryans themselves were not an undifferentiated community. They were divided into elites and commoners. The latter were called *vis* in the *Rig Veda*. This category later largely constituted the Vaishya community, the third stratum of the fully-developed varna scheme. The Vaishyas were the common peasants engaged primarily in agricultural practice. The Aryans tried to absorb the indigenous local tribes and communities and establish a workable relationship with them, but naturally from a position of strength. Some friendly tribes like the Sutas were even considered respectable (Jha 1975: 15). Rituals were profitably utilized to make allies for the Vedic Aryans from among the non-Vedic people (Sharma 1975: 11).

Members of several weak or unfriendly tribes who were unable to withstand the Aryan onslaught were enslaved by the Aryans or became a servile class in the Vedic economic structure. They were called the Dasas. The Dasa thus later came to mean, according to Kosambi, a helot of some sort. He had 'not the right to initiation, nor to bear weapons: he was property of the Aryan tribe as a whole, much in the same way as cattle.' (Kosambi 1975: 97.) And, like cattle, both male and female Dasas were objects of gift to the superior community (Chanana 1960: 21). The evidence that Kosambi and other historians have cited to show the absorption of Dasas into the Aryans fold leads one to believe that Shudras arose out of this servile population 'augmented also by such Aryans as were subjugated and enslaved in internecine warfare.' (Habib 1965: 23.)

A clear delineation of the four varnas is not evident in the *Rig Veda*, but appears in the *Purusasukta* which is a later addition. Further, the Brahmans, or the priestly class, did not constitute an exclusive community. In the

Vedic age priestly duties were not necessarily performed by men of priestly families (Apte 1951a: 388). Even in the later Vedic age of the *Yajur Veda*, where we find the Vedic Aryans in a settled community, and where the full elaboration of the four orders of the varna scheme had taken place, a conflict for supremacy existed between the Brahmans and Kshatriyas, as well as a considerable overlapping of duties between them (Sharma 1975: 10). Throughout the later Vedic age and up to the Upanishadic period, we find several instances of a Kshatriya's thirst for knowledge and increasing inquisitiveness to know the essence of nature and the world. Thus though the priest-king/warrior groups combined to form a composite ruling class, the distinctions between them were nebulous.

From the ancient texts it appears that the basic unit of Aryan social life was the patriarchal family. Their chief god was Agni (fire) while their other anthropomorphic deities were male, headed by the hard-drinking Indra (Kosambi 1975: 87). The Aryans were also pastoral people who had domesticated the horse and, as a result, had gained much mobility. Their indices of wealth accordingly were associated with cows, horses and other animals. The Aryans had also sought to combine pastoralism with agriculture and are said to have used the wooden plough to cultivate barley and other cereals. There were, however, no towns at this stage and the Aryans were in fact rather proud of the great destroyer Indra who had allegedly demolished the earlier pre-Aryan towns (Habib 1965: 23).

The Aryans in this stage had a simple social structure. They were divided among tribes which they called *jana* and lived in villages (ibid: 30). *Bali* was the recognized form of payment to the Brahman-Kshatriya combine and was more in the nature of an offering than a tax. There does not seem to exist any overlordship of land, but cattle and horses were owned by Brahmans and Kshatriyas.

It appears that most of the land was divided into fields cultivated by individual peasants who were regarded as *kshetrapati* or holders of the land. Lands as Kosambi said, 'were allotted to groups in rotation, and within the group by rank . . . Agriculture was so crude in any case that ploughed land had to be changed every year.' (Kosambi 1975: 111.) According to Habib, as the Aryans lived in 'semi-nomadic conditions, the conception of permanent occupation, let alone ownership of particular fields could not have possibly developed.' (Habib 1965: 24.)

In contrast to the earlier nomadic *Rig Veda* stage, the later Vedic phase, i.e., when the other three *Vedas* as well as the early *Brahmans* were composed, denoted a phase of great Aryan expansion (ibid: 23). According to Kosambi, this period, beginning more specifically from the Yajurvedic stage,

> seems nearer to that of Caesar's Gauls, who were Aryans too, softened from a recent martial past. They had developed settled agriculture, some trade and strong class structure within the tribe. The existence of still lower class of menials, the Sudras, made the position of the Vaishya easier. The two privileged class of druids and knights correspond exactly to Brahmans and Kshatriyas. (Kosambi 1975: 111.)

Also unlike in the Rig Vedic period, the Aryans now produced wheat, several kinds of pulses, rice (Sharma 1975: 1) and even sugarcane (Habib 1965: 66). Society was not pastoral as in the Rig Vedic age: the peasant now 'produced surplus to maintain priests, princes and their retinues' (Sharma 1975: 1), though the wooden plough was still in use. The peasants, Vaishyas, became increasingly subject to exactions of the superior class. Behind this class differentiation can be traced 'the growth of the power and pretensions of the ruler or chief'. (Habib 1965: 27.) The grain tithe of the Vaishyas served to maintain Brahmans and Kshatriyas, while the Shudras performed essentially menial tasks and were a domestic adjunct, small in number at this stage (Sharma 1975: 4).

In spite of such sharp differentiations, monarchy did not develop. Tribes took the form of oligarchies, where the undifferentiated superior community was maintained by the efforts of the Vaishya commoners and Shudra menials, or helots (Habib 1965: 66). The Vaishya community also served as artisans and provided the nobility with such services as carpentry, smithery, chariot making, etc. (Apte 1951a: 397). The tax collectors were generally related to the king, and force was used to collect taxes, the royal share being one-tenth or one-twelfth of the total produce (Sharma 1975: 6-8). 'The Vedic communities had neither a regular taxation system nor a standing army which was permanent, though one hears of *Sena, Senapati*, etc.' (Ibid: 12.)

Neither had the distinctions between artisans and peasants developed. They belonged to the undifferentiated Vaishya category of the varna scheme. This was probably due to the low level of productive forces of that period. Some iron weapons were made by smiths for the nobility, but they were few and of an inferior quality. This suggests that these artisans probably also had an additional stable means of livelihood, namely, agriculture. The utilization of wooden implements produced limited surplus, and this did not favour greater class differentiation either.

However, the priest-warrior/king combine undoubtedly constituted the nobility and there was no question of this class paying any taxes (Ghoshal 1972: 170). The Brahmans could hold land in the form of villages and fields without invoking the authority of the tribe and the clan (Kosambi 139).

The differentiation of the varna scheme into four broad categories was a reflection of the socio-economic formation of that period, namely, small peasant-predominated villages which used pre-iron agricultural equipment and gave up the surplus to the Brahman-Kshatriya combine. The latter directly collected the surplus from the peasantry and took advantage of the artisans' rudimentary skills. Exploitation, in other words, was general. As the *Satapatha Brahmana* states: 'The state authority feeds on the people. The state is the eater and people are the food: the states, the deer and people are the barley.' (See Sharma 1975: 6.) Likewise, the principal aim in the later *Vedas* is to sanction this exploitation. It is made clear that man is born with certain *rinas* (debts) and that he can overcome these *rinas* by following the injuctions laid down in the Vedic scriptures, by paying homage to the gods and the Brahman rishis, and by swearing allegiance solely to the lawmakers and the law-enforcers (Apte 1951: 445).

The entrenchment of the varna scheme may in no small measure be attributed to the fact that until the first half of the first millennium BC, the settled phase of Aryan society was prolonged on account of the persistence of pre-iron agriculture. India saw the advent of iron four centuries after Greece did and two centuries after Iran. 'Hence on account of low agricultural productivity, ritualism and ritualist class grew far more rapidly in India' (Sharma 1975: 13), rigidifying the ritual basis of the varna order as well. The tools and implements of the period throw light on the nature of the economic formation which, in turn, influenced the relations of production of that epoch, and profoundly affected the superstructure. As Emmanuel Terray states: 'It is not articles made, but how they are made, or by what instruments, that enables us to distinguish different economic epochs. Instruments of labour not only supply a standard of the degree of development to which human labour has attained, but they are also indicators of the social conditions under which labour is carried on.' (Terray 1972: 103.)

It may appear that the four-fold varna scheme was an outcome primarily of the low development of productive forces (and its corollary—the absence of extensive division of labour), and had nothing to do with generalized exploitation. But, as we hope to show, even in the succeeding post-Vedic Mauryan period which saw quite an extensive division of labour, the four-fold categories of the varna scheme still sufficed to guide social intercourse and ranking. So obviously the varna scheme was rooted in a deeper reality, namely the relations of production, or the character of exploitation, which as we shall see, remained largely unaltered from the later Vedic to the Mauryan period. There is nothing inherently contradictory between the existence of extensive differentiation and division of labour and a simple four-tiered stratification system, such as the varna system. The two can be reconciled, as it is here hypothesized they were, in the Mauryan period, if the logic of generalized exploitation is followed through. The following section hopes to deal with this problem.

The Mauryan Empire—Acme of Asiatic Society

The second phase of iron which began approximately around 550 BC made greater surplus expropriation possible by intensifying the prevailing structure of exploitative relations. Artisans and peasants, Vaishyas in their dual role, were still tied to the nobility with the difference that the petty oligarchies of Vedic Aryans had given way to powerful kingdoms beginning from the Magadha and climaxing with the Mauryan Empire. The release of productive forces with the more intense utilization of iron crystallized the formation of the state and its apparatuses such as the royal bureaucracy and a standing army.

For the appropriate utilization of this technological breakthrough, the state grouped different categories of artisans in separate guilds and directed their energies solely towards the production of superior agricultural tools and weapons. While the former augmented the agricultural surplus, the latter enhanced the instruments of coercion at the hands of the Mauryans. Several *srenis* were also composed of certain communities and tribes outside the empire who had been subjugated by the state. Through the *srenis* they rendered myriad services to the state. Book 2 of the *Arthashastra* mention *srenis* of *vratya* (non-Vedic) Aryans as well. Those guilds, or *srenis*, functioned primarily to meet the needs of the state and the nobility for their personal consumption, warfare and trade.

> The King as the successor to chiefs of many different tribes and as the recipient of great revenues in kind from harvested grain and from local manufacture, had to convert a substantial part of the grains into commodities to pay the army and the bureaucracy.

The state was therefore the great trader, the supreme monopolist. (Kosambi 1975: 216.)

Exploitation, thus still continued to be general.

The artisans in the guilds or *srenis* of the Mauryan period were probably members of the Vaishya community, who were alienated from agricultural practice as the art of smelting became widely known. But even so it included only a minority of the artisans in the Mauryan empire. Evidence suggests that certain artisans, such as smiths and carpenters, settled in villages composed only of members of their caste, and where they also had to, quite naturally, cultivate land for themselves (Habib 1965: 29). The artisans in the *srenis* were probably drawn from these villages. Such manufacturers' villages were a peculiarity of this period and may be explained by the fact that the artisan would not have been able to feed themselves without engaging in agriculture, indicating once again that strict occupational specialization resulting in exchange at the local level did not exist to a significant degree. Handicraft production had therefore not yet moved to the village in the sense that artisans, as a distinct occupational group, had not yet emerged, nor had they been integrated into a web of exploitation and exchange at the local village level. In subsequent epochs, when this was to become important, the possibility of artisans engaging in agricultural production was resisted by the peasantry and by the ruling classes (Chichirov 1971: 31).

But where do these guilds fall in the varna scheme? There is a tendency among certain scholars to dismiss every other group, tribe or community, and to believe that the four categories of the varna scheme were the only social divisions that existed. And on the other hand, because of the restricted nature of this differentiation, others believe that the varna system never existed at all. As we have already pointed out, there were numerous tribes, other than the Vedic, which were integrated in the Vedic Aryan society. Nevertheless, the four-fold varna scheme was still the dominant model of status and economic differentiation. As each community was largely self-sufficient, because agriculture was still open to all, and as exploitation was general, hardly any economic interaction among different groups and communities existed at the local level. This rendered further elaboration of the four-tiered varna scheme unnecessary. Other groups, tribes and *srenis* found their place in one of the four categories, more often at the bottom, but sometimes in the Kshatriya category, through various occupations prevalent in that period.

It is widely believed that these guilds crystallized into jatis (Ghurye 1969: 114). A nascent form of occupational specialization can be seen to have started here. But to believe that it was just a matter of time before guilds became rigid caste groups may not be quite correct. The complete elaboration and strict separation of the various orders denoting the rules of intercourse and exchange had to await a further development in the socio-economic structure. The ramifications of caste rankings among artisans, peasants and traders had not yet developed, nor had notions of superiority and inferiority bordering on competition amongst the erstwhile constituents of the Vaishya and Shudra communities. This was because they were all exploited by the state and had few, if any, rights and obligations towards each other.

From the Vedic age to the Mauryan period we find the gradual development of a monolithic, centralized authority. Though productive forces increased in this period with the second phase of iron, they did not bring about a qualitative change in the relations of production. Authority and ownership still lay with the state, and with the growth of powerful empires, exploitation became more general and more intensive. The Vedic rationale of superiority on an ascriptive criterion continued to serve in this period as well. It was a very vital element of the structure of power. Its dominance was an outcome of a stagnant economy with low rates of production in the pre-iron Vedic age. It is necessary to emphasize this aspect of the varna classification if one is to understand the peculiarities of the caste system as it developed over the ages.

The phase beginning from the Yajurvedic age to the fall of the Mauryan Empire, is in essence similar to Marx's Asiatic mode of production. Ownership and authority over land were vested with the state, which resulted in the second crucial characteristic, viz., that of the general exploitation of the peasantry and artisans by the state via the royal bureaucracy, or directly by the oligarchs of the Vedic era.

It was this system of generalized exploitation that brought about the varna order of differentiation wherein the various distinctions between the artisan and peasants had yet to develop. This was for two reasons. First, each community was largely self-sufficient, as agriculture was open to all. Secondly, exploitation was general. The subordinate communities were all exploited by the superior community, or the state. Together these did not demand further elaboration of obligations and duties beyond the four-fold varna scheme, which adequately defined the status and privileges of numerous communities and groups which accreted over a period of time to the Vedic and Mauryan societies.

This four-tiered differentiation is admittedly, a view from the top of the hierarchy, but the view from the bottom is no more varied, and may, in fact, appear less differentiated, because economic obligations were only directed vertically.

Transition to Feudalism

We shall try to highlight some of the contradictions and forces of change within the Asiatic mode of production, in the specifics of its Indian variant, which led to its gradual dissolution, albeit over centuries, resulting in far-reaching changes in the forms of stratification and property rights. What also seems analytically important in this connection is not to mistake a slow pace of change (as compared to the West) for no change at all.

The period ending approximately with the Mauryan Empire was characterized by substantial trade and mercantile activity. This is evident from the large number of coins available from the period, as well as by the presence of merchants, who, though despised by the state, were nonetheless quite powerful, and some even bore arms. Between the peasant mass and the monarchs were the *pauri janapadas* who were leaders of erstwhile tribal formations (Kosambi 1975: 223). These *janapadas* were in charge of certain districts, and were also ministers of the royal courts. According to the *Arthashastra*, they were paid salaries. The *janapadas*, at this stage, did not resemble feudal or private landlords. According to Kosambi, 'by tribal custom land had been apportioned by the chief or a council of elders whose authority had now passed to the king.' (Ibid: 222.) Authority had not devolved to the *janapadas*, even though they converted surplus produced by *janas* in their jurisdiction into private property. Moreover, the royal *sita* lands, which largely belonged to the king, and formed the bulk of arable land, 'could adequately explain the Greek report that in India all land belonged to the King.' (Habib 1965: 31.)

Mauryan society did, however contain within itself the seeds of its own destruction. This brought about a qualitative change in the production relations. The disintegrating forces of the preceding period were, firstly, the contradiction between private property and the property of the state. The early stirrings of landlordism emerged in the Mauryan period as the *janapadas* were able to convert surplus to private property, though during the reign of the Mauryas this contradiction was not allowed to develop (Kosambi 1975: 225). Moreover, the Mauryan Empire, due to its size, was susceptible to fissiparous tendencies where local officials began to assert themselves once the period of expansion and of powerful emperors was over. Secondly, the population of craftsmen increased and certain skills like smelting became widely known under the impetus of the growth of commerce and the centralized administration of the Mauryas. This meant that individual artisans could begin moving to villages (Habib 1965: 32). Thirdly, the forcible settlement of Shudras as cultivators, advocated by Kautilya, transformed a large number of Shudras from pure menials and servants of the nobility, to peasants and rural labourers (Habib 1965: 301; Ghoshal 1972: 194). This transformation also helped the subsequent growth of a village-based economy which characterized the period beginning around 200 AD These peasant villages were subordinated to local chiefs who had begun to assert their local authority and whose links with the emperor were tenuous and much weaker than in earlier times. This development is often characterized as feudalism which took on a more pronounced form during the Gupta (circa 400-500 AD) and the Harsha (circa 700 AD) periods, and continued down through the medieval age under different local economic formations.

According to R.S. Sharma, certain political and administrative developments tended to feudalize the state apparatus after the Mauryan period. The most striking development, he believes, was the practice of land grants made to Brahmans (*Brahmadaya*) which was sanctified by the injunctions in the *Dharmasastras* (Sharma 1965: 1-2). The *Mahabharata* which was written just prior to the Gupta period devotes an entire section to praising such gifts of land (ibid: 2). The practice of giving up administrative rights to the grantees was started probably during the reign of Gautamiputra, the Satavahana ruler in the second century AD. This became more frequent by the Vakataka period around the fifth century AD (ibid: 3). The Gupta period also affords instances of such transfer of powers to the grantees, however, they were not always Brahmans. They were also officers of the state (ibid: 7). Though there is no direct information, it appears that the office of the *bhogikas*, or administrative officer of the Gupta period, had become hereditary in some localities. Moreover, 'the village headman' (*gramadhipati ayuuktaka*) is represented in the *Kamasutra* (c.400-500 AD) as 'exacting unpaid labour from peasant women, and compelling them, among other things to fill his granaries and work on his own fields. The officials thus appear as having land of their own and enjoying semi-feudal rights over the peasantry.' (Habib 1965: 38.) According to the *Arthashastra*, the officials in the Mauryan period were paid salaries in cash, but by the time of Manu (circa

200 AD), they were paid in land grants, while in Harsha's time, they were paid a percentage of revenues (Sharma 1965: 11).

It is a reasonable assumption that by this time individual ownership of land was quite prevalent. The *Manusmriti* (9.44) also declares: 'The land belongs to he who first clears it, as the deer to him who gets in the first arrow.' This is in substantial agreement, as Kosambi points out, with the earlier *Milindipanha* text which states: 'When a man clears away the jungle and sets free (*niharti*) a piece of land . . . people say it is his land. It is because he has brought this land into use that he is called the owner of the land.' (Kosambi 1975: 257.) This would certainly not have been entertained in the *Arthashastra*.

A statement such as the one just mentioned in *Manusmriti* might lead one to believe that as land was abundant, it could be cleared and occupied directly by the individual peasant. This, however, seems unlikely for a number of reasons. Firstly, the individual peasant would be far too ill-equipped to clear the jungle without the help of the king or the superior class. According to Ghoshal, 'in so far as the settlers of new lands are concerned, it will be seen that they are required to furnish the necessary capital in the shape of provisions, implements and the like . . . (It) requires the king to make advances of money to the new settlers.' (Ghoshal 1972: 170-171.) Secondly, as Kosambi argued, 'the individual who cleared a patch of land would in general be a member of some community, based upon kinship and upon a village. A solitary cultivator in completely virgin wilderness is difficult to imagine.' (Kosambi 1975: 257.) It would appear then that the superior class cleared the forest land with the help of the general peasantry and menials, and exercised property rights over it by siphoning off the surplus produce, a portion of which was paid to the king.

The Jati System and Localized Exploitation

From the seventh to the twelfth century AD these features crystallized. Serfdom became a widespread phenomenon (Sharma 1975: 57-60). The erstwhile officials of the king now began to keep the entire revenue and for all practical purposes severed their ties with the monarch by totally usurping his administrative authority. The feudal elites such as the *samantas*, petty village chiefs, and lesser landholders began to exert greater rights over land (Yadav 1976: 45). This brought about the division of the entire territory of the kingdom, leading to several sub-divided clan monarchies of the Gujara Pratihara kind between the eighth and the tenth century AD, and the Cahamanas from the middle of the eighth century to the early 14th century AD (Chattopadhyaya 1976: 69).

> Here the territory was parcelled out by the ruler after retaining his own share among his kinsmen and clan chiefs. Each of the latter then set about dividing his territory among his own clansmen while retaining his own share, until by this process, every village was assigned to a particular man in return for a supply of troopers when needed by the assignor . . . The most common titles of the potentates i.e., the new landed aristocracies) are *samanta, ranaka, rauta, thakkura* and *rajaputra*. (Habib 1965: 41-42.)

The distribution of land among royal kinsmen and officers was a widespread phenomenon of this period (Gopal 1963-64: 75-103). The Harsha inscriptions of

973 AD at Jaipur are considered to be the earliest evidence of such distribution (Chattopadhayaya 1976: 71).

This period is also characterized by the breakdown of large-scale commerce and trade which is evident from the paucity of coins of the era (Sharma 1965: 270). The towns and large trading centres which dotted the earlier Buddhist and Mauryan empires had also disappeared. The ruralization of the ruling class was accompanied by the ruralization of the artisans and handicraft workers. Never before had the peasants and craftsmen been subject to such direct control by local chiefs, their intermediaries and clansmen. As Sharma said:

> The main characteristics of European feudalism, the self-sufficient economy, buttressed by lack of commercial intercourse and the rise of intermediaries leading to the subservience of the peasantry prevailed in India (and) the possessing class appropriated the surplus produce of the peasants by exercising superior rights over land and persons. (1965: 271-72.)

Moreover, in the feudal structure of exploitation, the subordinate communities were generally not linked directly to the state, but to the various local intermediaries and to the feudal lords. The officials of the Mauryan Empire were officials of the royal court, and the benefits they derived from the structure of generalized exploitation were routed *via* the state. In the feudal period, however, the intermediaries and clansmen of the overlords were paid not so much in cash by way of salaries, as in land grants. This led to a hierarchy of direct exploiters in feudal societies as the noblemen held differential sizes of land, depending on their rank and closeness to the overlord, and on their right to differential shares of the produce of the peasants, which they extracted through extra economic coercion in their respective demesnes.

In feudal societies all land generally did not belong to the overlord or to his intermediaries and clansmen. Some land was distributed to particular groups in return for their services during military campaigns. The rest was given over for peasant (*ryot*) cultivation. The landlord's own land was either cultivated by serfs, or by *ryots* who, in addition to giving up part of the surplus on their own allotments, were forced by the lords to render service.

This localization of exploitation had several consequences. First, as we have already mentioned, was the decline of trade. Second, the exactions by the overlords and the nobility from the serfs, peasants and artisans increased. This was possible as the former held juridical rights over their area. Third, as land became the index of wealth and power it was highly prized and cultivation emerged in this period as the only viable occupation for the people. Those peasants who had enough land to make a living out of agriculture were, as a consequence, held in greater esteem, than those who had to supplement agriculture by crafts and artisanry. This tied the *ryot* to the nobility. The nobility also took care not to dispossess or ruin the peasants uniformly, as they formed a guaranteed pool from where they could draw labour services. Fourth, not only did stratification increase and deepen among the ruling class, but it also in turn differentiated the subordinate community who served them. The peasants were split into grades depending on the type of allotment, differing amounts of payment, whether state peasant, or tied and taxed by the feudal lord (Sharma 1966: 183). A peasant's status also depended on the status of his feudal overlord (see also Breman 1974: 19).

Artisans were also ranked depending on the rank of their patrons or of their customers. An iron-smith, therefore, was lower than a goldsmith, a weaver even lower than an iron-smith, and so on. The other side of this tendency towards greater stratification in feudal societies, was the greater integration and interdependence in the local village between communities and occupational specialist. No longer were there villages belonging to any one artisan community: each village now had not only its lords and nobles, its *ryots* and officials, but also its complement of goldsmiths, weavers, iron-smith, potters, etc.

It was the progressive development of this economic structure of localized exploitation within the village nexus which bought about the elaboration of the jati, or what is popularly known as the Indian caste system. The dependence of the lower exploited classes on each other and on their masters in a closed society necessitated greater elaboration of the rules of exchange and intercourse. The rationale of 'natural superiority' which served the varna scheme so well was not abandoned. It worked effectively in a more differentiated fashion to underpin the regime of jatis. The general exploitation of the Asiatic mode of production of the previous epoch, whereby the obligations and duties of the artisans and peasants vis-à-vis each other had not been elaborated, now gave way to more clearly specified patterns of interaction due to the exigencies of localized feudal exploitation. Also the notion of 'untouchability' originated around 200 AD, especially in association with the Chandalas. This institution took on an extreme form by the twelfth century AD as revealed in the *Parasamriti*.

It is not merely the proliferation of numerous occupational groups that distinguishes jati and varna. As we have pointed out, the view that the Vedic age had only four orders of the varna schema is incorrect. This belief led one to question the veracity of the various occupational groups in Megasthenes' *Indica* (Kosambi 1975: 193). The Vedic society, however, did try to fit these diverse groups and communities into the procrustean bed of the varna schema, though not always very successfully. The failure to do so did not create any problems of controlling social relations of the period because exploitation was general and the exploited classes served the superior community with little economic intercourse among themselves. The status of numerous occupational groups of peasants, artisans, menials, etc, corresponded generally to that of either the Vaishya or the Shudra varnas. Further delineation of status and position among them was not necessary. The evolution to jatis was on account of the social transition to a closed village economy.

With the levels of productive forces remaining stagnant, any rise in population was accommodated in the feudal structure of medieval India at the cost of greater rigidification and further stratification of the jatis. As the facilities to utilize land were limited, and property rights over land were monopolized by a minority, population pressure did not expand the frontiers of land utilization, but led instead to greater differentiation within the confines of the feudal economy. This resulted in a plentiful supply of skilled labour which was intensively utilized for the expropriation of use values and also for commodity production (Habib

1971: 41). This inhibited productivity. Habib quite rightly says:

> While it is true that extensive development in technology can only occur when metal, particularly iron, replaces other materials, this change can be delayed in a particular situation for no other reason than that a tool of lower efficiency can be used to manufacture the same commodity by employment of cheap skilled labour. (Ibid: 38.)

Besides the abundance of skilled labour in a labour-intensive economy, the number of jatis was also enhanced by the continuing absorption of tribals, whose lands were annexed by the might of the nobility the village. nexus. They were forced to render certain services to meet local needs, and were likewise placed in the hierarchy, usually at the bottom. Conversely, those tribes that did not function within this nexus, due to either their inaccessibility or their indomitability, were driven to the extremities of established society and to the brink of survival. This can be seen even today in the tribal belts of India (Breman 1974: 7).

When trade resumed on a large scale in eleventh century AD; it did not disturb this village structure. Indeed, the needs of trade very often brought about new occupational groups, like the diamond miners of Karnataka (Habib 1971: 38). Similarly, during the Muslim period, the regeneration of powerful royal bureaucracies did not dismantle this feudal set-up (Singh 1973: 200), and contrary to popular beliefs, as Alavi points out, all land did not belong to the Mughal Emperor (1975: 186). Royal officials of the Muslim court were alternatively paid salaries in cash, or were assigned the revenues of a particular area over which they exercised superior authority, much in the manner of a feudal overlord. Such changes were rather abrupt if the earlier ruler was overturned by his successor, but none of this really altered the fundamental structure of economic relations; thus the village structure was left largely undisturbed (Siddiqi 1970: 17-40; Habib 1965: 54-55; 1971: 14-15; Hasan 1963: 118).

Conclusion: The Limits of Naivete

If anthropology and sociology turn through the pages of history it certainly helps in developing a sociology of knowledge. In our case, it is abundantly clear that the varna and jati systems did not just descend full blown, but gradually evolved over time. Whether or not the finer details of history are agreed upon, from the vantage point of sociology and anthropology there is enough to suggest that values and ideologies pertaining to varna and jati have roots in material history and in actual relations among people. Doubtless there will be disagreements about the minutiae of historical data, on apportioning responsibilities to different historical epochs, but we are not fundamentally concerned with them. As scholars trying to understand the present, endeavouring to piece together the social roots of ideologies and belief system, the heuristic tools afforded by the mode of production allow us to draw inferences which best explain the known facts about the contemporary caste system. We have approached history within the limits of our naivete, which is as it should be for anyone approaching any other discipline other than one's own.

9

Imagination Against Typification: On De-Exoticizing the Other

> . . . the organisation of mind is practically identical among all races of man, that mental activity follows the same laws everywhere but that its manifestation depends upon the character of individual experience that is subjected to the action of these laws.
> (Boas 1911: 99.)

> . . . it is really the same mental attitude which makes us value our heirlooms and makes the natives in New Guinea value their vaygu'a.
> (Malinowski 1922, 90-91.)

For an Intersubjective Sociology/Anthropology

The many advances in the study of the caste system have brought about an enrichment of sociological theory. Sanskritization has advanced our understanding of reference group behaviour and social mobility. Likewise, the relationship between ritual status and social power and privilege, should also help to broaden our appreciation of how social identities are formed and transmitted.

All this is possible only if we agree that what appears distant at first sight is really not all that fantastic and exotic after all. For example, the temptation to look at caste as a completely unique form of stratification makes it difficult for scholars to cross-culturally share their human predicaments with one another. Only strangeness is emphasized in grinding detail. Scholarship is rewarded for emphasizing the distance between cultures and not for building empathy and intersubjectivity.

When castes are viewed first as discrete entities then they do not seem that alien any longer. All abiding and durable identities are discrete phenomena. Identities affix values, quantification and degrees come later. If to give value is to hierarchize, then the caste system can be seen as yet another empirical variant of the general theory of stratification and differentiation. The extent to which castes hypersymbolize to express differences can also be illuminated by general theories of semiology. It is no doubt tempting to yield to popular temptation and type away the 'other'. Yet the fact remains that human beings have more things in common than what anthropology generally acknowledges, and what the popular mind routinely dismisses. This is because human beings spontaneously divide among themselves. The distinction between 'us' and 'them' is to be found everywhere. On every occasion those who are outside are never valued as highly as those within. The cultural 'others' are thus prone to caricature, and social differences are often posited as if they were in fact natural differences as well. This is not just true of the much talked about Chinese overestimation of themselves and of the 'middle kingdom' they occupy, but this also features among the Pueblos of North-West America, the

Kachins of Burma, and so on. Against this background it is important for anthropology and sociology to redress the tendency towards typification whenever the occasion arises.

The caste system has for a long time been a victim of such typifications and caricatures primarily because it is posited as such an alien construct that there is greater purchase in stoking curiosity than in examining data in an intersubjective framework. It is not as if caste loyalties have unchallenged authority in political and economic matters. The ways in which caste ideologies can be mutated and transformed to justify political or economic ambition is very well known. What needs to admitted alongside is that all this would not have been possible if castes were not discrete in character, with their own idiosyncratic hierarchies. Castes today have joined horizontally for mutually beneficial political purposes, but this coming together, as we have pointed out earlier, has nothing to do with caste logic as castes as hierarchically removed as Kshatriyas, Harijans and Muslims form the block called KHAM. Likewise, Ahir, Jats and Gujars comprise the AJGAR front. The Kurmi Association has disparate castes in it as well. There is no internal logic or ideological affinity that brings these castes together. In terms of inter-caste interaction, strictly, Jats and Gujars are bitter rivals, and there is obviously a deep chasm between Kshatriyas and Harijans, so also between Bareyas and Kolis. Yet in certain political situations they combine to share a common platform as allies.

We also recorded in the previous chapter how elections in India are misunderstood because it is assumed that political loyalties can only be informed by caste patriotism. If that were the case then it would have been difficult for any one to win elections on the basis of caste loyalties as no caste numerically preponderates over others. Even in the so-called Jat or Yadav areas the population of these castes are in a hopeless minority. So it is not just caste numbers or caste loyalty that accounts for electoral success, but the ability to organize and present oneself as a credible alternative in the political market place. To be mesmerized by the 'otherness' of caste, its exotic value too, have led to pure culturological analyses, which apart from being off the mark, separates humankind under the imprimatur of scholarship.

I have always considered anthropology and sociology at their best to be humanizing discipline, great 'levellers'. These are disciplines that knock the bottom out of all social manifestations of arrogance, obscurantism and prejudice and which assert the fundamental equality of humankind. This I believe is the principal task of sociology and anthropology. More important, I would opine, than providing delightful vignettes of different cultural traditions, mores, customs, which many sociologists think is the bread and butter of their discipline.

The problem, as I see it, is that the study of human diversity as an end in itself cannot function intrinsically as a 'leveller'. It does not see its eventual destination as that of demonstrating the equality of humankind, but as that of portraying, sometimes with a very fine nib, the minutiae of various social systems. Each such system is identified and insulated by the pervasive penetration of a typical cultural model which, it is believed, is diffused throughout society in all its institutions. Studying human diversity in this fashion leaves the popular consciousness unfettered and unembarrassed to go on with a construction of reality, where the 'other' is, according to

Berger and Luckmann, apprehended in a continuum of typifications, which are progressively anonymous as they are removed from the 'here and now' of the face to face situation (Berger and Luckmann 1971: 45-48).

It is this principle of typification that is being identified here as the source of human misunderstanding. It denies a universal view of humanity and orders it instead into categories that become more rigid and unyielding as the life situation of one section of humankind gets more distanced from the other. Once humanity is thus segregated in the popular construction of reality, the accession of inegalitarian ideological structures is legitimized on an ever-widening franchise. The 'sociological imagination' as C. Wright Mills described it, enters here to counter these typificatory schemes, not, as the following quote will show, as a compendium of arms and ammunition, but as a theory of warfare (Mills: 1970).

C. Wright Mills wrote:

> The sociological imagination enables its possessor to understand the larger historical scene in terms of its meaning for the inner life and the external career of a variety of individuals. It enables him to take into account how individuals, in the welter of their daily experience, often become falsely conscious of their social positions . . . We do not know the limits of man's capacities for supreme effort or willing degradation, for agony or glee, for pleasurable, brutality or the sweetness of reason. But in our time we have come to know, that the limits of 'human nature' are frighteningly broad . . . The sociological imagination enables us to grasp history and biography and the relation between the two within society, That is its task and its promise. (Ibid: 6.)

The role of the sociological imagination then is primarily combative, and it is in its application to the terrain of human diversity that the notion of the fundamental equality of man is won and asserted.

It is from here on that on several occasions I shall depart from both Mills and Berger and Luckmann in developing my argument. In the context of this paper, my disagreement with Mills is that he believes that 'ordinary men' feel the need for sociological imagination and hunger for facts which would allow them to develop their imagination most vividly. What they need, and what they feel they need, is a quality of mind that will help them to use information and to develop reason in order to achieve lucid summations of what is going on in the world and what may be happening within themselves. It is this quality, he contends, that journalists and scholars, artists, scientists and editors are coming to expect of what may be called sociological imagination (ibid: 5).

In my opinion the lay people do not ordinarily feel the need for sociological imagination for they have recourse to 'symbolic universes' which they have internalized and which provide them with the rationale for the popular construction of reality. And neither, I might add, are there moments of any significant duration either in the biography of an individual or in the history of the collective, where either feels hampered or crippled by the awareness that the knowledge possessed is not whole, and that it lacks a rigorous theoretical system.

I also disagree with Berger and Luckmann for they proceed in detailing the social construction of reality from its imputed pre-theoretical origin. Whatever might be the value of such an approach, it is entirely hypothetical and does not conform to the liveliness and depth of the ongoing process of the construction of reality at the social and popular levels.

The above, hopefully, illustrates why I have pitted imagination against social (or popular) construction of reality. The individual does not feel the need for sociological imagination (except for a few misfits) and neither is the *homo socius* ever at a loss for a theoretical system. It is precisely because the social construction of reality excels at typifications to order its social universe, that fellow humans are seen (in decreasing order of sophistication) either as unfortunately unequal, or as culturally unequal or as biologically unequal; or as a composite of all these formulations.

The eventual arrival at such higher-order typifications presumes a theoretical awareness, so that the typifications less general, are not a jumble of contradictory observations but are, on the contrary, constructed out of an ordered arrangement of observation. This is possible because they are imbued even at the lowest level, by a theory, by a grand design. To think that the process of social construction of reality is even remotely analogous to the inductive system would be to misunderstand and underestimate the fertility of the collective and subjective consciousness.

The people are not waiting for or wanting sociological imagination. This makes even harder the task of a sociologist who sets out to propagate a state of mind and a theoretical system which understands and relates inequality and diversity not to types of human beings, or at a higher level of sophistication, to types of human culture, but to socio-historical factors that dwell upon and fashion different contingent conditions.

Popular constructions of reality from the highest level of symbolic universe to the lowest level of typification refract and do not reflect reality. Reality thus refracted falls on the screen, like so many colours through a prism, only now human beings are distinctly categorized and typed. This classification is not a transitive one, that is one that bears the possibility of transition from one class to another, but is fixed and positioned in a culturological (more commonly, racial) trance.

When sociologists take up these constructions of reality as their sole domain of concern, or even as starting points, they leave the door wide open for insidious accretions from outside, and secretions from within, which mesh their scholarship with inegalitarian and obscurantist ideological formulations. The sociology thus generated would mix easily with the bric-a-brac of various typifications in the popular mind. Sociology would then be a gracious pastime with impeccable table manners. Some of its outpourings would no doubt be excellent and would be eagerly sought. They would be read and digested. And in each course, their data base, like nutrients, would add muscle and flesh to the dominating, that is the popular, intellectual constructs.

But sociological paradigms need not succumb to popular constructions of reality in such an obvious manner always. There are two major routes by which this might happen. First, and the most easily identifiable route, is when they adopt these constructions almost wholesale into the paradigms. The other less easily identifiable and more prevalent way is when, by scholarly acumen, societies or segments of societies are typed by sociologists into categories which, though unheard of in the non-academic world, still follow the principles of popular typifications.

These typifications again pronounce 'hermetically

sealed' cultures and indicate the range of culturally permissible (or tainted) responses to a variety of stimuli. These typifications, too, notwithstanding their nomenclatural acuity and the tautness of their conceptualization, rest, as do popular typifications, on a cultural determinant, and cannot be used combatively against the latter.

On the other hand, because their specific gravities are the same they intermingle easily and strengthen the current of inegalitarian ideologies flowing down their declivities to fill up their chauvinist and racist estuaries. If such an accusation seems unwarranted to some, sample the following quote from the greatest type builder of all, Max Weber: 'Only Master Races have a vocation to climb the ladder of world development. If peoples who do not possess this profound quality try to do it, not only the sure instinct of other nations will oppose them, but they will also come internally to grief.' (Quoted in Stammer 1971: 85.)

What the imagination is up against is, in short, ahistoric typifications of humanity. And the opposition is fairly stiff as sociologists in general have not shown the mettle to resist capitulating before the moral regime of the popular construction of reality and to shake off that 'culturological trance'. The temptation to use stereotypes, or invent new types, is very compelling for they suitably blank out problem areas, unlike scientific categories which throw them up and push them into focus.

Partly also it is a question of the cultural conditioning of sociologists and their susceptibility to be enthralled in the 'culturological trance'. Rather than shake it off consciously and invoke the imagination, for which they feel no need in this state of trance, it seems much more straightforward and legitimate for them to get bearings and reference points from popular constructions of reality, either of the members of the society, or of those outside regarding that society.

A culturological view would say of the caste system, for instance: If the people have a 'theory' such as the caste system, then it follows that the political and economic factors are secondary because the caste system says so. It is such a position that we specifically wish to impugn. It is one thing to know popular theories and it is quite another to see reality ordered by them. In which case then the sociology itself becomes redundant, and along with it the incessant demand to unravel the socio-historical bases of this peculiar theory. It is the spread of a peculiar symbolic universe (or theory) that determines the 'sociological' universe of one's academic pursuit. Each sociologist or anthropologist has a defined beat, clearly demarcated by the discontinuities in symbolic universe. We are thus left with a plethora of sociologies with no overlapping interests and consequently where no overlapping questions need be asked. Diversity, yes, there is abundant scope for that, but are we not in typing away humankind, the Hindus in this case, and submitting to the protocol of the popular construction of reality? How are we adding to that quality of mind that is so essential in demonstrating the fundamental equality of peoples all over the world?

It is not our intention here to legislate away the vast variety of societal arrangements in order to arrive at an abstract 'human nature'. Not at all. Our starting point as we said earlier, is that human beings are fundamentally equal and this has nothing to do with the ahistorical concept, 'human nature'. The task ahead is to explain the historical forces that have shaped human diversity.

This point is not new but was made earlier by C. Wright Mills when he said:

> The idea of some 'human nature' common to man as man is a violation of the social and historical specificity that careful work in the human studies requires . . . Surely we ought occasionally to remember that in truth we do not know much about man and that all the knowledge we do have does not entirely remove the mystery that surrounds his variety as it is revealed in history and biography. Sometimes we do want to wallow in that *mystery* . . . (but) we will inevitably also study human variety, which for us means removing the mystery from our view of it. (Mills 1970: 182, emphasis added.)

Sociology/anthropology hopes to study the totality and comprehend the relation of parts to the total in a larger dynamic historical conspectus. The 'mystery' that surrounds other cultures is specifically the conundrum we wish to resolve. For this purpose a historical and relational optic is ineluctable. Such an optic faces no difficulty, in integrating studies in various dimensions of human reality and offers the very real possibility of overlapping questions without resorting to perfunctory overlapping fabrications. Now, for instance, not only do dominant forms of social groupings become amenable to socio-historical investigation, but also the genesis of cultural patterns and their communal articulation become 'overlapping' concerns of the discipline.

The 'mystery' that was alluded to earlier, the mystery that patrols the region between different typifications, is pursued and hunted on a historical terrain, which is *terra incognita* so far as the popular constructs of reality go. Whereas the orthodox anthropological route at its best reconstructs, sometimes more, vividly, popular constructs, a de-exoticizing imagination demystifies them by locating them in their historical and relational environs.

The first tangible result of this demystification is the sociological awareness that human culture, broadly understood, is a 'highly mutable affair'. The sanctity of popular constructions of reality loses its aura, for the human mosaic is not longer predetermined, that is immediately knowable and cannot, like items in a dictionary, be listed. Human diversity is on the other hand being constantly enriched by human beings who refuse to submit to their imputed one-dimensional causality, who reach out for fresh social options with a rational calculus.

As Peter Worsley said in *The Third World:*

> For men are not determined entities, like rocks and trees. They have minds. Human beings can and do react against the past. They are affected by the past in so far as they absorb behaviour patterns of their culture. But they also have faculties of imagination and creativity; they innovate as well as receive and absorb, they revolt as well as continue. They step outside the structural framework of the existing order and the intellectual framework of received ideas to create new ideas and new ways of ordering their relationships with one another. In order, to understand human behaviour, then, we have to be sensitive not only to the past and the present, but also to the future. (Worseley 1967: 272.)

If the plasticity and malleability of cultures are not recognized, then great harm is done in all vital areas of human concern which cannot afford anything but intellectual integrity and responsibility. In the field of social medicine, for instance, the popular typifications of mankind and all the prejudices that go along with them obstruct any meaningful debate on health policy and medical care. In order to launch a meaningful discussion, on genuine humanist assumptions, one has to wade through tomes of culturological studies whose approach to the problem, is 'to blame the victim'.

Sectarianism then, as we understand it, is invested in the very origins of popular typifications. Part of the problem in understanding communalism is that it is recognized only when such popular constructions of reality climax in a collective orgiastic finale. For, the paradigm that generates communalism is the same paradigm that generates, at seemingly innocuous levels, scholarly and popular typifications. It is because the ripest derivative of this paradigm is seen in isolation from its quotidian manifestations that sectarianism appears on the intellectual horizons as a 'problematic' with special properties whose resolution can be achieved by a negative articulation of these properties, that is, by sheer 'will power', an exogenous determination not integral to the discipline.

It is then not only outright cases of sectarianism that the imagination resolves. It works consistently to bridge the interstices and uproot the barricades that impede the understanding of one section of humankind regarding another placed in a different socio-historical milieu. To give an example: the prosperity of the North West, say Punjab, and the poverty of the East, say Bengal, are often explained by, among other things, the hardiness and the entrepreneurship of the Punjabi peasants. Not discounting the fact that the weather may have something to do with the relentless robustness of the Punjab peasant, this supposed difference in characteristics has to be explained and analysed in a historical perspective.

Why, for instance, did so many Maharashtrians in Bombay, swayed by the Shiv Sena, pick on the South Indians? The question becomes all the more important as less than a decade ago the Maharashtrians viewed the Gujaratis as their main enemy. Why is it, for instance, that the caste Hindus in Marathwada attacked the Mahars of that region? Why in this case were the Hindu-Muslim contradictions not as dominant as the caste Hindu-Scheduled Caste contradictions? Why again were Mahars largely persecuted in three out of five districts in Marathwada? Why were those in the other two districts left relatively untouched? Finally, why was the brunt of caste Hindu wrath centred on the Mahars alone? Why not on the members of other Scheduled Castes and untouchable communities like the Mangs and Chamars who also live there?

These are questions that cannot be easily answered by the traditional sociological/anthropological route, which begins with the 'phenomenon' without paying too much attention to its context and background. Once these are factored in, the scholar can overcome the tendency to essentialize culture. If beef-eaters are considered at the popular level to be natural enemies of cow-worshippers and vice-versa, then how was it that they once lived in amity in the past? Not just that, why did beef-eaters fight among themselves? And why did cow-worshippers frisson into numerous warring sects that turned on each other? What clearly needs to be appreciated is the protean and changeable character of culture that sectarian fanatics and cultural virtuosos can never recognize.

It remains then for the sociologist/anthropologist to delegitimize cultural essentialism and to examine the selective nature of historical, economic and social factors which render a particular form of communalism its specifics and to be able to differentiate its scope and potentiality from other proximate and potential varieties of the same phenomenon. By insisting on the examination of historical deposits on structural faults, the sociologist shifts the primary focus from categories thrown up and defined by ripened sectarianism or communalism. To understand communalism in this sense is also to destroy it with a finality that cannot be approximated by well meaning scholarship which works within the boundaries of the traditional sociological/anthropological route.

Imagination and Humanism

The early anthropologists such as Tylor, Boas down to Malinowski, in an almost uninterrupted tradition, were interested primarily in the study of man—the universal Man. Their primary concern was to demonstrate that 'primitive' human beings shared with so-called 'civilized' peoples a common mental apparatus. They then analysed, through diverse theoretical perspectives, how in spite of this fundamental unity, societies were so diverse. An analysis of the social structure became essential, not in itself, but to drive home the larger point. For Malinowski, in particular, any analysis that was undertaken at the level of social structure was also intended to debunk the search for exotic items while stressing the need to understand such exotica in terms of the total system of relationships existing in that society (Malinowski: 1922). This allowed him to argue that what appeared strange, unfamiliar and exotic can be made more accessible if parallels were drawn between them and institutions and customs that the so-called civilized also cherish. He went on to say:

'To pause for a moment before a quaint and singular fact; to be amused by it, and see its outward strangeness; to look at it as a curio and collect it into the museum of one's memory or into one's store of anecdotes—this attitude of mind has always been foreign and repugnant to me. Some people are unable to grasp the inner meaning and psychological reality of all that is outwardly strange, at first sight incomprehensible in a different culture. These people are *not born* to be ethnologists. It is in the love of the final synthesis . . . that lies the test of the real worker in the true science of Man.' (Ibid: 517; emphasis added). Strong words, and yet how soon after Malinowski, anthropology continued to be defined not as the study of Man, but largely as the study of primitive societies. This entailed that anthropology was about recording strangeness rather than exploring the diverse ways through which the fundamental unity of humankind could be demonstrated.

Consequently, the approach towards primitive societies became excessively formal. Every ceremonial custom was seen as formally fulfilling some essential functional imperative of the social structure. Durkheim's rigid insistence that social facts are external to individuals (Durkheim 1966: 3) while it did provide a secure emplacement from which the sociologist could combat idealism, methodological individualism and unexamined prejudices, nevertheless also reduced human beings to the status of an unreflective subject of the social structure (Durkheim 1966: Lvi). 'It would thus appear' as Yogendra Singh writes,

> that functional sociology both in its systematic postulates such as those of Parsons and Merton, or in its micro-systemic form as in Homans, has rendered man a peripheral concept. Man is treated

not in the fullness of his existential being, but as an
abstraction or as a process. (Singh n.d.: 16.)

Each cultural institution, rite, custom and belief was
deemed to exist in a rather stylized fashion such that
their influence on social action appeared predetermined
to a large extent. Brilliant, though Durkheim's
contributions were—indeed it is difficult to think of
sociology today without Durkheim, yet there was a
major drawback in his style and method. As Adam
Kuper correctly pointed out in the case of Radcliffe-
Brown, but equally applicable to Durkheim too, what is
missing is that 'whiff of reality' that is to be found in
Malinowski's brilliant essay *Baloma*, or in his magnum
opus *Argonauts of the Western Pacific* (Kuper 1973:
59). The logical order of symbolic representations were
considered to be 'so rigid, the power of constraint of
these categories on the mind . . . so strong' (Durkheim
and Mauss 1970: 16) that 'the individual . . . at every
moment of time conforms to it. These ways of thinking
and acting exist in their own right. The individual finds
them completely formed and he cannot evade or change
them.' (Durkheim 1966: vi.) Durkheim's enormous
reputation succeeded in giving anthropologist a certain
academic bent that favoured rules over actual action.
Humankind became differentiated on a cultural
determinant, and the search for exotic items was never
quite delegitimized.

The anthropological imagination which begins with
the fundamental concern of demonstrating the unity of
human beings is forever perceptive in noting how customs
and traditions do not exercise a permanent and undiluted
influence over people. It examines, on the other hand,
how these customs are modified, altered, bypassed,
subverted and resisted when social actors find it in their

interest to do so. This would bring in cross-cultural comparisons and de-exoticize 'strangeness'. As Marret said, 'The immobility of custom, I believe, is largely the effect of distance. Look more closely and you will see perpetual modification in process.' (Quoted in Kuper 1973: 31.) This could stand, as Kuper observed as the 'motto to any of Malinowski's Trobriand monographs.' (Ibid.) In fact Malinowski himself wrote that 'the description in familiar terms of exotic customs' is the task of anthropologists, and only then will come the recognition that what may seem 'strange at first sight are essentially cognate to very universal and fundamentally cultural items.' (Malinowski 1944: 41.) Elsewhere he said that 'whenever the native can evade his obligations without loss of prestige, or without the prospective loss of gain he does so exactly as a civilised business man would.' (Malinowski 1926: 30.) Where Radcliffe-Brown would have stressed the unquestioning attitude of the 'primitives' towards their customs and rules, Malinowski detailed how it was typical that 'a rule very stringently formulated by all informants when you ask about it, yet in reality often observed with laxity.' (Malinowski 1922: 30.) For Malinowski then 'man was down to earth, reasonable, rather unimaginative, perhaps, but able to discern his long term interests.' (Kuper 1973: 40.) To appreciate this and to utilize it requires, I believe, an essential quality of mind which is crucial to anthropology, and which I call the anthropological imagination.

Anthropological Imagination and Social Structure

Sartre once said: 'We do not wish the dialectic to become a divine law again, a metaphysical fate, it must proceed from individuals and not from some kind of supra-individual ensemble.' (Sartre 1976: 36.) This statement might easily arouse fears of a voluntaristic, privatized, solipsistic and a purely ethical intercalation of the individual into the objective science of society. But Sartre put his finger quite accurately on the failure of many Marxists who view social processes as a concatenation of necessary events, almost as if they were emanations of the logic of the structure itself. Conscious intervention is viewed then simply as 'chance' or accident, and as occurrences outside the scientific dialectical tempo of necessity. The emphasis on matter to the exclusion of everything else, and the consequent slogan—'the insurmountable character of historical laws'—negates the very essence of human praxis in which lies the true dialectical moment. As Marx said: 'The materialist doctrine that men are the product of circumstances and education, that changed men are therefore products changed circumstances and of a different education, forgets that circumstances in fact are changed by men and that the educator must himself be educated.' (Marx 1969: 14.)

It is not as if by bringing in back the anthropological human being we are forgetting the epochal constraints of society. Or that we are going back again to methodological individualism and forcefully conjuring up a relation between it and sociology/anthropology. Or even that we are denying that the individual in society is really the historically conditioned individual.

All these objections are false though the concern with epochal constraints and with the historically conditioned individual, is valid. The legitimacy of this concern is unquestionable. Social sciences rest on the principle that human beings are neither automatons or autonomous. It is true that what separates the entire range of sociological theories from Marx to Durkheim to Parsons to Mead from idealism and positivism is the insistence on epochal constraints and the reflexivity of social action. While considerations of the historical individual are central, it is not as if this individual is not denied practical and sensuous dimensions. Individuals interrogate their own social existence, reflect on it, and maximize their options. It is incorrect then merely to uphold historically determined individuals and then to predetermine them as subjects of unbending material forces. The conception of historically determined individuals (or classes), tells us what is structurally foreclosed without dictating what is structurally allowed. Causality, in other words, cannot be stated in advance. The reflexive individual is constrained but not determined.

Sartre critiques a variety of Marxists for reducing the individual either to an accident or to an objective interpolation necessitated by the diktat of structures. But does Sartre's understanding of the individual ignore the fact that social action cannot occur in isolation and that praxis is always social praxis. If placed in its proper context, one notes that Sartre's individual is already integrated into the dialectic (Sartre 1976: 80-81). This individual is not an isolate, but is a practical sensuous person whose activities presume an internalization of the total with its interstices. By constantly reflecting upon the totality, individuals attempt to transcend and transform their environment to their advantage. In realizing these ambitious individuals work through groups, or even singly, but through instrumentalities that are available and accessible. The transcendence and transformation of the given is always from the vantage point at which individuals find themselves. And 'in the course of this transformation', as Lukacs points out, 'pure' economics are naturally transcended though this does not mean we must appeal to transcendental forces.' (Lukacs 1971: 15.) But Sartre is not fully able to overcome the lingering remains of solipsism even in *The Critique of Dialectical Reason*. This is probably because he defines praxis as serialized individual praxis, and thus opens himself to criticisms. When Sartre set out to reconquer the individual within Marxism, he would have been less equivocal and solipsistic had he begun with the unconscious infrastructure and the 'give' that it allows in its dialectic with social actors. Instead, he advanced via the existentialist schemata, which even in its sophisticated form, considers praxis as a plural inflexion of individual praxis. By underplaying the role of the infrastructure which unites heterogeneous elements in its field of force, Sartre, who has come a long way since his postulation 'hell is other people' now apparently believes that 'structure is other people'. The dialectic, undoubtedly, is there in Sartre. But the dialectic is now between individual praxis and serialized praxis, which without the unconscious infrastructural logic that Marx himself repeatedly emphasized, still leans towards solipsism. But Sartre certainly succeeds in bringing about the reappearance of the individual by focusing attention on the reflexivity, freedom as well as the constraints on action imposed by other people. The difficulty with Sartre is that his individual is advised to abandon 'other people' in order to experience true existentialism, while the anthropological imagination exerts itself to understand how through other people, and in their midst, individual ambitions and goals are sought to be realized. In this process nothing is really the same, even if this quantum of change is microscopic in its initial effects.

There is a greater urgency in adopting such a perspective when studying traditional, or 'pre-modern' societies in view of the careless manner in which the members of these societies are generally characterized by scholars. It is the anthropological imagination alone which helps one capture the essence of dialectics. The imagination underpins and informs (or should in any case), the friction between necessity and freedom and between structure and the individual. The fact that human beings believe they are free, and yet behind their backs the structure bends to assert a finality to their actions, without ever fully determining them, gives space to individuals to assert themselves as social actors.

Structure, Typification and Anthropological Imagination

In the Durkheimian understanding of structure, observed behaviour is standardized to become the objective determinant of human behaviour. In an extreme form this could degenerate into positivistic determinism or causality. Even Malinowski in his later period, when he was unexpectedly appreciative of Durkheim, complained against his 'sociological one-sidedness . . .' (Malinowski 1944: 24). This sociological one-sidedness of Durkheim leads to an understanding of social structure which, to steal a phrase from Simmel, is actually 'the lowest common denominator of individuals'. But whereas Simmel scorned society, Durkheim rightly upheld it. But his underlying 'sociologism' empowered the issual of a comprehensive protocol for human behaviour. So along with societies, individuals also received their appropriate classificatory labels.

The constraints of the structure of any historical

period can be compared to the social structure of Durkheim, as can the open-ended paradigm of Kuhn (Kuhn 1970: 23). Structural constraints are like an open-ended paradigm for they do not enable one to project what would be the concrete character of the whole social formation. The paradigm provides the underlying logic of the system. In abstraction it is made to stand apart, but in reality it forms the limits consequent upon the determinate relations people enter into in producing and reproducing material life. This logic loops the multitude of social actions with centripetal and conservative pressure, but it has also constantly to shift its position and enlarge its options in order not to destroy itself. Social action is therefore always burdened with this logic, but never fully determined. From any point in the social formation social actors are both dependent and independent, but their energies are more frequently concerned with the area of independence that logic grants them—the 'give' so to say of the logic itself. The anthropological imagination emphasizes the attributes of freedom, of decision and of choice, which become relevant and assume importance because the logic of the system curtails sizeable chunks of these. A pure free individual is not only conceptually a sociological absurdity but would also empirically be a mentally certifiable case. It is because there is no complete freedom in society, it is because choices are limited and options mostly closed, that individuals must exercise their faculties. It is in this process that universal attributes of humankind become salient in a cross-cultural and comparative perspective. The ability to empathize is heightened even though the scholar and the field may belong to very diverse cultural provenances.

But this has not always been considered by

sociologists and anthropologists in their understanding of social structure. An outcome, as we have tried to show earlier, of denying praxis its rightful position at the core of sociological analysis, When this happens, individuals become only standard bearers of structure.

They are capable of neither reflection nor contemplation. After this is done, it matters little whether it is the economy or culture that does all the determining of social action: for on all occasions people are only there to fulfil their mute roles. If human beings are mute bearers of structures (plural), the distinction between culture and structure loses its significance. And as is often the case, for e.g. Dumont (1972) or Godelier (1977, 1978) culture plays as determinate a role as the economy did with 'vulgar Marxists'. In fact Godelier concedes as we noticed earlier, that superstructure can act as infrastructure, particularly in 'primitive' societies. Beginning by granting superstructural moments their own levels and autonomy, we end up by positing the two as interchangeable. In between, as we have not managed to locate the subject of the various structures we have also moved towards ideationalism and structural functionalism (see Thompson 1978: 237-253, 268 and *passim*).

Structure, Superstructure and the Anthropological Imagination

It is from material foundations, Marx said, that specific ideas, beliefs, values, etc. emerge. The superstructure does not have an independent existence, but grows out of the material relations people enter into in concrete historical situations. This methodological starting point towards an epistemological theory should not however be construed to mean that at any given point in a concrete social formation, every superstructural element has a one to one origin in the base. To stress an obvious Marxian platitude, elements in the superstructure are not outgrowths of the pure mind, but of the mind contemplating and ratiocinating on and within given social conditions. As Althusser said, 'Human societies secrete ideology as the very element and atmosphere indispensable to their historical respiration and life.' (Althusser 1969; 232.)

If individuals are only supports for structures and superstructures then we can again type them off in a manner not unlike the exotic hunting anthropologists that Malinowski despaired of. For once again these structures are insurmountable and impervious to human agency, and individuals must therefore constantly submit to them. Louis Althusser's treatment of 'survivals' is also instructive in this regard (Althusser 1969: 118-19).

Though Althusser concedes that ideological elements and ideological systems, needless to say, are outgrowths of the material world, yet at no one point can they become fully autonomous. They can however live beyond the conditions that give them birth. But these elements live on and are structured and restructured, built and shattered, to express and articulate the lived-in conditions of people in society. As Boas said long back: '. . . mythological worlds have been built up, only to be shattered again, and that new world were built from the fragments.' (quoted in Lévi-Strauss 1966: 21.) This is why, as Althusser argues, ideological and cultural elements are not univocal (Althusser 1969: 209). They have many voices, but are not equivocal either. In different social contexts these cultural elements can articulate themselves differently. Thus, for example notions of racial superiority can be expressed in a

variety of ways from the 'White man's burden' to
straight apartheid. Likewise caste can be activated as a
vertical system of integration (as in tradition) or as
horizontal blocs as in contemporary caste politics. There
is therefore a constant play, or dialectic, between culture
and context—a reality that cultural determinists tend to
ignore. It is because the human mind cannot fully grasp
its surroundings, that it treasures the ideological elements
of the past, hordes them as one would ancient heirlooms,
not knowing when, nor for what reason, their value
would appreciate. This is what leads to what Althusser
calls 'the reactivation of older elements.' (Althusser
1969: 116.)

This is where the anthropological imagination
becomes active. It heightens the realization that human
beings are reviewing and revising their strategy towards
this end continuously. In this process new alliances are
created, new obstacles are detected and within the range
of novelty that historical conditions allow newer
ideological structurations emerge. These aspire to explain
such large questions as the purpose of life, contemporary
conditions of existence, as well as how to cope with the
world and strategize options to one's best advantage.

Seen in this light the Althussian structuralist thesis is
not inconsistent with the argument that cultural elements
can live beyond conditions that gave them birth, and
that they can respond to changed conditions on account
of being multivocal. Not only are elements of the
superstructure outgrowths of the basis, but a particular
ideological structuration, or expression, is the result of
human strategizing during determinable moment in social
history. The articulation and acclaim of the ideological
structure rests primarily on its ability to aspire towards
a world view and to project, by condensation,

experimental reflexes learnt from the lived-in world as knowledge. But as the lived-in world also changes in small microscopic doses, so do experiences. The ideological structure is then a protean phenomenon and therefore it cannot be said that a class has a fixed ideological structure composed of a fixed number of elements. It is only in the structuration that ideological, or superstructural elements, get a semantic content and meaning. This structuration makes sense because of the *selective manner* in which certain elements are given salience to provide a charter for action. At another point, different aspects of these non-univocal elements can be activated, or wholly new elements may be brought in. To give an example: sometimes 'casteism' expresses itself in the form of a war between the upper castes and some (not all) members of the untouchable castes, whereas the logic of pure casteism should not have distinguished between different sections among the 'untouchables'. At other times 'casteism' finds expression in a situation of hostility between Hindus and Buddhists, while at other times 'untouchables' and Hindus bury their differences and have a face off with the Muslims. Yet again, two dominant castes are antagonistically ranged against each other with the lower and middle castes either left out of the picture or drawn in at different points; and so on it goes. This holds true for nativism, chauvinism, regionalism, racism, etc. Also from casteism, the same protagonists, may move over to some other idiom to express their mutual hostility. In this process they may draw in other allies or drop their previous ones. The models change, the elements undergo transformation, depending entirely on the manner in which people in society give meaning to them, in order to maximize their conditioned options.

This understanding should hopefully take us away from two types of errors. The error of the first type occurs when 'survivals' are believed to be phenomena with a past, but with little future ahead of them. In India, for instance, we are often told that communalism and casteism are precapitalist and feudal, and if only the Indian economy had been a really developed capitalist one they would have withered away. This is a form of evolutionism which was long ago effectively debunked by Malinowski. Criticizing A.A. Goldenweiser, Malinoswki said: 'There is no doubt that the survival endures because it has acquired a new meaning, a new function . . . Antiquated types or automobiles are never used simply because they have survived, but because people cannot afford to buy a newer model. The function is economic.' (Malinowski 1944: 29.) The same is expressed elsewhere when he said, 'Much has been said and written about survivals. Yet the survival character of an act is expressed in nothing so well as in the concomitant behaviour in the way in which it is carried out. Observe and fix the data of their behaviour, and at once the degree of vitality of the act will become clear.' (Malinowski 1922: 30.) To return to our problem, elements of the 'superstructure' do not just wither away. They are part of the historic memory to be used and revitalized just when they were about to be considered as defunct.

The error of the second type occurs when it is believed that culture and ideology have a clear run, propelled either by their own mode or by the logic of their autonomous production. But as social actors are constantly straining against sociological constraints they are compelled to, at the same time, to apply and reapply, ideological elements to express themselves, their ambitions, hopes and fears. Just as given historical conditions curtail freedom they also open up options which are often accessed by rearticulating elements in the inherited storehouse of ideas and beliefs.

Let us return now to our anthropological imagination. Once it is acknowledged that neither structure nor superstructure can determine causality in society we are close to an appreciation of the various ways by which human beings manipulate their social environment to their advantage. We then also hesitate to designate a prefixed set of behaviour patterns for those belonging to different societies with differing social structures. Nor can we say that the ideological level exists in any one form but that human beings manipulate their ideological heritage in consonance with their 'lived in' relation in the world. From this friction emerges a particular ideological structuration. If one grants the ideological level complete autonomy then it would be tantamount to taking away the autonomy of social actors. For how else can ideology express itself but through live human beings? If we believe on the other hand that the social structure is close ended, then men and women are again bearers of a preordained 'transcendental dialectic'.

The Unconscious Structure and its Methodological Relevance

Lévi-Strauss used the deep structure of the mind which functions on the principle of binary oppositions to understand 'how the human spirit works' (Glucksmann 1974: 87), notwithstanding the social diversity of human existence. His studies focused especially on the superstructure, i.e., on myths, totemism, 'savage' thought, etc. According to Lévi-Strauss, 'Without questioning the undoubted primacy of infrastructures, I believe that there is always a mediator between praxis and practices, namely, the conceptual schema . . . It is to this theory of superstructures, scarcely touched upon by Marx, that I hope to make a contribution.' (Lévi-Strauss 1966: 130.) But this superstructure is not a defined and conscious structure. Lévi-Strauss sharply distanced himself from Balzac who wrote that '(i)deas form a complete system within us, comparable to one of the natural kingdoms' (ibid). As Lévi-Strauss puts it, Balzac's enterprise would require 'more madness than genius to accomplish.' To continue with Lévi-Strauss, 'If, as I have said, the conceptual scheme governs and defines practices, it is because these, which the ethnologist studies as discrete realities placed in time and space and distinctive in their particular modes of life and forms of civilisation are not to be confused with praxis which—and here at least I agree with Sartre—constitutes the fundamental totality for the science of man.' (Ibid.)

It is sometimes falsely construed that for Lévi-Strauss the social structure is derived from the structure of the mind (Glucksmann 1974: 72). Such as interpretation occurs because of insufficient attention paid to the methodological principles of the Lévi-Straussian method. Glucksmann cites Lévi-Strauss's studies on kinship to make this point (ibid). But if one looks a little closely at Lévi-Strauss's study on kinship it will be noticed that what Lévi-Strauss is actually doing is using linguistic theory, and the theoretical insights of linguistic theory—the distinction, for instance, between *langue* and *parole*—to bear upon the ordering of authority and joking relationships in kinship studies. In this process Lévi-Strauss hopes to undermine the counter-emphasis on conscious interventions in the detailing of kinship relations (Lévi-Strauss 1968: Chapter 1).

Our earlier quotation from Lévi-Strauss makes clear that he has no intention of trifling with the economic infrastructure of Marx. His search is for the common properties of the mind. To quote him again: 'If as we believe to be the case, the unconscious activity of the mind consists in imposing form upon content, and these forms are fundamentally the same for all minds—it is necessary and sufficient to grasp the unconscious structure underlying each institution and each custom, in order to obtain a principle of interpretation valid for other institutions and customs.' (Lévi-Strauss 1968: 21.) It would appear then that Lévi-Strauss's object of analysis is to study the universality of the human mind via a variety of customs, institutions and practices, and not to emphasise or demonstrate either that the structure of the human mind determines concrete socio-economic environs, or that myths, customs, etc., constitute the social infrastructure. His search is for the deep structure behind the superstructure which would explain the universal attributes of the mind, and also the principle that keeps ordering and reordering the cultural world with its many diversities. All this is important if one is to understand the methodological foundations and aims of Lévi-Straussian structuralism, and distinguish it from the structuralism of Louis Dumont. Dumont's structuralism, as we have already noticed, posits a perennial empirical separation between binary opposites. The pure and impure, *homo hierarchicus* and *homo aefuilius* are fixed empirical stations incapable of structural transformations (of the Lévi-Straussian variety) that bring about different combinations. The 'untouchable' may become a priest, or the priestly class as such might disappear, or the category of untouchability too might become redundant. All of this can happen and indeed do happen, but Dumont's system cannot accommodate them because his methodology is premised on the conscious model. This model assumes that what exists at any point of time is because of a grand ideological design, and that each such design is deliberately arrived at.

What escapes the attention of the conscious model, such as of the Dumontian variety, is that superstructure is a vast store house. There are far too many elements in it to make possible an empirical inventory even of the worst sort. But only certain elements of the superstructure are more directly related to the basis, or to the infrastructure, than others. These more directly relevant ones are those which best hide the basic contradictions in the infrastructure and therefore recur constantly in that epoch. But it is not enough to stop here in one's examination of the superstructure for this would truncate its vast epistemological sweep. Certain elements, it is true, occur again and again in an epoch. Yet any of their specific articulations (and they are capable of several, as it was maintained earlier) must combine with other elements borne more directly out of mundane experiences. These experiences in turn have the mnemonic effect of revitalising certain other items from collective memory, which also go into the combination to form an ideological structuration.

The process of ratiocination of the lived-in world, changes the world itself, albeit gently. To add to this the several fractures that exist at the level of culture-ideologies and beliefs, makes this phenomenon extremely dynamic and fluid. As social actors are constantly straining to optimize and maximize their opportunities the symbolic universes too undergo significant modifications. Nevertheless, the fact that the unconscious structure is invisible and hidden compels human beings to comprehend only the sensible world in sensible terms. This assures the continuation of the infrastructural logic, for its deep secret is well-hidden and never consciously comprehended in its entirety.

But the superstructures of each epoch have a definite quality about them, with enough diacritical marks to distinguish them from the superstructures of other epochs. It is by the elaboration of these diacritical notations that we are able to talk of the existence of such superstructural themes as the belief in the caste system, in democracy, in paternalism, etc. The governing elements of each such superstructural theme are intimately related to the basic contradictions of the infrastructure, in the sense that they most effectively conceal these contradictions. But as these elements are finite and not equivocal, it is only within certain limits that they can be used. But as long as they are in existence they do strive to perpetuate the internal logic of the system, and hence material reproduction, though never in a uniform or clearly knowable way. For the anthropological subject is ubiquitous and perpetually present with all faculties intact, reinterpreting elements of any structuration to personal advantage. This happens by bringing in different elements, or reviving dormant themes, and altering the assembly in such a manner that not only explains the present, but also provides hope and a raison d'être for the future.

The superstructure, if the analysis thus far is accepted, does not have its own autonomous level. It enjoys a relative autonomy of course, but this relative autonomy does not have abundant ideological free space. The reason why earlier elaborations of this theme sounded so implausible was because the logic of the economy was supposed to govern to the last detail every element of the superstructure and even its structuration, *ab initio*. This not only obfuscated a close study of the peculiarities of the material basis and its prior history, but also standardized the superstructure on a dogmatic principle leaving little for human agency to design and fashion.

How can Dumont and Godelier Think Alike?

In bringing Dumont and Godelier together the intention is primarily to demonstrate that once human beings are susceptible to being culturally typed and separated, then no matter how diverse one's stated methodological preferences, the conclusions are going to be very similar. Dumont in *Homo Hierarchicus* (1972) tries to demonstrate how inadequate Marxism is for the study of Indian reality. And yet Godelier, from a clearly stated Marxist position, finds it possible to appreciatively quote Dumont, and also to utilize Dumont's formulations as theoretical stepping stones. This unity between Dumont and Godelier, which might otherwise seem baffling, can however be understood by the commonality, of their respective orientations towards the understanding of human agency. For both of them human beings are *determined* by structures. For Dumont the 'conscious model' is the most important level of reality determining in detail how people are to act in a variety of situations. For Godelier, too the conscious structure of ideologies and beliefs acts as infrastructure in pre-capitalist societies, and hence constitutes the most important level of reality in these societies. Consequently, neither Dumont and Godelier considers the anthropological subject, that is the actor, to be capable of functioning as a 'reflexive cognito.' Why do the Indian tribes in the Inca state formation hand over part of their surplus to the gods? Because, according to Godelier, their religion commands them to do so (Godelier 1977: 35). It is the religious idea that 'causes things to happen.' (Godelier 1978: 90.) Therefore, politico-religious ideas exist at the level of infrastructure in the Inca empire. In spite of the demonstrable reliance on Marxist terminology, the substance is really quite culturological. Let us move on to Dumont. Why do Hindus still remain backward in spite of the great strides taken by industrialization elsewhere in the world? Because, Dumont avers, the caste system determines just how much to give in to industrialization without endangering its hierarchical principle. The Hindus are allowed to avail of the benefits of industrialization only in areas which the caste system considers unimportant (Dumont 1970: 228). Relying on Dumont's considered opinion on this subject, Godelier moves swiftly and claims caste as infrastructure as well (Godelier 1978: 89; Godelier 1972: ix).

It cannot be denied that beliefs play a role in human behaviour. This is a truism that need not be stated. But what is being disputed here is that these beliefs, in the hands of sociologists and anthropologists, become absolute determinants of human behaviour and prescribe a set rule of action. Thus, in spite of Dumont's and Godelier's rather diverse theoretical starting points, they quite unambiguously come to similar conclusions—only the terminologies are different.

Though Malinowski's work was constantly devalued by later anthropologists who only saw him as a crude functionalist with somewhat naive predilections towards an analysis of social phenomena in terms of psychology and human needs, Malinowski continued to provide massive doses of inspiration to all those who were interested in the study of conflict and tension in social formations. Max Gluckman and Edmund Leach were the foremost in this regard. But because of the complexity of their material, and of their arguments, most anthropologists preferred to take up the simpler, almost rule of thumb and sociologistic approach which resonates well with popular constructions of cultures. This precluded a full elaboration of Malinowski which would have thrown up some of his theoretical weaknesses more fully without losing out on his core concern and without abjuring what I have called the anthropological imagination.

It was with Lévi-Strauss that the anthropological imagination which was made vulnerable after Malinowski was reassembled again. The impact was devastating. Here was a man able to move freely between Marx, Jakobson, de Saussere, as well as Boas and Kroeber. Not many perhaps understood what was happening, a state of incomprehension that at times Lévi-Strauss seemed deliberately to inspire by his equivocation on some vital issues, and also by the subtle dislocations effected by the translation of his works. Also, and most importantly, he chose for himself the study of 'cold societies' and of their myths, beliefs, to arrive at the structure of the superstructures of these societies. All this demanded a great deal of mental agility, as such 'cold societies' are no longer in existence. But, I think Lévi-Strauss also implies, that this past can only be forgotten if we are determined to misunderstand ourselves in the present.

As was mentioned earlier (recall Lévi-Strauss's comment on Balzac), Lévi-Strauss had no intention of suggesting that conscious models determine actual social relations. Also Lévi-Strauss was actually searching for invariant principles behind all conscious models and nothing more. Two simple quotes from Lévi-Strauss and Dumont should make clear their vast theoretical differences. To quote Lévi-Strauss first:

> I do not, at all mean to suggest that ideological transformations give rise to social ones. *Only the reverse is in fact true.* Men's conception of the relations between nature and culture is a function of modification of their own social relations. But since my aim here is to outline a theory of superstructures, reasons of method require that they should be singled out for attention and that major phenomena which have no place in this programme should seem to be left in brackets or given second place. We are however merely studying the shadows on the wall of the cave forgetting that it is only the attention we give them lends them a semblance of reality. (Lévi-Strauss 1966: 117, emphasis added.)

In direct contrast to Lévi-Strauss's method, Dumont writes that the 'caste system is a state of mind, a state of mind which is expressed by the emergence, in various situations, of groups of various orders generally called "castes".' (Dumont 1972: 71.) The state of mind therefore expresses itself by giving rise to concrete social formations. This is exactly the kind of position Lévi-Strauss opposed strongly while criticizing Balzac. For Lévi-Strauss 'the relation between the "representation" of the object to the real non-conceptual object is always transcendental, but not centred in consciousness. The relation between the categories of thought with the elements of reality is transcendental precisely because

. . . it is not an empirical relation of thought to its object—nor can experience ever provide its status as a conceptual object.' (D'Amico 1973: 89.) This summing up by D'Amico most accurately represents Lévi-Strauss's methodological position regarding the relationship between the categories of the mind and empirical reality which again demonstrates the distance between him and Dumont.

Finally , when Lévi-Strauss employs a binary model for grasping the hidden structure behind the superstructures, he is not thinking of the 'content of mind' but of the 'capacity of mind'. (Needham 1970: xxcv.) Nor does he posit that the elements which express these oppositions have an innate quality as such which attach them to either pole of the opposition. The oppositions only make sense in a system of internal homology and transformations. The semantic content of the superstructure is related to empirical reality only in so much as it permits human beings to overcome the very unsatisfactory contradictions on which their societies rest. For Dumont, on the other hand, the opposition between the pure and impure, by virtue of being an empirical opposition cannot bear a transcendental relation between categories of thought and empirical reality. There is no system of internal homology or transformations in Dumont. It is the opposition alone which is on its beat, searching the society, differentiating it, imprinting it, and constantly adding, over the years, to its combined stockpile of things pure and impure. In this method, loaded semantic categories operate which then raise tricky analytical problems. From one point of view the opposite of pure, is: not pure. Anything that is not pure need not be impure and so on. Moreover, whether or not a certain object should be designated as pure and another as impure, cannot, in the Lévi-Straussian sense, be understood simply in terms of their innate properties, but only in a system of internal homology and of structural opposition. This would then allow structural transformations, which in turn would demonstrate the versatility of the human subject.

Conclusion: The Sociological and Anthropological Imagination

The sociological imagination primarily demands a conjuncture between historical and biographical investigation whereby one is able to understand the social and historical processes that separate individuals and alienate them from one another. This at least is the way I read C. Wright Mills's *The Sociological Imagination*. An imaginative analysis of this sort, Mills believed, would cross-illuminate the method and logic of seemingly timeless, faceless, inert social institutions which conceal the relations that bind human beings, sectorized and atomized as they are at different, often remote points on the scatter diagram of society.

The sociological imagination brings one to an understanding of our common fate, and to the multiple social forces in history which shape institutions and classes and separate them from our common consciousness. The anthropological imagination works in a complementary mode, and indeed encompasses all of the insights of the sociological imagination. It starts however, from the realization that 'at the root of man is man himself'. Social forces must work through the human agent, the social actor, who is essentially, a 'reflexive cognito'. This person contemplates and thinks, rationalizes and maxmizes, such that no social force is left entirely in its pristine form once it has undergone such active human mediations. This dynamic is propelled in fact by the rational energies invested in human kind which allows the social actor to contend against the circumscribing logic and constraints of the social order for self-realization, in however incomplete a fashion. The anthropological imagination that proclaims at the start that '(t)he organisation of mind is practically identical among all races of man' (Boas 1911: 99), and which focuses on human universals, is deeply suspicious of anthropological exotica and constantly strives to normalize them. The anthropological imagination is committed to deep intersubjectivity to see 'the them in us'. Only then can the unfamiliar be made known in familiar terms and aid in human understanding across cultures.

If any overwhelming point needs to be reiterated, after all that has been said, admittedly in a discursive manner, it is that academics cannot imitate the mode of discourse prevalent in popular constructions of reality, if sociology and anthropology are to act as 'levellers' and as humanizing disciplines. Aimless studies of culture not only sediment around typifications which divide humanity in the popular consciousness, but often even substantiate them. To be able to ask 'overlapping questions' the sociologist will have to look take a long self-critical at every step. The 'culturological trance' is then broken. Diversity is no longer a cut-off point of sociological investigation whose origins reside in a never-never world. It now demands an explanation in a historical and relational perspective, a perspective that bathes all of humankind in the same light and then discovers its potentiality as a creator of social diversity.

Bibliography

Alavi, Hamza, 1975, 'India and the Colonial Mode of Production', in *Socialist Register*, edited by Ralph Miliband and John Saville, London, Merlin Press.

Althusser, Louis, 1969, *For Marx*, Harmondsworth, Penguin Books.

Appadurai, Arjun, 1974, 'Right and Left Hand Castes in South India' in *Indian Economic and Social History Review*, Vol. 11, pp. 216-260.

Apte, V.M., 1951a, 'Political and Real Institution (The age of Rig Samhita)' in *History and Culture of the Indian People, Vol. 1: The Vedic Age*, eds., R.C. Majumdar and A.D. Pusalker, London, George Allen and Unwin.

————1951b, 'Religion and Philosophy in the Age of the Later Samahitas', in *History and Culture of the Indian People, Vol. 1: The Vedic Age*, eds., R.C. Majumdar and A.D. Pusalker, London, George Allen and Unwin.

Aronson, Ronald, 1978, 'The Individualist Theory of Jean Paul Sartre', in *Western Marxism: A Critical Reader*, London, New Left Books, Verso Edition.

Arthashastra, 1960, ed., R.P. Kangle, Bombay, University of Bombay Press.

Atyachar Virodhi Samiti, 1979, 'The Marathwada Riots: A Report', *Economic and Political Weekly*, Vol. 14, pp. 845-52.

Avineri, Shlomo, 1969, 'Introduction' in *On Colonialism and Modernisation*, New York, Anchor Books.

Babb, L.A., 1998, 'Rejecting Violence: Sacrifice and the Social Identity of Trading Communities', in *Contributions to Indian Sociology* (N.S.) Vol. 32, pp. 387-407.

Banks, Michael, 1969, 'Caste in Jaffna,' in E.R. Leach, ed., *Aspects of Caste in South India, Ceylon and North West Pakistan*, Cambridge University Press.

Barzun, Jacques, 1965, *Race: A Study in Superstition*, New York, The Macmillan, Harper and Row.

Bayly, C.A., 1983, *Rulers, Townsmen and Bazaars: North Indian Society in the Age of British Expansion, 1770-1870*, Cambridge, Cambridge University Press.

Beck, Brenda, E.F., 1970, 'The Right-Left Division of South Indian Society', *Journal of Asian Studies*, Vol. 29, pp. 779-798.

Behera, Sanjeeb, K., 1999, *Data Base on Scheduled Caste Literacy (Based on Census Data 1991)*, New Delhi, Indian Social Institute.

Berger, Peter and Thomas Luckmann, 1971, *The Social Construction of Reality*, Harmondsworth, Penguin.

Berreman, Gerald, 1991, 'The Brahmanical View of Caste', in Dipankar Gupta, ed., *Social Stratification*, Delhi, Oxford University Press.

Béteille, André, 1977, *Inequality Among Men*, Oxford and London, Basil Blackwell.

Blunt, E.A.H., 1960, *The Caste System of Northern India with Special Reference to the United Province of Agra and Oudh*, Delhi, S. Chand & Co.

Boas, Franz, 1911, *The Mind of Primitive Man*, New York, Macmillan Company.

Bose, N.K., 1960, *Data on Caste*, Calcutta, Anthropological Survey of India.

————1961, *Cultural Anthropology*, Bombay, Asia Publishing House.

————1975, *The Structure of Hindu Society*, (translated with an introduction by André Béteille), Delhi, Orient Longman.

————1975, 'Some Aspects of Caste in Bengal', in Milton Singer, ed., *Traditional India: Structure and Change*, Jaipur, Rawat Publications.

Bose, Pradip Kumar, 1992, 'Mobility and Conflict: Social Roots of Caste Violence in Bihar', in Dipankar Gupta, ed., *Social Stratification*, Delhi, Oxford University Press.

Bougle, C., 1991, 'The Essences and Reality of the Caste System', in Dipankar Gupta, ed., *Social Stratification*, Delhi, Oxford University Press.

————1992, 'The Essence and Reality of the Caste System,' in Dipankar Gupta, ed., *Social Stratification*, Delhi, Oxford University Press.

Bourdieu, Pierre, 1984, *Distinction: A Social Critique of the Judgement of Taste*, Cambridge, Massachusetts, Harvard University Press.

Breman, Jan, 1974, *Patronage and Exploitation*, Berkeley, University of California Press.

Brihadarnakeya Upanishad, 1965, Harmondsworth, Penguin.

Briggs, Geo, W., 1920, *Chamars*, London, Oxford University Press.

Brouwer, Jan, 1997, 'The Goddess for Development. Indigenous Economic Concepts Among South Indian Artisans', *Social Anthropology*, Vol. 5, pp. 69-82.

Burghart, Richard, 1996, *The Conditions of Listening: Essays on Religion, History and Politics of South Asia*, ed., C.J. Fuller and Jonathan Spencer, Delhi, Oxford University Press.

Census of India, 1931, Bihar and Orissa, 1933, Patna, Superintendent Printing and Stationery.

Census of India, 1931, Bombay, Government Central Press.

Census of India, 1931, United Province of Agra and Oudh, Allahabad, Superintendent Printing and Stationery.

Census of India, 1991, New Delhi, Registrar General of Census.

Chanana, Dev Raj, 1960, *Slavery in India*, Delhi, Peoples Publishing House.

————1961, 'Sanskritisation and Westernization in India's North West', in *Economic and Political Weekly*, Bombay, Vol. 8, pp. 409-414.

Chatterji, S.K., 1951, 'Race Movements in Pre Historic Culture', in *History and Culture of the Indian People, Vol: 1, The Vedic Age*, ed., R.C. Majumdar and A.D. Pusalker, London, George Allen and Unwin.

Chattopadhyaya, B.D., 1976, 'Origin of the Rajputs: The Political Economic and Social Processes in Early Medieval Rajasthan', in *Indian Historical Reviews*, Vol. 3, pp. 59-82.

Chattopadhyaya, Debiprasad, 1977, *Science and Society in Ancient India*, Calcutta, Research India Publications.

————1978, *Lokayata: A Study in Ancient Indian Materialism*, Delhi, Peoples Publishing Huse.

Chichirov, A.C., 1971, *Indian Economic Development in the 16th and 18th Centuries*, Moscow, Nauka Publishing House.

Cohen, M.T. Nagel and T. Scanlon, eds., 1977, *Equality and Preferential Treatment*, Princeton, Princeton University Press.

Cohn, Bernard, 1987, *An Anthropologist among Historians*, Delhi, Oxford University Press.

Colletti, Lucio, 1978, *From Rousseau to Lenin*, Delhi, Oxford University Press.

Cox, Oliver Cromwell, 1970, *Caste Class and Race: A Study in Social Dynamics*, New York, Monthly Review Press.

Crooke, William, 1906, *Things Indian*, London, Methuen.

D'Amico, Robert, 1973, 'The Contours and Coupures of Structuralist Theory', *Telos*, No. 17, pp. 70-79.

Das, Veena, 1982, *Structure and Cognition: Aspects of Hindu Caste and Ritual*, Bombay, Manohar.

de Reuck, Anthony and Julie Knight, eds., 1968, *Caste and Race: Comparative Approaches*, London, J.A. Churchill Ltd.

de Tocqueville, Alexis, 1969, *Democracy in America*, ed., J.P. Mayer, New York, Doubleday.

Deliege, Robert, 1992, 'Republication of Consensus: Untouchability, Caste, and Ideology in India', *Man* (N.S.), Vol. 27, pp. 155-173.

Desai, I.P., 1976, *Untouchability in Rural Gujarat*, Bombay, Popular Prakashan Pvt. Ltd.

Dhar, Hiranmoy, et. al, 1982, 'Caste and Polity in Bihar', in Gail Omvedt, ed., *Land, Caste and Politics in Indian States*, Delhi, Authors Guild Publications.

Dirks, Nicholas B., 1987, *The Hollow Crown: Ethnohistory of an Indian Kingdom*, Cambridge, Cambridge University Press.

Douglas, Ann, 1977, *The Feminization of America*, New York, Avon Books.

Douglas, Mary, 1972, '*Introduction*' in Louis Dumont, *Homo Hierarchicus*, London, Paladin.

Dumont, Louis, 1960, 'World Renunciation in Indian Religions', *Contributions to Indian Sociology*, Vol. 4, pp. 33-62.

————1970, *Homo Hierarchicus: The Caste System and its Implications*, London, Weidenfeld and Nicholson.

————1971, *Homo Hierarchicus*, Delhi, Vikas Publication.

————1972, *Homo Hierarchicus*, London, Paladin/1970 Edn. Delhi, Vikas.

————1988, *Homo Hierarchicus: The Caste System and its Implications*, London, Weidenfeld and Nicholson.

Dumont, Louis and David Pocock, 1960, 'For a Sociology of India', in *Contributions to Indian Sociology*, Vol. 4.

Durkheim, Émile, 1966, *The Rules of Sociological Method*, New York, Free Press.

Durkheim, Émile and Marcel Mauss, 1970, *Primitive Classifications*, London, Cohen and West.

Enthoven, R.B., 1975, *The Tribes and Castes of Bombay*, 3 Vols., Bombay, The Times Press.

Fox, Richard G., 1969, *From Zamindar to Ballot Box: Community Change in a North Indian Market Town*, Ithaca, Cornell University Press.

Frankel, Francine, R., 1989, 'Caste Land and Dominance in Bihar: Breakdown of the Brahmanical Social Order', in Francine R. Frankel and M.S.A. Rao, eds., *Dominance and State Power in Modern India: Decline of a Social Order,* (Vol. 1), Delhi, Oxford University Press.

———1990, 'Conclusion', in Francine R. Frankel and M.S.A. Rao, eds., *Dominance and State Power in Modern India: Decline of a Social Order,* Vol. 2, Delhi, Oxford University Press.

Fuchs, Stephen, 1946, *The Children of Hari: A Study of the Nimar Balahis in Madhya Pradesh*, Ahmedabad, New Order Book.

Fuller, C.J., 1979, 'Gods, Priests and Purity: On the Relation Between Hinduism and the Caste System', *Man,* (N.S.), Vol. 14, pp. 459-76.

———1984, *Servants of the Goddess: The Priests of a South India Temple*, Delhi, Oxford University Press.

———1992, *The Camphor Flame: Popular Hindus and Society in India*, Princeton, Princeton University Press.

Ghosh, B.K., 1951, 'The Aryan Problem', in *History and Culture of the Indian People, Vol. 1: The Vedic Age*, eds., R.C. Majumdar and A.D. Pusalker, London, George Allen and Unwin.

Ghoshal, U.N., 1972, *Contribution to the History of the Hindu Revenue System*, Calcutta, Saraswati Library.

Ghurye, G.S., 1969, *Caste and Race in India*, Bombay, Popular Prakashan.

Gluckman, Max, ed., 1964, *Closed Systems and Open Minds: The Limits of Naivete in Social Anthopology*, Chicago, Aldine Publishers.

Glucksmann, Miriam, 1974, *Structuralist Analysis in Contemporary Social Thought: A Comparison of the Theories of Claude Lévi-Strauss and Louis Althusser*, London and Boston, Routledge and Kegan Paul.

Godelier, Maurice, 1965, 'The Notion of the "Asiatic Mode of Production" in Marx and Engels', *Enquiry*, (N.S.), Vol. 2, pp. 28-48.

———1972, *Rationality and Irrationality in Economics*, New York, Monthly Review Press.

———1977, *Perspectives in Marxist Anthropology*, Cambridge, Cambridge University Press.

———1978, 'Infrastructures, Society and History' in *New Left Review*, London, No. 112, pp. 84-96.

Goffman, Erving, 1961, *The Presentation of Self in Everyday Life*, Harmondsworth, Penguin.

Goldthrope, J.H., C. Llewellyn and C. Payne, 1987, *Social Mobility and Class Structure in Modern Britain*, Oxford, Clarendon Press.

Gopal, K., 1963-64, 'Assignment to Officers and Royal Kinsmen in Early Medieval India (C. 700-1200. AD), Allahabad, University of Allahabad Studies (Ancient India Section).

Gore, M.S., 1993, 'Social Movement and the Paradigm of Functional Analysis: With Reference to the Non-Brahmin Movement in Maharashtra', in Yogesh Atal, ed., *Understanding Indian Society: Festchrift in Honour of S.C. Dube*, Delhi, Har-Anand Publication.

Gough, K., 1969, *The Social Structure of a Tanjore Village in India*, ed., M.N. Srinivas, Bombay, Asia Publishing House.

Gramsci, Antonio, 1971, *Selections from the Prison Notebooks*, ed. and translated by Quentin Hoare and Geoffrey Nowell Smith, New York, International Publications.

Guirand, Pierre, 1975, *Semiology*, London, Routledge and Kegan Paul.

Gupta, Dipankar, 1979, 'Understanding the Marathwada Riots: A Repudiation of Ecletic Marxism', *Social Scientist*, No. 82, 3-22.

————1992, 'Continuous Hierarchies and Discrete Castes', in Dipankar Gupta, ed., *Social Stratification*, Delhi, Oxford University Press.

————1997, *Rivalry and Brotherhood: Politics in the Life of Farmers of Northern India*, Delhi, Oxford University Press.

Gupta, Dwarkanath C. and S. Bhasker, n.d., *Vyasas—A Sociological Study*, New Delhi, Ashish Publishing House.

Gutman, Herberg, G., 1976, *The Black Family in Slavery and Freedom, 1750-1925*, New York, Pantheon Press.

Habib, Irfan, n.d., 'An Examination of Wittfogel's Theory of Oriental Despotism', *Enquiry*, Vol. 6, pp. 54-73.

————1965, 'Distribution of Landed Property in Pre-British India', *Enquiry*, Vol. 2, pp. 21-75.

————1971, 'Potentialities of Capitalist Development in the Economy of Mughal India', *Enquiry*, (N.S.), 3, pp. 1-56.

Harriss, John, 1979, 'Why Poor People Stay in Rural India', *Social Scientist*, No. 85, pp. 20-47.

Hasan, S.N., 1963, 'The Position of Zamindars in the Mughal Empire', *Indian Economic and Social History Review*, Vol. 1, pp. 107-109.

Hazelhurst, Leighton, W., 1968, 'Caste and Merchant Communities', in Milton Singer and Bernard Cohn, eds., *Structure and Change in Indian Society*, New York, Werner Gren Foundation.

Heesterman, H.C., 1985, *The Inner Conflict of Tradition: Essays in Indian Ritual, Kingship and Society*, Chicago, University of Chicago Press

Hegel, G.W.F., 1944, *Philosophy of History*, Trans, by J. Sibereo, New York, Willey Book Co.

Hitchcock, John, T., 1975, 'The Idea of the Martial Rajput', in Milton Singer, ed., *Traditional India: Structure and Change*, Jaipur, Rawat Publications.

Hocart, A.M., 1945, *Caste: A Comparative Study*, London, Methuen.

Horowitz, David, 1985, *Ethnic Groups in Conflict*, Berkeley, University of California Press.

Hutchinson, Harry, 1957, *Village and Plantation Life*, Seattle, University of Washington Press.

Hutton, J.H., 1963, *Caste in India: Its Nature, Function and Origin*, Bombay, Oxford University Press.

Jassal, Smita Tewari, 1980, 'Agrarian Conditions and Resistance in Faizabad District of Oudh (India)', *Journal of Peasant Studies*, Vol. 7.

Jay, Martin, 1976, *Dialectics of Imagination*, London, Heinemann.

Jha, Vivekanand, 1975, 'Stages in the History of Untouchables', *Indian Historical Review*, Vol. 2, pp. 14-31.

Khare, R.S., 1970, *The Changing Brahmans: Association and Elites Among the Kanya Kubja of North India*, Chicago, University of Chicago Press.

———1978, 'Structuralism in India: Some Issues and Observations', *Contributions to Indian Sociology* (N.S.), Vol. 12, pp. 253-278.

Kilson, Martin, 1983, 'The Black Bourgeoisie Revisited', *Dissent*, Winter, pp. 85-94.

Klass, M., 1980, *Caste: The Emergence of the South Asian Social System*, Philadelphia, Institute for the Study of Human Affairs.

Kosambi, D.D., 1975, *An Introduction to the Study of Indian History*, Bombay, Popular Prakashan.

———,1988, *The Culture and Civilization of Ancient India in Historical Outline*, Delhi, Vikas Publishing House.

Kramrisch, Stella, 1975, 'Traditions of the Indian Craftmen', in Milton Singer, ed., *Traditional India: Structure and Change*, Jaipur, Rawat Publicatons.

Kuhn, T.S., 1970, *The Structure of Scientific Revolutions*, Chicago, University of Chicago Press.

Kuper, Adam, 1973, *Anthropologists and Anthropology: The British School 1922-72*, London, Penguin Books.

Leach, E.R., ed., 1960, *Aspects of Caste in South India, Ceylon and Northwest Pakistan*, Cambridge, Cambridge University Press.

Lele, Jayant, 1981, *Elite Pluralism and Class Rule: Political Development in Maharashtra-India*, Toronto, University of Toronto Press.

————1990, 'Caste, Class and Dominance: Political Mobilization in Maharashtra', in Francine R. Frankel and M.S.A. Rao, eds., *Dominance and State Power in India: Decline of a Social Order*, Delhi, Oxford University Press.

Lenin, V.I., 1960, *The Development of Capitalism in Russia, Collected Works*, Vol. 3, Moscow, Foreign Language Publishing House.

————1976, *The Agrarian Question and the 'Critics of Marx'*, Moscow, Progress Publishers.

Lévi-Strauss, Claude, 1966, *The Savage Mind*, London and Chicago, University of Chicago Press and Weidenfeld and Nicholson.

————1968, *Structural Anthropology*, London, Allen Lane, The Penguin Press.

Lipset, S.M. and R. Bendix, 1957, *Social Mobility in Industrial Society*, Glencoe, Illinois, The Free Press.

Lowie, Robert H., 1934, 'Social Organization', in *Encyclopaedia of Social Sciences*, Vol. 14, New York, Macmillan.

Luhmann, Niklas, 1982, *The Differentiation of Society*, New York, Columbia University Press

Lukacs, George, 1971, *History and Class-Consciousness*, London, Merlin Press.

Lynch, Owen, 1972, 'The Politics of Untouchability in Agra', in Milton Singer and Bernard Cohn eds., *Structure and Change in Indian Society*, New York, Werner and Gren Foundation.

Malinowski, Bronislaw, 1922, *Argonauts of the Western Pacific: An Account of Native Enterprises and Adventure in the Archipelegoes of Melanesia*, New Guinea, London, Routledge and Kegan Paul.

———1926, *Crime and Customs in Savage Society*, London, Routledge and Kegan Paul.

———1944, *A Scientific Theory of Culture and Other Essays*, University of North Carolina Press.

———1948, *Magic, Science and Religion and Other Essays*, Glencoe, Illinois, Free Press.

Mannheim, Karl, 1960, *Ideology and Utopia: An Introduction to the Sociology of Knowledge*, London, Routledge and Kegan Paul.

Manor, James, 1977, 'The Evolution of the Political Arena and Units of Social Organization: The Lingayats and Okkaligas of Princely Mysore', in *Dimensions of Social Change in India*, ed., M.N. Srinivas, S. Seshaiah and V.S. Parthasarthy, Bombay, Allied Publishers.

Manusmriti, 1971, translated by Arthur Coke Burnett, completed and ed., Edwar H. Hopkins, New Delhi, Oriental Books Reprint Centre.

Marglin, Fredrique Appfel, 1977, 'Power, Purity and Pollution: Aspects of the Caste System Reconsidered', *Contributions to Indian Sociology*, (N.S.), Vol. 2, pp. 245-70.

Marriot, McKim, 1959, 'Interactional and Attributional Theory of Caste Ranking', *Man in India*, Vol. 39, pp. 92-107.

Marriot, McKim and Ronald B. Inden, 1977, 'Towards a Ethnosociology of the South Asian Caste System', in Kenneth A. David, ed., *The New Wind: Changing Identities in South Asia*, Chicago, Aldine Publications.

Marx, Karl, 1969, 'Theses on Feuerbach', in Karl Marx and Frederick Engels, *Selected Works,* Vol. I, Moscow, Progress Publishers.

Marx, Karl and Frederick Engels, 1962, 'Manifesto of the Communist Party', in Karl Marx and Frederick Engels, *Selected Works*, Vol. 1, Moscow, Foreign Languages Publishing House.

Marx, Karl and Frederick Engels, 1950, *Selected Works, 2 Vols.* Moscow, Foreign Language Publishing House.

————1945, *Selected Correspondence 1846-1895*, Calcutta, National Book Agency.

————1973, *Grundrisse*, Harmondsworth, Penguin Books.

————1965, *Pre-Capitalist Economic Formations*, ed., E. Hobsbawm, New York, International Publishers.

Means, Gordon P., 1986, 'Ethnic Preference in Malaysia', in Neil Neville and C. Kennedy, eds., *Ethnic Preference and Public Policy in Developing States*, Boulder Lynne Reinner Publications Inc.

Mencher, J.P., 1975, 'The Caste System Upside Down or the Not So Mysterious East?' *Current Anthropology*, Vol. 15, pp. 469-94.

Mehendale, M.N., 1951, 'Language and Upanishad (The Age of Upanishads and Sutras)', in R.C. Majumdar and A.D. Pusalker, eds., *History and Culture of the Indian People, Vol. 1: The Vedic Age*, London, George Allen and Unwin.

Mills, C. Wright, 1970, *The Sociological Imagination* Harmondsworth, Penguin Books.

Milner, Murray Jr., 1994, *Status and Sacredness: A General Theory of Status Relations and an Analysis of Indian Culture*, New York, Oxford University Press.

Moffat, Michael, 1979, *An Untouchable Community is South India: Structure and Consensus*, Princeton, New Jersey, Princeton University Press.

Mullick, Promatha Nath, 1969, *History of Vaisyas of Bengal*.

Myrdal, Gunnar, 1962, *An American Dilemma*, New York, Harper.

Nanjudayya, H.V. and L.K. Anantha Krishna Iyer, 1928, *The Mysore Tribes and Castes*, Mysore, Mysore University Press.

Needham, Rodney, 1970, 'Introduction', in Émile Durkheim and Marcel Mauss, *Primitive Classification*, London, Cohen and West.

Nehru, Jawaharlal, 1960, *Discovery of India*, New York, Anchor Books.

Nesfield, John C., 1885, *The Caste System of North West Province and Oudh*, Allahabad Government Press.

O'Malley, L.S.S., 1932, *Indian Caste Customs*, Cambridge, Cambridge University Press.

———1975, *Indian Social Heritage*, London, Curzon Press.

Omvedt, Gail, 1978, 'Class Struggle or Caste War', *Frontier*, Vol. 11.

Ortner, Sherry B., 1991, 'Reading America Preliminary Notes on Culture and Class', in R.G. Fox, ed., *Recapturing Anthropology*, Santa Fe School of American Research.

Parry, Jonathan P., 1978, *Caste and Kinship in Kangra*, London, Routledge and Kegan Paul.

———1985, 'Ghosts, Greed and Sin: The Occupational Identity of the Benares Funeral priests', *Man*, (N.S.) Vol. 15, pp. 88-111.

———1986, 'The Gift, the Indian Gift and the Indian Gift', *Man*, (N.S.), Vol. 21, pp. 453-73.

———1990, 'Death and Digestion: The Symbolism of Food and Eating in North Indian Mortuary Rites', *Man*, (N.S.), Vol. 20, pp. 13-30.

Polanyi, Karl, 1944, *The Great Transformation*, New York, Rinehart.

Pusalker, A.D., 1951a 'The Indus Valley Civilization', in *History and Culture of the Indian People, Vol. 1: The Vedic Age*, eds., R.C. Majumdar and A.D. Pusalker, London, George Allen and Unwin.

————1951b, 'Traditional History from the Earliest Times to the Accession of Parikshit', in *History and Culture of the Indian People, Vol. 1: The Vedic Age*, eds., R.C. Majumdar and A.D. Pusalker.

Quigley, Declan, 1993, *The Interpretation of Caste*, Oxford, Clarendon Press.

Raheja, Gloria Goodwin, 1988, *The Poison in the Gift: Ritual, Presentation, and the Dominant Caste in a North Indian Village*, Chicago, University of Chicago Press.

Rex, John, 1971, *Key Problems of Sociological Theory*, London, Routledge and Kegan Paul.

Risley, H.H., 1891, *The Tribes and Castes of Bengal*, 2 Vols., Calcutta, Bengal Secretariat Press.

Rowe, William L., 1968, 'The New Chauhans: Caste Mobility in North India', in James Silverberg, ed., *Social Mobility and the Caste System in India: An Interdisciplinary Symposium*, Mouton, The Hague.

Rowe, W., 1968, 'Mobility in 19th Century Caste system', in Milton Singer and Bernard Cohn eds., *Structure and Change in Indian Society*, New York, Werner Gren Foundation.

Rudolph, Lloyd I., and Sussanne H. Rudolph, 1969, *The Modernity of Tradition*, Bombay, Orient Longman.

Russel, Kathy, Midge Wilson, and Ronald Hall, 1992, *The Colour Complex: The Politics of Skin Colour Among African Americans*, New York, Anchor Books, Doubleday.

Sacks, Karen Bodkin, 1994, 'How did Jews Become White Folks?' in Steven Gregory and Roger Sanjek, eds., *Race*, New Brunswick, Rutgers University Press.

Sanjek, Roger, 1994, 'Intermarriage and the Future of Races', in Steven Gregory and Roger Sanjek, eds., *Race*, New Brunswick, Rutgers University Press.

Sartre, Jean Paul, 1976, *Critique of Dialectical Reason*, London, New Left Books.

Schurmann, F., 1971, *Ideology and Organization of the Communist Party of China*, Berkeley, University of California Press.

Shah, A.M. and G. Shroff, 1975, 'The Vahivanca Barots of Gujarat, A Caste of Geneologists and Mythographers', in Milton Singer, ed., *Traditional India: Structure and Change*, Jaipur, Rawat Publications.

Shah, Ghanshyam, 1982, 'Rural Politics in Gujarat', in Gail Omvedt, ed., *Land, Caste and Politics in Indian State*, Delhi, Guild Publications.

Sharma, R.S., 1965, *Indian Feudalism C. 300-1200*, Calcutta, University of Calcutta Press.

——1966, *Light on Early Indian Society*, Bombay, Manaktalas.

——1975, 'Class Formation and its Material Basis in the Upper Gangotri Basin (c. 1000-500 BC)', *Indian Historical Review*, Vol. 2, pp. 1-13.

Shastri, Dakshinaranjan, n.d., *A Short History of Indian Materialism, Sensationalism and Hedonism*, Calcutta, Bookland.

Shiva Rao, B.D., (ed.) 1968a, *The Framing of India's Constitution: Selected Documents (Vol. II)*, Delhi, Indian Institute of Public Administration.

——1968b, *The Framing of India's Constitution: A Study*, Delhi, Indian Institute of Public Administration.

Siddiqui, N.A., 1970, *Land Revenue and Administration Under the Mughals (1700-1750)*, Bombay, Asia Publishing House.

Siddiqi, Majid H., 1978, *Agrarian Unrest in Northern India: The United Provinces, 1919-22*, Delhi: Vikas Publishing House.

Silversten, Dagfinn, 1963, *When Caste Barriers Fall: A Study of Social and Economic Change in a Small Indian Village*, New York, Humanities Press.

Singer, Milton, 1972, *When a Great Tradition Modernizes: An Anthropological Approach to Indian Civilization*, New York, Progress Press.

Singh, H.D., 1996, *543 Faces of India*, New Delhi, Newsman Publishers.

Singh, Yogendra, 1969, 'Social Structure and Village Panchayat', in *Rural Sociology,* ed., A.R. Desai, Bombay, Popular Prakashan.

———1973, *Modernization of Indian Tradition*, New Delhi, National Book Trust.

———(n.d.), *The Concept of Man in Sociology* (Mimeo), Centre for the Study of Social Systems, Jawaharlal Nehru University, New Delhi.

Sorokin, Pitrim, 1967, 'Social Stratification' in Talcott Parsons, Edward Shils, K.D. Naeghle, and J.R. Pitts, eds., *Theories of Society: Foundations of Modern Sociology*, Vol.1, Glencoe, Illinois, The Free Press.

Sowell, Thomas, 1995, *Preferential Policies*, New York, Walter Morrow & Co.

Srinivas, M.N., 1962, *Caste in Modern India and Other Essays*, Bombay, Popular Prakashan.

Srinivas, M.N., ed., 1996, *Caste: Its Twentieth Century Avatar*, New Delhi, Viking, Penguin.

Stammer, Otto, ed., 1971, *Max Weber and Sociology Today*, Oxford, Oxford University Press.

Stark, Werner, 1962, *The Fundamental Forms of Social Thought*, London, Routledge and Kegan Paul.

Steinberg, Stephen, 1989, *The Ethnic Myth: Race, Ethnicity and Class in America*, Boston, Beacon Press.

Subramanian, K., 1974, *Brahmin Priests of Tamil Nadu*, New York, John Wiley.

Terray, Emmanuel, 1972, *Marxism and 'Primitive' Societies*, New York, Monthly Review Press.

Thapar, Romila, 1975, *The Past and Prejudice*, New Delhi, National Book Trust.

————1978, *Ancient Indian Social History: Some Interpretations*, Delhi, Orient Longman.

Thompson, E.P., 1978, *The Poverty of Theory and Other Essays*, London, Merlin Press.

Timberg, Thomas A., 1978, *The Marwaris, From Traders to Industrialists*, Delhi, Vikas Publishing House.

Van Woodward, C., 1951, *Origins of the New South, 1877-1913*, Baton Rouge, Louisiana State University.

Veltmeyer, Henry, 1974-75: 'Towards an Assessment of the Structuralist Interpretation of Marx, Claude Lévi-Strauss and Louis Althusser', *Science and Society* Vol. 38, pp. 385-421.

Wagle, Naren K., 1998, *Customary Law Among the Non-Brahman Jatis of Pune*, (Mimeo), Toronto University of Toronto, Centre for South Asian Studies.

Wagley, Charles, 1959, 'On the Concept of Social Race in the Americas', in *Congresso Internocional de Americanistas*, Vol. 1, Lehman San Jose.

Warner, Lloyd, Marchia Meeker and Kenneth Eels, 1949, *Social Class in America*, Chicago, Science Research Associates.

Weber, Max, 1946, 'Class, Status and Party', in *From Max Weber Essays in Sociology*, eds., and translated by H.H. Gerth and C. Wright Mills, New York, Oxford University Press.

Weber, Max, 1958, *The Religion of India*, Glencoe, Illinois, Free Press.

Wittfogel, Karl, 1970, *Oriental Despotism: A Comparative Study in Total Power*, New Haven, Yale University Press.

Wilson, William Julius, 1978, *The Declining Significance of Race: Blacks and Changing American*, Chicago, University of Chicago Press.

Worseley, Peter, 1967, *The Third World*, London, Weidenfeld and Nicholson.

Wright, Erik Olin, 1979, *Class Structure and Income Determination*, New York, Academic Press.

————1985, *Classes*, London, Verso.

Yadav, B.N.S., 1976, 'Problems of Interaction Between Socio-Economic Classes in Early Medieval Complex', in *Indian Historical Review*, Vol. 3, pp. 43-58.

Yalman, Nur, 1969, 'The Flexibility of Caste Principles in a Kandyan Community', in Edmund Leach, ed., *Aspects of Caste in South India, Ceylon and North West Pakistan*, Cambridge, Cambridge University Press.

Index